P9-BTX-922

CUISINE SANTÉ

The New French Cooking
for Healthy Gourmet Eating

CUISINE SANTÉ

Christophe Buey

and L'École de Cuisine Française Sabine de Mirbeck

VIKING

Dedication

To Sabine and Patrick Brassart, who
supported me and treated me like a son.
Thank you for these eight years of trust;
may this continue throughout our lives.

VIKING
Viking Penguin Inc., 40 West 23rd Street,
New York, New York 10010, U.S.A.
Penguin Books Ltd, Harmondsworth,
Middlesex, England
Penguin Books Australia Ltd, Ringwood,
Victoria, Australia
Penguin Books Canada Limited, 2801 John Street,
Markham, Ontario, Canada L3R 1B4
Penguin Books (N.Z.) Ltd, 182–190 Wairau Road,
Auckland 10, New Zealand

First published in 1987 by Viking Penguin Inc.
Published simultaneously in Canada

Conceived and produced by
Swallow Publishing Limited
Swallow House
11-21 Northdown Street
London N1 9BN

Editors: Susan Fleming and Carole Clements
Art director: Elaine Partington
Designers: Judith Robertson and Su Martin
Photographer: Tim Imrie
Home economist: Mandy Wagstaff
Assistant editor: Catherine Tilley
Studio: Del & Co

Library of Congress Cataloging-in-Publication Data
Buey, Christophe.
    Cuisine santé.

    Includes index.
    1. Cookery, French. I. École de cuisine française
Sabine de Mirbeck. II. Title.
TX719.B924 1987   641.5944   87-40118
ISBN 0-670-81792-9

Typeset in Garamond Original by
Bournetype, Bournemouth
Color origination and printing in
Hong Kong by Imago Publishing

Title page The vegetable garden at Clapham House,
home of l'École de Cuisine Française Sabine de Mirbeck.
Page 1 Clapham House. Page 30 *Gougère* and
Pissaladière à la Niçoise. Page 46 *Peperonata, Terrine
de Foies de Volaille, Tourte aux Épinards* and *Potage Crécy.*
Page 80 *Bar Farci en Chemise, Huîtres au Gratin* and
Filets de Sole Pochés au Vin Blanc.
Page 104 *Ballotine de Faisan, Poulet Sauté à l'Estragon*
and *Escalope de Veau Woronoff.*
Page 150 *Salade de Champignons de Sabine, Salade Niçoise*
and *Salade d'Endives.* Page 164 *Tarte aux Fraises.*

~ CONTENTS ~

$\backsim$ FOREWORD $\backsim$

CHRISTOPHE BUEY AND SABINE DE MIRBECK-BRASSART

All art evolves constantly, and the art of French cooking would be lost if French chefs did not move with the times. Cooking methods must be adapted to suit changes in lifestyle, and that means finding a way to accommodate today's stressful and sedentary habits. In short, modern food must be lighter and healthier than before.

So the concept of cooking traditional French food with health and nutrition in mind was developed in our school, not as a break with traditional French cuisine, but as a continuation of it, modified to today's tastes and demands. We teach both traditional French recipes and their Cuisine Santé counterparts at our cooking school as part of our courses, and comparisons between the two have fascinated both staff and students.

Although the concept of Cuisine Santé is not the invention of a single person, its development owes considerably to our head chef, Christophe Buey. When my husband Patrick Brassart (who was a member of the board of the Cordon Bleu de Paris) decided to open a cooking school in England, I was happy to become *directrice*, but I was faced with the important and delicate task of appointing a teacher. Should I, as they did at the Cordon Bleu de Paris, appoint a well-known chef with an international renown, such as Monsieur Pellaprat, or should I choose a more academic sort of person who would lack the knowledge and experience of a great chef but have the communicative flair of a teacher?

Despite his youth — he was twenty-six at the time — we decided to give this opportunity to Christophe, who had earned the Diplôme de l'École Hotelière de Lausanne, and allow him to create his own methods of teaching our students the classic techniques and skills. We felt that his original approach would open the doors of the French culinary arts to competent amateurs as well as to those who wanted to become professional chefs.

At the time, this choice was very much a gamble, but one we have never regretted, as Christophe has made an invaluable contribution to the formation of what we hope is a truly professional cooking school. Not the least of it is his role in the development of a new form of cooking which we hope will affirm the flexibility and continuing supremacy of French cuisine.

To him, to the rest of the excellent staff at our school, and to everyone else involved in the production of this book, I should like to say, "*Merci beaucoup, et bonne santé!*"

Sabine de Mirbeck Brassart

SABINE DE MIRBECK-BRASSART

INTRODUCTION

Everyone involved in and concerned with food has long been aware of a major shift in dietary habits — a shift toward food that not only tastes good but which is also good for the health of the body. The bourgeoise and haute traditions of classic French cuisine have been the first to fall from grace because of their use of ingredients which contain saturated animal fats, salt, sugar, and a lot of alcohol — all now disapproved of by the medical establishment — and too little dietary fiber. Nouvelle and other related cuisines have attempted to redress the balance by limiting or entirely omitting potentially harmful ingredients, but in so doing have been criticized for concentrating on appearance at the cost of quantity — and, occasionally, even of flavor.

Cuisine Santé, which has been especially evolved to satisfy the concerns and desires of the most health-conscious gourmet, is an alternative to all of these — while, at the same time, it retains many of the principles, techniques and flavors which have for so long characterized the very best of French cooking. Cuisine Santé is a well-balanced cuisine that favors the use of fresh fruit, fresh vegetables, the very best of white meat, fish and whole-foods, and avoids foods that have been artificially flavored, processed and refined. Fats too are avoided where possible: oils high in polyunsaturates are used in place of the butter of traditional French cuisine; low-fat strained yogurt is used instead of cream — and if cream *is* called for, we use the lighter whipping or single rather than double cream. Herbs are important for their wonderful aroma, delicious flavors and their general beneficial effects, and many of them reduce the need for salt — another potentially harmful ingredient which we overuse these days. Our desserts rely more on fruit, thus they contain more fiber, and much less flour, sugar and cream.

Many of the Cuisine Santé recipes are versions of the traditional classic cuisines, redesigned so that they are healthier without sacrificing flavor. The favored cooking methods are also those which retain the maximum freshness and nutritional value of foods — poaching, steaming, sweating, braising and casseroling.

Cuisine Santé is not a diet book. It does not involve calorie counting, but examines every recipe for its fat, sugar, salt and fiber content. To show more clearly what the Cuisine Santé concept does and what it can achieve, we have in fact compared Cuisine Santé recipes with their classical counterparts. The comparison of ingredients, and the calorie, protein and fat contents (in grams), will illustrate much more vividly than can even the most enthusiastic words, just how "derivative" in one way, but "revolutionary" in another, Cuisine Santé is.

CUISINE BOURGEOISE

Cuisine bourgeoise is family cuisine of good, satisfying, honest — and substantial — home cooking. Cuisine Santé can also be good, satisfying and honest — but without the calorie-rich substance of many bourgeoise dishes, as below. The original recipe for *Potage Orge Perlé Brunoise* contained butter and flour, as well as the barley to thicken. A lot of double cream would also have been added; in the Cuisine Santé version we are quite happy with a little single cream mixed with Greek yogurt.

POTAGE ORGE PERLÉ BRUNOISE

Cuisine bourgeoise original	Cuisine Santé version
1 oz. butter	*1 tbsp. grapeseed oil*
4 oz. onions	*4 oz. onions*
4 oz. leeks	*4 oz. leeks*
4 oz. carrots	*4 oz. carrots*
4 oz. celery	*4 oz. celery*
4 oz. pearl barley	*2 oz. unrefined barley*
1½ quarts stock	*1½ quarts stock*
salt	*salt*
freshly ground black pepper	*freshly ground black pepper*
¾ cup double cream	*¼ cup single cream*
1 egg yolk	*2 oz. Greek yogurt*

Cuisine bourgeoise original		Cuisine Santé version	
Proteins	= 39.12	Proteins	= 39.41
Fats	= 103.34	Fats	= 26.38
Carbohydrates	= 182.82	Carbohydrates	= 122.10
TOTAL CALORIES	2055.69	TOTAL CALORIES	1831.25
CALORIES PER PERSON	513.92	CALORIES PER PERSON	457.81

HAUTE CUISINE

Haute cuisine was the cuisine of the city restaurants of France — the cuisine of the chef with his kitchen brigade of *sous-chefs* and their individual specialities. Most of the ingredients used were expensive and rich — truffles, *foie gras*, etc. — and the presentation was elaborate and time-consuming, often to the detriment of the food itself. Cuisine Santé has absorbed the techniques and presentation skills of haute cuisine but has cut out the rich ingredients and substituted lighter and less refined ones, and concentrated on healthier methods of cooking.

BALLOTINE DE FAISAN

Haute cuisine original	Cuisine santé version
1 pheasant, about 1½ lb.	*1 pheasant, about 1½ lb.*
4½ oz. pork fat	*1½ tsp. grapeseed or safflower oil*
salt	*salt*
freshly ground black pepper	*freshly ground black pepper*
1 cup Madeira	*1 cup Madeira*
MIREPOIX	**MIREPOIX**
1 thyme sprig	*1 thyme sprig*
1 bay leaf	*1 bay leaf*
1 cup stock	*1 cup stock*
¾ oz. butter	—
¾ oz. flour	—
STUFFING	**STUFFING**
1¼ oz. pork fat	—
1 shallot	*2 shallots*
2¼ oz. foie gras	*pheasant liver*
¾ oz. mushrooms	*4 oz. mushrooms*
3 oz. veal	*5 oz. lean veal*
4 oz. forcemeat	*4 oz. pork tenderloin*
4 egg yolks	*1 egg*
½ cup white sauce	*¼ cup Greek yogurt*
—	*a pinch of ground allspice*
—	*pheasant fillets*

Proteins	= 229	Proteins	= 216
Fats	= 181	Fats	= 37
Carbohydrates	= 52	Carbohydrates	= 18
TOTAL CALORIES	2684	TOTAL CALORIES	1546
CALORIES PER PERSON	671.11	CALORIES PER PERSON	386

NOUVELLE CUISINE

Nouvelle cuisine was the response of chefs to demands — from businessmen and regular restaurant eaters in the main — for lighter, less rich food. Technically speaking, it is not a "*nouvelle*" (new) cuisine, as it is soundly based on classic French cuisine, but it places more emphasis on healthier methods of cooking and preparation, and uses unusual and fashionable ingredients which did not have a place in traditional French cuisine. It has also led to the emergence of the chef as artist, arranging foods to make a feast for the eye as well as the palate. However, many chefs and restaurant proprietors have taken advantage of the new cuisine's popularity, serving ridiculously small portions at astronomical prices, and breaking the sensible and appropriate balance of ingredients. Cuisine Santé, however, has embraced all the original precepts of the nouvelle cuisine, while serving decent portions and concentrating on the highly important matter of keeping a correct and sensible balance of flavors and nutrients.

FILETS MIGNON DE PORC À LA NORMANDE

Nouvelle cuisine original	Cuisine Santé version
14 oz. pork tenderloin	*1½ lb. pork tenderloin*
salt	*salt*
freshly ground black pepper	*freshly ground black pepper*
1 tbsp. oil	*grapeseed or safflower oil*
1 oz. butter	
1½ oz. each of carrot, turnip, leek and celery	*7 oz. each of carrot, turnip, leek and celery*
—	*1 cooking apple*
1 shallot	*1 shallot*
2 tbsp. Calvados	*2 tbsp. Calvados*
⅔ cup hard cider	*⅔ cup hard cider*
2 cups stock	*2 cups stock*
½ cup double cream	*½ cup whipping cream*

Proteins	= 107.77	Proteins	= 178
Fats	= 315.07	Fats	= 107.05
Carbohydrates	= 293.12	Carbohydrates	= 183
TOTAL CALORIES	3239	TOTAL CALORIES	2425
CALORIES PER PERSON	810	CALORIES PER PERSON	606

To conclude, Cuisine Santé is no passing or dictatorial culinary fad — abolishing certain ingredients, insisting on the use of others. It is a sensible, highly professional and affectionate rethinking of the best cuisine in the world — and has the potential to be the next great movement in culinary history.

Christophe Buey

CHRISTOPHE BUEY

HOW TO USE THIS BOOK

This section is designed to help you — the cook — to use this book as efficiently as possible. Even though the recipes are not difficult, there are certain "lessons" to be learned before they should be attempted. In fact, the recipes have been especially evolved so they can be easily understood and followed — even the ones which require up to three days and three stages of preparation (don't panic, each day's work only takes up to an hour at most). But these lessons are necessary because we have used a form of shorthand in describing certain ingredients, techniques, pieces of equipment, and so on. You need to know, for instance, what is different about Greek yogurt (and how to manufacture an alternative if that is unavailable); you need to know the constituents of *fines herbes*, a *bouquet garni* or a *mirepoix*; and once you know that "cut into *chiffonade*" means simply "cut into thin strips," you can cook the Cuisine Santé way with the ease of a professional!

There are four essential elements in cooking, all four as important as one another, and they are closely interlinked.

The first element is *the cook*, with his or her interest in and love of palatable, good and healthy food.

Equipment is the second element, through which the cook can apply his or her knowledge with confidence. This equipment should be the very best you can afford, and we have prepared a list of what we consider vital for good Cuisine Santé cooking. A fat-separator, for instance (see page 13), is a necessity for all our fat-free, *santé* dishes. You may also need scales when making pastry as the right mix of flour to fat is obtained by a formula using weight (see page 44).

The ingredients, the third element, are obviously highly important. All foods — meats, fish, fruit, vegetables and oils, flours, etc. — should be the very freshest and best possible to produce the highest quality and healthiest dish or meal. "Choose the best or refuse" would be our motto, except that compromise might occasionally be necessary — when, say, you have to use dried herbs because fresh ones are not available. The more often we, as consumers, insist on the best, the more suppliers will be forced to supply just that! Make sure you read the Ingredients section that follows before you start any of the recipes — it contains helpful shopping tips as well as cooking and nutritional information.

The techniques are the final element — the cooking techniques favored by Cuisine Santé, and the cutting, chopping, preparation and garnishing techniques which are basic to French cuisine in general. Many of these we have illustrated as well as described in words so that you can fully understand what the recipe means and demands.

Finally, it should be understood that Cuisine Santé is not a dogmatic cuisine — nothing can ever be exact or final in a recipe. We have found at the School that although every student receives exactly the same tuition and uses exactly the same basic ingredients, the results always taste slightly different. Each student will have added to a dish his or her own individual attention, interest and love — with perhaps a pinch more of this or that — and this is what we should like you to do too. Add your own "signature" to our basic recipes — and live and cook happily, wisely and healthily!

You do not have to be an expert gardener to grow your own herbs. This contains a basic selection: parsley, sage, rosemary, thyme, sweet marjoram, chives, mint and fennel.

INGREDIENTS

Allspice The dried berry of a tropical plant, used with cloves to give a strong and spicy taste to a stock, sauce, or stew. To be used sparingly.

Apple juice Buy sugar-free juice with no additives or preservatives.

Asparagus Look for freshness. Stale or old asparagus spears appear dry and have droopy, soggy tips. Rich in vitamins A, B, B_2 and C.

Baking powder A mixture of acid and alkaline substances which, when heated and/or moistened, produces carbon dioxide gas, which helps cakes rise.

Barley Unrefined barley is high in vitamin B and full of protein. It is the oldest of the cereal crops and has a slightly nutty taste.

Basil A very important herb used mostly in dishes from the Mediterranean, where it grows well. Available in more northerly climates in spring and summer. It grows well in a sheltered south-facing spot. Preserve it for the winter in jars of olive oil. The oil, in small quantity, can also be used to prepare salad dressings. Basil is a natural tranquilizer, and is good for stomach troubles.

Bass, sea As with all fish, look for bright eyes, shiny and firmly attached scales, firm flesh and a pleasant smell. Sea bass is costly, but has a lovely flavor. Eat as fresh as possible.

Bay leaf The Romans used it as a symbol of peace, victory and triumph, thus the "laurels" of success, the wreaths of leaves with which they crowned the heads of caesars. However, it is most efficient used in cooking: its strong aroma gives flavor, and it is also antiseptic and digestive. Used mostly in stocks, sauces and stews, and in a *bouquet garni*.

Beans French beans or dwarf green beans. Simply top and tail, and de-string if tough. Cook very quickly. Buy small, crisp regular-sized beans which break easily when raw. Rich in vitamin C, potassium, calcium and iron.

Belgian endive A slightly bitter vegetable. Can be eaten raw or cooked. Look for white, firm, crisp plants.

Broccoli Look for bright compact tight buds; yellowing buds indicate poor quality. Cook in very little salted boiling water for a minimum time to retain color. Contains vitamins A, B and C.

Butter We always use the unsalted kind.

Cabbage, red Available all year around. Rich source of vitamins B and C. Like all cabbage, it loses a lot of its nourishment during cooking, so cut finely to keep cooking time short.

Cabbage, savoy Rich in vitamins A and C. Buy tight, firm heavy ones. The winter variety has wrinkled leaves. Remove outer leaves and stem before using.

Calvados Apple brandy from Normandy, France.

Caper Small immature flower buds of a tree which grows all around the Mediterranean, which are pickled. Look for large soft gray-green capers. Always keep in liquid as, uncovered, they develop a nasty taste.

Caraway A very strongly flavored seed used as an aromatic in a *court-bouillon*. Cooked with cabbage, it helps certain disorders.

Carrots Buy young, small ones which are best washed and cooked unpeeled. Used in *mirepoix* as well as stocks, vegetable garnishes, etc. Very versatile. They contain a little iron, phosphorus, vitamins A, B and C, and the carotene content is reputed to strengthen the eyes!

Cauliflower Buy ones with good white/cream color with little foliage, and which are heavy for their size. Cook with care as they are easily ruined if overcooked.

Celeriac (celery root) Same family as stalk celery, and has similar taste. Knobbly root vegetable, best to peel with knife, discolors when exposed to air, so rub with lemon to stop oxidation. Excellent puréed as a vegetable, or grated and marinated for salads.

Celery Choose crisp, tight heads. At its best after frosts have started.

Champagne Sparkling wine from the Champagne region of France — the area around Reims and Epernay. Only wine made in this area and using grapes from this region can be called "champagne." Other so-called champagnes are made by the "*méthode champenoise*," and are often good substitutes, especially in cooking.

Chard, Swiss Popular in Mediterranean countries as it continues to produce during winter and spring. Similar to spinach, which is a good alternative. Difficult to find in supermarkets.

Chervil A constituent of *fines herbes*. Delicate taste of anise. Stimulating, diuretic, good for blood circulation and weak livers. Always use fresh as cooking destroys its virtues.

Chicken If you don't eat the skin, chicken, like all white meats, is much healthier than dark red meats. Try to buy a whole chicken with giblets — useful for sauces, etc. Clean well before cooking.

Chicken livers A very rich source of iron. Can now be bought frozen in supermarkets. Remove the tubes and membranes before cooking.

Chives A member of the onion family, it is a perennial plant which grows well in temperate climates. Leave a few flowers to grow and bloom, but remove most to produce more leaves. Cut often to obtain a regular supply. A constituent of *fines herbes*.

Cinnamon A good antiseptic as well as natural preservative, it is best fresh in sticks of bark. Cut a piece off and cook with it. Remove after cooking. Mostly used in sweet dishes but can also be used to flavor a savory sauce and give an unusual flavor.

Cloves The flower buds of an Asian tree dried in the sun. Extremely strong. A very good antiseptic and a well-known natural preservative. Use in casseroles, soups and stocks as well as in pickles, chutneys and preserves. For stews, prick into a small onion so they are easier to retrieve after cooking.

Cognac A brandy distilled from wine, made around the town of Cognac. Use a relatively cheap French brandy for cooking — a 3-star for instance.

Coriander Used either as a fresh herb like parsley for its unusual flavor, or as seeds mixed in with peppercorns and ground as a flavoring, seasoning agent. Sometimes used in *fines herbes*.

Cream We only use whipping or, occasionally, single — both lower in fat than double — and we use only a little.

Cucumber A very refreshing vegetable because of its high water content. Always buy young ones. Cooked cucumber is an interesting alternative to zucchini or squash.

Dijon mustard Pale-colored, prepared mustard with vinegar and spices. A speciality of Dijon in the heart of France. The whole–grain version is delicious too!

Dill Sweet anise-flavored herb which is antiseptic and helps digestion. Excellent with fish but delicious, too, added on its own to a sauce. The seeds can be crushed like pepper to season a dish.

Dover sole Best of the flat fish. Its flesh is white, firm, delicate and easily digestible. Unlike with other fish, the flavor of sole (and skate) can be enhanced by keeping the fish for a couple of days after landing.

Eggs We cook with "large" grade A fresh eggs.

Eggplant Look for fairly heavy ones with bright shiny skins without blemishes. Salt, leave for half an hour and rinse, to remove excess water. When cooking in oil, be careful, as they will absorb all the oil that you give them.

Emmenthal A hard, cooked Swiss cheese, with mild flavor, distinctive because of its holes.

Endive A slightly bitter vegetable. Endive can be eaten raw or cooked. Look for white, firm, crisp plants. A popular variety is Belgian endive.

Fennel The bulb fennel — Florence fennel — is delicious raw or cooked. The herb fennel, like dill, has a strong anise flavor; it also has the same antiseptic and digestive qualities as dill. Fennel seeds are also used in cooking.

Fines herbes Consists of a mixture of parsley, chervil, tarragon, chives and coriander in equal proportion, to taste. Adds iron, calcium and vitamins (especially C). Best used raw and chopped at the last moment onto any savory dish or sauce. The combination depends on the availability of the herbs, but each addition makes its own flavor contribution.

Flour We generally use all-purpose whole-wheat flour and a higher gluten flour for bread making.

Garlic Strong flavor, and size of cloves vary, so use to taste. Easy way to peel them is to crush cloves gently with the hand or flat of a knife. Has disinfectant properties and thus is good for cleansing the blood, as well as for a lot of ailments.

Gelatin Protein substance used to set liquids. Sprinkle powdered gelatin over a small amount of cold liquid in a shallow bowl or ramekin. Let stand a minute until transparent, then heat the liquid over (or in) hot water, stirring constantly until the gelatin has dissolved.

Gherkins These are not necessarily baby cucumbers, but a special variety of cucumber found in the Caribbean. Pickled in vinegar, and used as a condiment or garnish, or to flavor in sauces.

Grand marnier Orange-flavored liqueur.

Grapeseed oil Very pure and light in polyunsaturated fats.

Greek yogurt This is a thick, smooth type which normally has some whey running out. It also contains more fat than ordinary yogurt, so use as we do instead of cream and not instead of yogurt! If none is available use ordinary live yogurt and leave overnight to thicken in a sieve lined with cheesecloth on top of a bowl to drain off the whey.

Green beans In Europe we have tiny French beans and green dwarf beans. Buy small, crisp regular-sized beans which break easily when raw, and are rich in vitamin C, potassium, calcium and iron. Simply top and tail, and remove string if tough. Cook very quickly.

Green onions Whatever their alternative name, spring onions, might imply, these can in fact be bought all year around. Mild onion flavor.

Gruyère A hard, cooked Swiss cheese, with strong flavor, with holes like Emmenthal.

Haddock fillets, smoked Look for fillets that are pale yellow in color; a bright yellow means dyes have been used. Also known as Finnan haddie, after the village of Findon, near Aberdeen, Scotland.

Hake A member of the cod family, easily boned. Best from May to September.

Hard cider A fermented apple drink. Like wine it can be dry or sweet, still or sparkling.

Herbes de Provence A miraculous blend of dried Mediterranean herbs such as thyme, bay, oregano, rosemary, and savory. Add sparingly to meat, fish and vegetable dishes, as it is very strong. Its wonderful aroma will evoke the evening smells of Provençal wild herb fields!

Herbs, fresh Now available in supermarkets – but it is easy to grow your own! Use dried if necessary, rehydrating them if necessary first, or allowing time for them to do so in a sauce. Use half quantities of dried as they are stronger than fresh.

Honey Different honeys (from various regions and flowers) have slightly different tastes. Clear liquid honey is easier to use.

Lamb Do not buy muddy looking meat. Look for bright, firm textured meat which does not smell and has a deep, even, rose color.

Leek Member of onion family, often called the "asparagus of the poor." Rich in vitamin C, iron and fiber. It needs very careful washing to remove dirt and grit trapped between layers. Buy fresh young, small leeks with a large proportion of white. The "wrapping" of a *bouquet garni*.

Lettuce Rich in vitamins A and C, iron and minerals. Many varieties are available. Wash and dry well, and keep in the refrigerator to crisp. Low in calories, less than 20 per 4 ounces.

Madeira A fortified wine. Buy either Sercial (slightly nutty, dry, light blend) or Verdelho (sweeter, and better with cakes or soup). Use sherry or port as an alternative.

Milk A range of milk is available, from full fat to skim. A general good balance is semi-skim (2%) which has half the fat of whole milk.

Mint A deliciously aromatic herb — refreshing, antiseptic, and digestive (thought to be aphrodisiac too!). Makes a good tea.

Mushrooms Buy small, tight button mushrooms, often called "Paris mushrooms." Cultivated mushrooms never have the flavor of wild ones. The large open cap mushrooms have a better flavor but don't look as good if needed for a garnish.

Nutmeg A tropical "nut" or "kernel," best grated fresh. Use sparingly in soufflés and stews as it is very strong. (It's also said to be soporific and digestive.)

Olives We use the black, ripe ones (green are unripened olives that are pickled, having been split and soaked to remove bitterness). Drain and wash well to remove brine or vinegar flavors. The best are those from the South of France, Italy or Greece, marinated in olive oil. Add a little *Herbes de Provence* and leave to marinate for a couple of weeks before eating or using!

Olive oil Buy the cold press, first pressing, virgin oil. It is expensive to buy, but only a little is needed. Combine it with grapeseed or safflower oil.

Onion One of the most basic ingredients in all cooking. A useful tip if they make you cry is to wash your hands and knife under running cold water.

Oregano This herb is more usually available dried. It is widely used in Italian cuisine where the fresh sun-cultivated herb is very strong. Delicious in sauces and stews and on our *Pissaladière*.

Parsley Rich in iron, calcium and vitamins. Use raw for best results. The stalks are used in a *bouquet garni* and to flavor stocks and sauces, and the leaves or sprigs chopped or whole, are added at the last moment to the dish. A constituent of *fines herbes*.

Partridge When buying, choose plump birds with supple skin and smooth, firmly attached feathers. Avoid badly shot birds and ones which have an unpleasant smell.

Passion fruit juice If not available use the "tropical" blend available in supermarkets.

Peas, tiny Frozen ones are easier to come by and in fact are often better than old peas bought in the market. However, fresh garden peas have an inimitable flavor.

Peppers, sweet Peppers change as they ripen from green through yellow to red. Little food value, more prized for their flavor, although those grown under glass are rather insipid.

Pernod French anise-flavored alcohol.

Pheasant Normally sold in a brace (hen and cock). The hen is the better eating bird. Always hang a bird unplucked, for 2–3 days maximum. Young birds have pliable beaks and the wing tip feather is pointed.

Pine nuts From the stone pine, a Mediterranean tree. They have a slightly buttery taste, especially when roasted.

Pistachio nuts Edible and expensive green nuts easily removed from the shell. They have a mild, sweet, nutty taste.

Pork The tenderloin or fillet has the lowest fat content.

Port A full-bodied red wine fermented with brandy.

Potato Many different varieties. Buy

potatoes that are heavy for their size. When fresh they are rich in vitamin C and potassium. Steaming helps retain these. Peel very thinly if at all. Potatoes are easily frost and light-damaged, so be careful about storage.

Potato starch Non-wheat flours are richer in protein and are good in gluten-free diets as a substitute for flour. Useful thickening agent for soups and casseroles.

Rabbit A white meat, now becoming fashionable again. Unlike hare, it ought to be eaten within days of being caught or shot. It is a cheaper and healthier alternative to other meats.

Rice flour Ground rice, useful thickening agent. Gluten-free.

Ricotta A very good Italian low-fat soft cheese. Push through a sieve to eliminate lumps. If not available, use sieved cottage cheese.

Roquefort Blue-veined cheese made from sheep's milk. Strong, sharp taste, but creamy texture.

Rosemary A constituent of the *herbes de Provence* mix, it is a strongly flavored evergreen herb. It is antiseptic and a stimulant. Especially good with lamb and other meat dishes. It can be used also as part of a *bouquet garni*.

Rum A spirit distilled from sugar cane residues. Use the darker varieties, they have a better flavor.

Rutabaga These are sometimes called yellow turnips. Generally yellow, and larger than a turnip and totally smooth. They are also sweeter and drier than turnips. Make sure not to choose spongy ones when buying.

Safflower oil A very pure oil, low in polyunsaturated fats.

Sage Coming from the Latin word meaning to save or heal. It has an aromatic, slightly bitter and very powerful flavor. Dries very well. A pinch of sage infused in boiling milk helps prevent the start of a cold. It also helps digestion of fatty meats. Do not use with parsley or chervil as they do not combine well. Slight camphor flavor.

Salmon, fresh Buy as Bass.

Salmon, smoked Buy the wild kind rather than those from fish farms, it is worth the extra expense. If buying to use as a flavoring, as for a soufflé or quiche, try to buy trimmings, often a lot cheaper. When buying, look for firm flesh which is moist and has a true smoked color, not bright and artificial.

Salt Use reduced salt blends or raw gray sea salt, very little of it.

Savory A constituent of the *herbes de Provence* mix, it is excellent for the digestion (it is thought to be an aphrodisiac too!) Its taste is very similar to

that of thyme, and can be used similarly.

Shallot A variety of onion with red-brown papery skins, about the size of pickling onions — in fact, they make the *best* pickling onions. They have a lovely, special flavor and are particularly nice in sauces.

Skate Flat, cartilaginous fish which is kite shaped, hence the use of the wings only. The taste is improved by hanging for a couple of days. Very gelatinous.

Snow peas A variety of pea. The pods are topped and tailed and eaten whole when young. Buy bright green, young, crisp ones.

Soft cheeses Soft unripened cheeses, made from pasteurized milk, including cottage, farmer's and pot cheeses, Ricotta, Petit Gervais and cream cheese.

Sorrel A vegetable, but usually thought of as an herb. Its acidity adds flavor, but use only a little as it can affect those with rheumatism or gout. It is delicious in combination with spinach, or stuffed inside a fish.

Spinach Rich in vitamins and iron, and contains more calcium than most vegetables. Buy young, glossy, green leaves. Wash thoroughly. Best cooked by dry steaming; place in pan with *nothing* else — the moisture from the washing makes the steam.

Star anise A very pretty star-shaped spice, widely used in Chinese cooking (and available in Chinese shops). A strong anise flavor for stocks, sauces and stews.

Sugar For general use we prefer "superfine" granulated sugar, which is very fine and dissolves quickly. Confectioners' sugar is used for cake decoration and in some desserts. Muscovado or molasses sugar is very dark, with an almost licorice-like taste.

Sweet marjoram A similar sweet and spicy flavor to oregano, but milder. Helps digestion.

Tarragon A constituent of *fines herbes*. It has an anise flavor. A perennial plant, the French variety is better than the Russian, which differs in flavor and is not as strong. A good substitute for salt in a recipe, as well as vinegar because of its acidity.

Thyme Best used in dishes that involve long, slow cooking. Major ingredient in a *bouquet garni*. Thyme is a strong antiseptic, stimulating good breathing and helping blood circulation and digestion.

Tomato Buy firm, smooth-skinned tomatoes — sun-ripened, if possible.

Tomato paste One of the few canned products we use. A great standby that adds good flavor to stocks, sauces, etc.

Trout Buy as Bass.

Turbot An expensive flat fish as it is difficult to catch. Large with lean, white, firm flesh and a good flavor.

Turnips An under-appreciated vegetable

in the US. However, small baby turnips have a lovely flavor. Buy small, unbruised ones.

Vanilla The pod of a tropical climbing orchid. It is very aromatic, and is used mostly in sweet dishes, split in half. It can be used more than once: rinse the pod well after use and store in a tightly closed jar of sugar. The pod imparts its flavor to the sugar.

Veal The best veal comes from animals several months old, which have been milk fed. May be difficult to obtain — most veal seems to go to France, where the demand is high.

Verbena A lemon-flavored herb. As an alternative, use a little lemon zest.

Vermouth Slightly fortified wine infused with herbs, spices, etc. Many different flavors and sweetnesses.

Vinegar Always try to use wine vinegar. A good quality vinegar, like oil, makes all the difference, particularly in dressings and sauces. Tarragon vinegar is particularly flavorful.

Vine leaves If fresh ones are not available, don't bother. The leaves cured in brine are not as good.

Watercress Use in soups, salads or garnishes. It's best raw, though, as like chervil it loses its goodness during cooking. It contains iron, copper, calcium, potassium, and iodine.

Wine Use a good table wine for general cooking. A better wine gives better results for sauces.

Zucchini Low in calories, 90 percent water, rich in vitamin C. Often need to be sprinkled with a little salt to remove some of this water in order to cook properly. Do not forget to rinse well before using.

⚍ EQUIPMENT ⚎

SMALL EQUIPMENT

1 set of saucepans, cast-iron enameled or copper (approx. 5½, 6½, 7, 8 and 9 inches), complete with lids.

1 cocotte/casserole, 10-inch cast-iron enameled, complete with lid. Some come with a concave lid in which water can be placed to give extra moisture inside the dish (the hot steam inside the dish condenses into extra moisture on contact with the cold).

1 set of skillets, cast-iron — approx. 6½, 8 and 10 inches — enameled or not. Essential when braising/wet roasting meats or vegetables using both the top of the cooker and the oven.

1 8-inch heat dissipater, either a cast-iron plaque or a wire one which, when fitted between a low flame/burner and a saucepan or casserole, will considerably reduce the amount of heat permeating through to the food, therefore allowing the cooking to be more succulent and avoiding any burning or sticking at the bottom.

1 wok about 16 inches in diameter, either in carbon steel with a wooden handle which diffuses the heat very evenly, but requires special care to avoid rusting, or a lighter weight one, Teflon-coated with a flat bottom.

1 steamer, if not a component of the wok; either stainless steel or wood. The base should be large enough to contain at least 2 quarts water/liquid. A "*couscoussier*" is ideal — this has a large top and a narrow base, or invest in a steamer basket which fits inside a saucepan.

1 set of mixing bowls, approx. 3, 4, 6, 8 and 10 inches. Earthenware ones can be used at the table as well as in the kitchen, and can be fitted into a saucepan of water to use as a bain-marie. Stainless steel bowls are good too, but don't look as attractive on the table!

1 flat sieve made of stainless steel — essential for straining vegetables and rinsing them under the tap.

1 conical sieve — essential for puréeing or sieving those sauces full of skin and seeds, into a thin stream.

1 food mill — still the best piece of equipment ever invented. It is versatile (except for chopping) and does the job of a food processor or blender and strainer combined. Very useful for fruit with seeds or pits, for vegetables with skins and seeds.

1 salad/herb spinner — essential for cleaning and drying salads and herbs, as well as vegetables. A small easy-to-use version is available for herbs.

1 scale — preferably graduated from ½ ounce to 1 pound in ½-ounce gradations.

Look for one of the new electronic scales which are designed for dieters (the gradations are lower and more accurate).

1 fat separator — which is a pitcher with the spout starting at its base. When liquid is poured into it, the fat rises to the surface, leaving the useful — and healthy — part of the liquid at the bottom of the jug. Stop pouring when the fat reaches the spout. This is *vital* for Cuisine Santé!

1 measuring cup which will accommodate a conical sieve, through which sauces can be strained, which is also marked to measure liquids.

Miscellaneous:

2 balloon whisks, one of 8 inches, the other larger (about 16 inches) for use only in combination with a copper bowl.

2 wooden spoons.

2 wooden spatulas.

1 rubber spatula.

1 plastic dough scraper (corne) — useful for making pastry using the flat edge, and as a bowl cleaner using the rounded edge (like a rubber spatula).

1 slotted spoon.

1 ladle.

1 cheese slicer — slices cheese very thinly and make *Lichettes de Légumes* (see page 24).

2 peppermills, one containing a combination of white and black peppercorns and coriander seeds, the other containing *herbes de Provence*.

1 rock salt mill.

1 salt box with loose cooking salt.

ELECTRICAL EQUIPMENT

1 electric hand mixer — useful but not essential for beating egg whites; making salad dressings; mayonnaises, etc. Choose one with variable speeds.

1 food processor is very useful for chopping a *mirepoix* quickly and finely. Remember to run it only for a few seconds at a time when chopping, so as not to purée the food.

1 blender — better than a food processor for soups.

1 mini chopper/coffee mill — very useful for chopping herbs and grinding coffee beans.

1 plunger mill — combines well with a food processor and blender (choose either as both might be extravagant!)

1 ice cream machine — a good investment for easily prepared granités, sorbets, and ice creams. I could not be without it!

PASTRY MAKING EQUIPMENT

1 rolling pin, 20 inches long, without handles. Do not leave in water or it will warp and roll pastry unevenly.

3 tart pans, with removable bottoms — 8, 9½, 11 inches. All are not essential, and the 9½-inch one is most versatile.

6 tartlet molds of 3 inches and **6 oblong barquette molds** of 4 inches. Care for as above.

1 pie plate with straight edges, 7 inches in diameter and 1¼ inches deep. Care for and clean as for tart pan above.

1 timbale mold, 8 inches in diameter and 2 inches deep.

1 cake pan (génoise), Teflon coated, 7 inches in diameter, 2 inches deep.

1 oblong cake pan (useful also as roasting pan, Teflon coated, tin or stainless steel, 6 × 9½ inches and 2¼ inches deep.

2 pyrex loaf pans or terrine molds, one 4 × 8 inches and 2¼ inches deep, the other 5 × 10 inches and 2½–3 inches deep.

1 ring mold, 9 inches in diameter.

12 ramekin dishes, pyrex or china, 3¼ inches in diameter.

1 cooling rack, rectangular, 10 × 16 inches.

1 cooling rack, round, 11 inches in diameter.

1 set of assorted small cutters, aspic and pastry cutters in all shapes.

1 pastry brush, flat, ½ inch.

CUTTING EQUIPMENT

1 set of knives: carbon steel is the best, and easy to sharpen, but they need attention or they rust — don't put them in the dishwasher! Or stainless steel with a good sharpening tool. You'll need 1 each of 4, 6, 8 and 10-inch filleting knives, 6-inch boning knife, 1 zester and 1 decorator (or 1 "decozest" combining the two tools in one), 1 peeler, 1 6-inch metal spatula, 1 apple corer, 1 6-inch trussing needle, 1 6-inch larding needle. If using all carbon steel, buy a 4-inch stainless steel knife to use on acid food like citrus.

Techniques

In the following pages are illustrated and described many of the more complicated or characteristic techniques for preparation, cooking, mixing and garnishing, which recur throughout the book. Specific references to the individual techniques are given as necessary in the recipes.

Baking Blind

This is the best way to avoid a soggy tart or quiche crust. Line the tin with the rolled dough and prick lightly all over the bottom with a fork (to prevent the dough from rising). Cover the bottom with a circle of parchment paper (see page 29), and rest in the refrigerator for 10 minutes. Cover the paper with baking beans (any dried pulse, for instance kidney beans or peas) and bake for 10 minutes at the recommended temperature. Remove the beans and paper and continue baking until the bottom is well dried and starts to brown. Brush with egg wash (see below) to fill in the holes in the pricked pastry, and cook for 2 minutes. Repeat this once or twice until the pastry is well glazed.

Egg Washing

Egg wash is a versatile and edible kitchen glue! Mix a whole egg with 1 teaspoon of water in a ramekin with a fork. For a glossier look, add another yolk or use yolks only. Follow instructions for brushing it on

(with a pastry brush) in each recipe. Glazing a blind-baked pastry case is essential to prevent liquid added later from seeping through and making the pastry soggy.

Feuilletés
BUTTERFLY CASES

These cases make a wonderful presentation for a variety of fillings (see Feuilletés aux Champignons, *page 72, for baking and filling instructions).*

1 Roll out the *Pâte Feuilletée*, trim to a 16-inch square, and cut into sixteen 4-inch squares.

2 Fold each square in half diagonally and cut through the two layers from the outer edges to the point. Leave the point uncut on both sides.

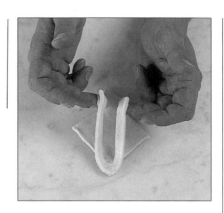

3 Open out the whole square and egg wash the edges lightly. Lift the two cut corners and bring together.

4 Pass one corner under the other to meet the opposite corner, and press the layers together to seal. Mold the outside edges together with the back of a knife.

Poaching Eggs

Bring a saucepan of water to the boil, adding about ⅓ cup white vinegar per 2½ cups water. Break an egg into a small cup and drop the egg gently into the slowly simmering water. Repeat the operation, but increase the heat slightly each time another egg is added. The water should be simmering all the time. If the white does not cling immediately to the yolk, help it along with a wooden spoon and increase the heat. Cook for 3 minutes, then lift out with a slotted spoon. Check for doneness by pressing with a finger: it should be soft for a runny yolk, firmer for a semi-hard yolk. Serve immediately or transfer to a bowl of cold water to stop cooking. Poached eggs can keep in water, in the refrigerator, for up to 3 days. To reheat, trim off the excess white and plunge into a bowl of hot water for 2–3 minutes, then drain and serve. Poached eggs can be used in various ways with different sauces — as starters or light supper dishes (*Oeufs Pochés à la Chantilly* and *Oeufs Pochés Colombo*, pages 63 and 55).

Boning a Round Fish

*R*ound fish include cod, mullet, trout (pictured below) and salmon.

1 First, slit open the belly from the head to the rear. Remove viscera and any blood and rinse well.

2 Using a knife, ease all the bones away from the fillets on each side, working from backbone to belly.

3 Using kitchen shears, snip open the flesh from anus to tail, and snip *through* the backbone at the tail. Pull this up gently and pull toward the head. Snip at the head and remove the backbone.

4 Cut through the skin in between the two fillets to remove the dorsal fins from the fish, then trim off all the other fins and discard.

5 Finally, feel for any missed small bones with your fingers, and remove with tweezers.

Dégorger

This is a term meaning to soak a food in cold water to remove impurities. Sweetbreads, for instance, are soaked to remove blood and to whiten them. Fish bones, too, are cleaned in this way before going into a *fumet*: put them in a bowl and run cold water from the tap over them for 20 minutes.

Skinning and Filleting a Flat Fish

*F*lat fish include flounder, turbot and Dover sole (pictured below).

1   First, lay the fish white side down on your work surface. Using a sharp filleting knife with a flexible blade, cut through the dark skin at the tail, and then, starting from the tail, carefully scrape the skin off the flesh, working toward the head. Ensure that the whole of the tail skin is lifted.

2   Holding the tail with a cloth in your left hand, grab the flap of skin with your right (using the cloth) and pull the skin off toward the head.

3   When the skin reaches the head, pull down (taking care around the mouth) the other side of the fish, thus removing the skin in one movement.

4   To remove fillets, cut next to the backbone from head to tail and insert the tip of the knife between bones and flesh on one side of the fish at the head (see step 1 below). Slowly work the knife down toward the tail, keeping it as close to the bones as possible. Turn the fish around and remove the second fillet, then turn the fish over and remove the remaining two fillets.

Stuffing a Flat Fish

*I*f stuffing a whole flat fish, as in Sole Farcie Soufflée *(see page 86), do not remove the fillets.*

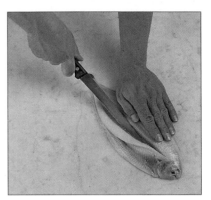

1   Cut along the backbone of the skinned fish as above, and free the flesh from the bones — but keep the outside edges of the fillets attached.

2   Fold the fish in half, with the open fillet side up, until the backbone snaps. Ease the bones away from the bottom fillets along the length of the fish with a filleting knife. Snip through the backbone at head and tail with scissors, and remove.

3 Holding the pastry bag in your left hand, fold back a cuff, and then fill the bag with *mousseline* filling.

4 Unfold the cuff and force the filling down in the bag with your right hand.

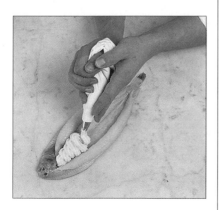

5 Pipe the *mousseline* carefully into the opening in the fish, and continue as directed in the recipe.

Poaching a Fish

*P*oaching is particularly good for large fish such as salmon, as pictured below. Properly poached, a salmon will not fall apart, so it can be cooked the day before and served cold. Either follow the instructions here or those in the recipe for Saumon à la Riga (see page 90).

1 If your fish is particularly large, truss the head so that it holds its shape and the mouth remains closed. Criss-cross a length of string over the head, under the chin and behind the gills. Put the fish on the rack in a fish poacher.

2 Either prepare enough *court-bouillon* (see page 32) for the size of your fish, or put 2–3 sliced

carrots, a couple of roughly chopped leeks, a leafy stalk of celery cut in chunks, a little salt, 6 black peppercorns, a bay leaf and a pinch of thyme into a large pan. Cover with about 2½–4 quarts water and bring rapidly to the boil. Simmer for 30 minutes, cool a little, then strain through a conical sieve over the fish.

3 Pound together a handful of black peppercorns, a teaspoon each of fennel, coriander and caraway seeds and sea salt using a pestle and mortar. Fill the poacher with white wine and/or water, according to the recipe, so that the fish is completely covered with liquid. Add the spice mixture from the mortar.

4 Add a sliced half lemon, 2–3 bay leaves, some parsley sprigs and 2–3 large dill sprigs.

(continued)

Poaching (continued)

5 Put the poacher on the burner and bring to the boil.

6 As soon as it boils, remove from the heat and cover with a clean dish towel.

7 Secure the dish towel with the lid. If you want to serve the fish cold, leave off the heat for 12—15 hours in a cool place. The fish will poach in the stock. Lift the rack with the fish on it from the poacher and let it drain for an hour. The fish is then ready to be prepared for serving.

8 If you want to serve the fish hot, return it to the heat as soon as you have put the lid on the poacher (see above). Simmer for a further 5–6 minutes. Be very careful to ensure that no part of the towel hangs near the heat source. Remove the poacher from the heat and let the fish "cook" for a further 20 minutes. Remove the rack and let the fish drain for 2–3 minutes. The fish is then ready to be prepared for serving.

Boning a Chicken

1 Place the chicken breast up on a chopping board and insert a large knife inside the chicken and cut through, downward on one side of the backbone.

2 Turn the chicken over, and finish cutting next to the backbone to open up the bird.

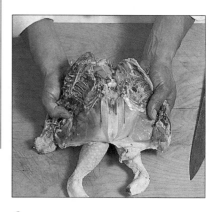

3 Spread the bird open so that the breastbones are exposed and point upward.

4 Cut out the backbone, including the tail.

5 Cut through the thighbone joints and remove the bone attached to the thighs.

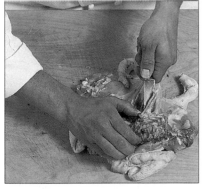

6 Insert a small knife under the rib cage and remove all the bones on both sides.

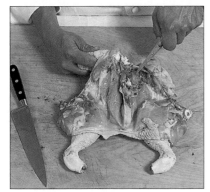

7 Ease the joints of the collarbone and remove the wishbone carefully so as not to damage the flesh.

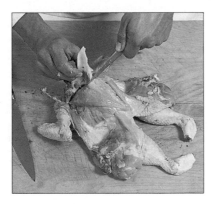

8 Ease the flesh from the breastbone on both sides and gently pull away the breastbone.

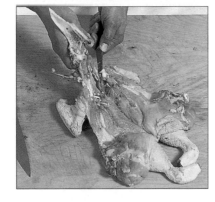

9 Completely free the breastbone and collarbone. Search all over with your fingers for any remaining bones (apart from thighs and drumsticks) and remove.

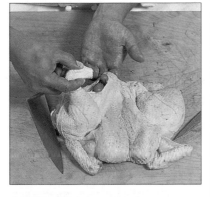

10 Turn the chicken over, pierce a hole through the skin near the thigh and tuck the drumstick through the hole. The

chicken is now ready for marinating (see *Poulet Grillé au Citron Vert*, page 134) or for stuffing.

11 For stuffing, have the chicken breast side toward you and insert two fingers between the skin and the flesh to ease open a space for stuffing. (Be careful not to break the skin in between the two breasts.) Separate the skin and flesh of the thighs and drumsticks and stuff these in the same way (see *Poulet Farci Fendu au Four*, page 131).

Deglazing

To deglaze means to add a liquid (usually wine, alcohol or stock) to a hot pan after meat or fish has been seared in it. The liquid dissolves the juices and crusty bits that form in the bottom of the pan and transfers the flavor to the liquid.

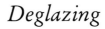

Disjointing a Chicken

*D*isjointing a chicken is simple once you know how, and it is a very useful technique to learn. You no longer need to rely on the butcher — and it is cheaper to buy whole chickens than portions.

1   Place the whole chicken on a chopping board, with legs nearest you, and grasp the left leg in your left hand. With a sharp knife cut through the skin, and on toward the joint.

2   Cut the white tendons between thigh and body, twist the joint, and then pull the leg free. Turn the bird over and repeat on the other side.

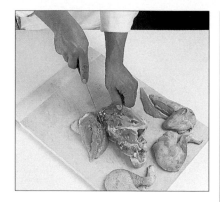

3   To remove the breasts, carefully cut down each side of the breastbone using a sharp knife. Cut along the breastbone toward the wishbone and right down to the wing joint. Cut down through this to free both breast and wing. Repeat on the other side of the bird.

4   Cut the wingbone and the wing tips from the carcass and use for stock. Remove the fillets from the breasts and cut the breasts in half. Divide the legs into thighs and drumsticks by bending each leg back until the skin is taut, then cutting right down the middle.

Boning a Turkey Thigh

*T*his is vital for a recipe such as Gigot de Dinde Farcie (*see page 142*).

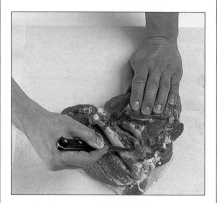

1   Lay the turkey thigh on a board and cut through the skin and flesh lengthwise to expose the bone. Cut in next to the bone to release the flesh. Remove the bone, and any sinews or tendons.

2   Trim any ragged pieces from the meat so that the bulk of the meat is as flat as possible. Use the trimmings in the stuffing.

Disjointing and Boning a Rabbit

*T*he most important thing to remember when disjointing a rabbit is not to cut through the bones if possible. The bones splinter very easily and are extremely sharp.

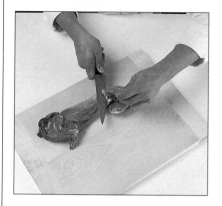

1   Lay the rabbit on a board and work the blade of a sharp knife around each of the four leg joints. Separate each leg from the body.

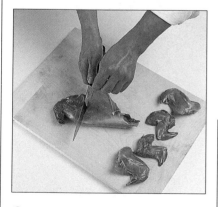

2   Cut the rabbit in two where the saddle meets the ribs. (Reserve the rib cage for stock.)

3   Cut away the two small fillets from the saddle. Then bone the saddle by easing the flesh away from the saddle bone. Use a sharp knife, but be careful not to cut through the flesh.

4   Bone the four legs as described in boning a turkey thigh (see above). Keep the bones for stock.

Sweating

This is a method used mainly for vegetables, so that they can cook in their own moisture without browning, and with hardly any fat.

Start by preheating the cooking vessel slowly over low heat. Add a very little fat (usually 1 teaspoon butter or olive oil), and then the prepared vegetables. Toss well and cover immediately to keep in the moisture. If more than one vegetable is to be sweated, add them one at a time, starting with those with the highest water content (usually onions). It is essential to cover the pan, as it is the steam created inside which cooks the vegetables. Toss once in a while, keeping the cover on, and always keep the heat on very low. The sweating is finished when all ingredients are soft but not browned.

Braising/ Wet Roasting

This method combines the moisture-retaining quality of braising with the browning quality of roasting, and is more usually used for meat. First, season with a little salt and pepper and then sear very quickly in a thoroughly preheated skillet, in a little oil. This retains the moisture, and browns the outside. Then put the meat aside, wipe the skillet and put it back on the heat. Sweat a *mirepoix* in the skillet, then deglaze with stock and/or white wine. Put the meat back in the skillet with the *mirepoix* and place, uncovered, into the oven. During cooking, any fat in the meat, will run down into the juices; these should be degreased and reduced before serving.

Washing Herbs and Leaves

All herbs and leaves should be washed this way before use. Place in a bowl of cold water and leave to soak for 5 minutes. This should be enough time for the grit and dirt to settle on the bottom of the bowl. Pick leaves or sprigs up delicately so as not to disturb the grit, and repeat the procedure once or twice with clean water.

Bouquet Garni

A fresh bouquet garni *is called for in a great number of traditional recipes and, although packaged versions are available, the flavor is not nearly as good.*

Cut the green of a leek — or the whole leek if you like — in half lengthwise. Remove a few center leaves from each side to make a groove, then fill one groove with about 10 black or white peppercorns, cracked. Top with some parsley sprigs, a thyme sprig and a bay leaf, and cover with the other half of the leek. Tie together with string.

Chiffonade

*C*hiffonade *is a word describing vegetable leaves cut into fine strips or ribbons — especially spinach (pictured below), lettuce and sorrel.*

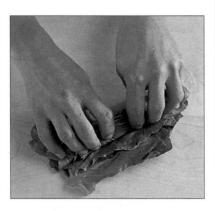

1   To cut spinach into *chiffonade*, wash it well first, then drain. Remove the stalks. Lay several leaves at a time on a board, and loosely roll them up into a cigar shape.

2   Holding the shape firmly with one hand, slice into strips crosswise with a sharp knife.

Chopping an Onion

*I*t *may be something you do every day, but this is the* correct *way to do it.*

1   First peel the onion *without* trimming the root and shoot ends. Cut in half lengthwise through the root then place one half, cut side down, on a board. Slice from the root end to the stem with a sharp knife, but do not cut *through* the root.

2   Keeping the onion in same position, cut in toward the root with the knife, parallel to the cutting board, still not cutting through the root.

3 Cut down through the onion to form cubes. The size of the cubes will depend on the width between cuts.

Peeling Tomatoes

Pull off the stalk and cut around this end — with a small sharp-pointed knife, and remove it. Cut a shallow criss-cross on the other end of the tomato and plunge into a saucepan of boiling water. Leave for 10–30 seconds (the time depends on the size and ripeness of the tomatoes), then remove immediately with a slotted spoon to a bowl full of extremely cold water. The difference in temperature will help removal of the skins and preserve the firmness of the tomato.

Skinning Peppers

Preheat the broiler and cut out the stem end of the peppers. Remove the pith and seeds, then broil the peppers until their skins brown and blister. Wrap in a wet dish towel or place in a plastic bag, where they will steam slightly, and cool. When almost cold, the skins will peel off very easily and the peppers will be nearly cooked.

Crushing Garlic

This is the best way to extract all the flavor from garlic.

Peel a clove by crushing it first with the palm of your hand on the counter. Remove the inner green "seed" (which is difficult to digest) and place the white flesh inside a garlic press. Squeeze the handles together over a plate, distribute the remains evenly inside the press and squeeze again. Remove shreds from the press and add to the dish.

Duxelle of Mushrooms

Heat a skillet and sweat a chopped shallot in 1 teaspoon grapeseed or safflower oil for 1 minute. Add a crushed garlic clove and sweat for 1 minute longer. Add the finely chopped mushrooms (according to the recipe) and season with a little salt and pepper and 1 teaspoon lemon juice. Place over high heat, tossing well, and when the juices of the mushrooms start to run, reduce the heat to medium. Allow to reduce until nearly dry, then add 1 tablespoon tomato paste. Stir well over the heat for 1 minute and then reserve on a plate.

Cutting Vegetables

Vegetables for any dish should always be cut into uniformly sized pieces so that they cook evenly. Vegetables cut in the ways described here also make attractive garnishes for sauces and soups. Always wash the vegetables well before use, and reserve any trimmings for stocks, sauces, mirepoix, *etc.*

JULIENNE

Julienne *vegetables are mostly used for garnishing. Many vegetables and some meats can be cut into* julienne, *or long, thin strips resembling matchsticks.*

First, wash and trim the vegetable, then square off and cut lengthwise into thin ⅛-inch slices (discard the rounded outside slices). Slice lengthwise into tiny matchsticks and cut in half if necessary. The vegetable *julienne* pictured here are (clockwise), carrot, asparagus, turnip, zucchini and leek.

BRUNOISE

Brunoise *vegetables make attractive garnishes for soups, particularly if made with many different colored vegetables.*

Cut the vegetables into *julienne* as above, and then chop the matchsticks into very fine dice. The vegetable *brunoise*, pictured here are (clockwise), carrot, asparagus, turnip, zucchini and leek.

PAYSANNE

Paysanne *vegetables can also be used to garnish soups.*

Trim and cut the vegetables into ⅛-inch slices as described for *julienne* above. Then cut into small squares. The vegetable *paysanne* pictured here are (clockwise), carrot, zucchini, leek, turnip and asparagus.

MIREPOIX

A mirepoix *is a mixture of onion, carrot and celery which is used in many meat and fish dishes to enhance the flavor, and as a bed upon which to braise meat or fish.*

Mirepoix can be roughly (*paysanne*) or finely (*brunoise*) chopped, depending on the recipe, but it is usually 1 part onion to 1 part carrot and 1 part celery.

Lichettes de Légumes

Simply peel or prepare the vegetables according to the recipe, and drag them across the back of a sharp cheese slicer or vegetable mandolin. The vegetable *lichettes* pictured here are zucchini, carrot and turnip.

Turned Vegetables

These are vegetable chunks carved into barrel shapes which make attractive garnishes.

Cut larger prepared and peeled vegetables (like potatoes, turnips and carrots) into fairly uniformly sized rectangles, and then carve with a sharp knife to a rounded barrel or oval shape. For large zucchini, cut into quarters lengthwise, then carve as shown. You can use any discarded trimmings in stock, or for a vegetable purée or soup.

Onion Leaves

*T*hese are easy to prepare and make a delicious and unusual casing for vegetable or meat fillings (see Oignons Farcis, pages 60 and 62).

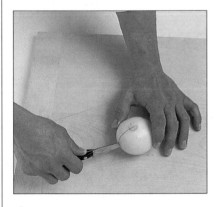

1 Make a single cut into a whole peeled onion from the stalk to the root end, cutting right into the core of the onion.

2 Place the onion in boiling water and simmer for 10 minutes, then refresh in cold water. Cut off the root end with a sharp knife and discard, then separate the onion into leaves.

3 Chop the heart of the onion to use in the filling, then stuff some filling into each leaf. Curl the leaves around the filling to close.

Garnishes

CROÛTONS

To make 2 cups, stack ½-inch slices of bread and trim off the crusts. Cut into ½-inch cubes and place on a baking sheet. Toast in a preheated broiler, shaking the sheet occasionally to turn the cubes and brown every side. These are much healthier than those fried in fat.

GLACÉ MINT LEAVES

These are ideal as a garnish for a fruit dessert or sorbet. Dip the leaves in a little beaten egg white and dip again in a bowl with either granulated, or confectioners' sugar. Let stand in a cool dry place, or in the freezer, to set for 3 minutes.

CAPER FLOWERS

To make a caper flower garnish, simply peel back the leaves of the caper very carefully. These flowers are an attractive garnish for many fish dishes.

ONION FLOWERS

*S*mall onions and green onions can both be cut to blossom forth into flower shapes.

Take a small peeled onion and stand it on its root. Make a series of narrow vertical cuts into the onion toward the root, but do not cut through the root. Turn the onion 90°, and make another series of cuts at right angles to the first ones. Again, be careful not to cut through the root. Place in ice water for about 1 hour to open out the onion flowers.

For green onions, remove the root and trim off most of the green. Either cut the bulb alone, as the onion above, or cut the bulb and the green stalk, leaving the middle section uncut. Leave in ice water as above.

TOMATO ROSES

Take a firm tomato and a small knife. Starting from the end opposite the stalk, and working around the tomato, peel off the skin carefully to make a continuous strip of skin about ½-inch wide. Start from the end first cut and curl the skin (flesh-side inward) into a rosebud, and finally into a fully-opened rose.

Quenelles

Y ou can shape almost any kind of soft food — a vegetable purée (as pictured here), ice cream, sorbet or meringue — with the aid of 2 tablespoons.

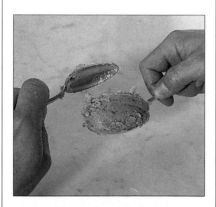

1 Take a spoonful of the mixture in one of the spoons. Place the second spoon over the

mixture in the first and slide it between the mixture and the bowl of the first spoon. Scoop the mixture toward you to transfer it to the second spoon. Continue until the mixture is well shaped.

2 Transfer to the plate by inserting one spoon underneath the mixture on the other spoon, and easing off gently.

Fruit Garnishes

ZESTING A CITRUS FRUIT

Either use a zester to remove very fine strips, or use a potato peeler to remove larger *julienne* strips.

SCORING LEMONS (OR CUCUMBERS)

Use a citrus scorer or decorator, or a cannelator, and cut along the sides of an unpeeled lemon (or cucumber) at regular intervals. When the lemon (or cucumber) is sliced, the grooves create a decorative effect (see lemon below).

LEMON GARNISHES

A selection of various lemon garnishes for meat, fish or salad dishes (clockwise from top): a wedge of lemon, the peel slightly separated from the flesh top and bottom, slotted onto the side of an individual salad bowl; a half lemon which has been scored, with the scoring tied in a knot, inserted in the center of the cut face; a lemon twist made from a slice of scored lemon, cut halfway through its diameter and twisted; a half lemon with a knot of peel — remove a narrow strip from around the diameter of a lemon half in one continuous piece, leaving ½ inch attached, and tie in a knot; a lemon basket — cut a thin slice off the bottom for stability and mark a ½-inch wide strip from the equator over the top of the fruit for a handle. Slice away the wedges on each side of the handle and remove the flesh to reveal the handle.

Cutting a Pineapple

T hese are just two of the ways in which to prepare pineapple decoratively, to serve on its own or to use in Ananas Princesse *(see page 180) and* Sorbet à l'Ananas *(see page 173).*

ANANAS PRINCESSE

Cut the leafy top off the pineapple and reserve. Cut a thin slice off the bottom for stability but do not expose the flesh. Run a long, sharp and thin-bladed knife all the way down from the top to within 1 inch of the bottom of the pineapple, between the flesh and the shell. Continue to cut all around the top. Insert the knife through one side of the shell, about 1 inch up from the base. Slice horizontally inside the shell, then remove the knife, turn the knife over and re-insert into the same hole. Slice across in the opposite direction, trying not to enlarge the hole in the shell too much. Repeat the operation on the other side of the pineapple and, if you cut in the right places, when you invert the pineapple, a cylinder of flesh will slide out! Remove the eyes and slice the flesh into rings and replace, in their original order, in the shell. Dust the leafy crown with confectioners' sugar and place on top. By using this method, the fruit does not become dry before serving.

SORBET À L'ANANAS

Cut the pineapple into quarters through the leafy top. With a small sharp knife, cut between the flesh and skin at a good distance from the skin to avoid the eyes (check there are no eyes before continuing). Cut across the width of the quarters in thick slices. For an attractive presentation, push the slices outward alternately to right and left.

Sectioning Citrus Fruit

This technique is ideal for preparing fruit salads and desserts (see Gratin d'Oranges à la Maltaise, *page 167).*

1 Cut a slice off the top and bottom of the fruit to make it stable, then cut down the side of the fruit, to remove the peel and pith, following the curve of the fruit with the knife.

2 Holding the peeled fruit in your left hand over a bowl, slice down as closely as possible between the membrane and flesh on both sides of each section. Let the freed sections and juice drop into the bowl, then squeeze in the juice from the remaining membrane.

Bain-marie

A *bain-marie* is a double boiler consisting of a pan of water for the base with another pan on top in which to gently cook, reheat or to keep warm a fragile substance like a sauce. Often, a roasting pan filled with hot water, into which a bowl or pan of food is placed, will work as well.

To Purée

When puréeing a soup, for instance, always put the solid ingredients into the machine first, using a slotted spoon, then pour in enough liquid just to cover them. Purée, adding the remaining liquid in a steady stream while the machine is running.

Correcting a Sauce

MAYONNAISE OR VINAIGRETTE: If either has curdled, place 1 teaspoon Dijon mustard (as an alternative to an egg yolk) in another bowl. Slowly add the curdled mixture, whisking vigorously.

YOGURT SAUCE: If this has curdled, purée in a food processor for 1 minute.

Folding

When folding mixtures of different consistencies as for a soufflé, first mix a spoonful of the thinner mixture into the stiffer one to lighten and thin it. Then put all the thinner mixture on top of the stiffer one and gently cut, scoop and turn the mixture over, using a rubber spatula, while rotating the bowl with the other hand. Never *over* fold — a soufflé mixture will lose all its lightness.

Papillotes

A papillote *is a well-sealed envelope of parchment paper, usually used for meat or fish. The advantage of cooking with* papillotes *is that they concentrate the aromas and flavors, and the meat or fish cooks in its own juices. Fold a 16-inch square of parchment paper in half, cut a half-heart shape from it and unfold.*

1   Open the paper and place all the recipe ingredients on the half of the heart nearer you, next to the crease. Spread a stiff flour and water paste in a ½-inch border along the edge of one side of the heart.

2   Fold in the far half toward you. Starting from the broader end, fold over the pasted border twice to seal, making little tucks around the curve.

3   Brush oil over the top of the *papillote* and place, oiled side up, in the oven.

Chop Frills

*T*hese are used to garnish the ends of chops or poultry bones.

1   Cut parchment paper into strips 10 inches long and 5 inches wide. Fold in half lengthwise. Cut into the folded edges at ⅛-inch intervals about halfway through the width.

2   Unfold, and open out flat, pressing against a table or counter edge to erase the fold.

3   Re-fold inside out, lining up the edges, then roll around your finger. Secure with a stiff flour and water paste or with tape.

Parchment Paper Circles

*T*hese are used to line the bottoms of cake pans for greater ease of turning out and to line the bottom of a tart or quiche so that the baking beans do not touch the dough.

1 Start with a square of paper considerably larger than the diameter of the pan. Fold it in half diagonally, then in half again, and again. Continue folding over from the center point of the square until you can no longer fold the paper.

2 Measure the radius of the tin against the paper holding the point of the folded paper in the *center* and mark the location of the pan edge. Cut along the mark, then open the paper into a circle.

Napkin Gondola

*T*his is the best way of presenting large, round fish, for instance, Saumon à la Riga (see page 90). You will need three large napkins.

1 Lay a napkin flat on a flat surface and cover with a square of foil. Fold in half horizontally, folding away from you.

2 Fold one side into the center of the fold, followed by the other side, to form a large triangle. From the point, fold twice more in the same way on each side.

3 Bring the two sides together for the last fold.

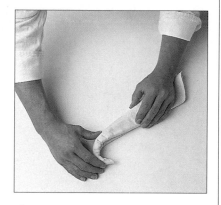

4 Hold the napkin with your left hand and shape the point to form the curved end of the gondola.

5 Repeat with a second napkin and lay them at opposite ends of a platter. Place a third napkin folded into quarters in the center.

STOCKS, SAUCES AND DOUGHS

French cuisine is built upon several important bases: stocks, sauces and doughs. Usually these traditional building blocks have been very high in fat, but here we have shown you how to make delicious alternatives that are much lighter. In the sauces, we have replaced cream either partially or completely with Greek yogurt, and the doughs use smaller quantities of butter, which can be further reduced by using semi-hard polyunsaturated sunflower oil. Our stocks not only use less fat than traditional recipes, but are then left overnight, and skimmed of the fat that forms on the top.

Fonds de Volaille

CHICKEN STOCK

There is no good cuisine which does not rely on good stocks. This basic stock is used in most main course and starter recipes and is a vital ingredient to prepare regularly and freeze as recommended below. For a rich, flavorful stock, never skimp on the recipe.

Whenever you have a chicken carcass, clean it well and discard all the fat along with the tail. Place it in the freezer for later use or prepare a stock immediately. In order to ensure a regular supply of carcasses, prepare healthy recipes such as Poulet Farci Fendu au Four *or* Poulet Sauté à l'Estragon *(see pages 131 and 135) frequently.*

This stock freezes well. Place in ice cube trays or small containers to freeze. Store the blocks of frozen stock in freezer bags ready to be used in small quantities when needed. Most stocks can be kept for up to 2 days in the refrigerator.

GLUTEN FREE
MAKES 3½ CUPS

1 chicken carcass plus neck and wing tips, washed
mirepoix *(1 carrot, 1 onion and 1 celery stalk)*
1 quart cold water
salt
freshly ground black pepper
1 bouquet garni
1 bay leaf
1 sprig thyme

1   Drain the chicken bones, then cut into small pieces and place in a saucepan.
2   Place the roughly chopped *mirepoix* in the saucepan with all the remaining ingredients.
3   Bring to the boil slowly, skimming off the impurities as they rise to the surface.
4   Simmer, partially covered, over low heat for 1 hour. Frequent skimming is very important for the clarity of the stock. Cover and leave to cool, then refrigerate overnight.
5   The next day, remove the layer of fat set on the surface. Bring to the boil again and skim off the impurities. Simmer for 5 minutes, then strain.

Court-Bouillon
VEGETABLE STOCK WITH WINE

A court-bouillon *is a wine-flavored vegetable stock. It is very useful for poaching or steaming fish. For vegetarians, it is particularly valuable, as is the plain vegetable stock following, which should be used whenever a stock is called for in the various vegetarian recipes in the book. Don't use this* court-bouillon *as the basis for a reduced sauce, as the wine will make it too acid.*

This stock can be frozen, like Fonds de Volaille *on page 31.*

GLUTEN FREE
MAKES 3½ CUPS

mirepoix *(2 carrots, 2 onions and*
   2 celery stalks)
1 cup white wine
3 cups cold water
salt
freshly ground black pepper
1 bouquet garni

1   Place the finely chopped *mirepoix* in a saucepan with the wine, water and the remaining ingredients.
2   Bring to the boil slowly, skimming off all the impurities as they rise to the surface.
3   Simmer over low heat for 20 minutes. Cover and cool before straining.

Bouillon de Légumes
VEGETABLE STOCK

T his stock, as useful as the court-bouillon *for vegetables, is also delicious and beneficial when used as a soup. Drink it, minus the vegetables or with them puréed into the liquid, to help a cold, an upset stomach, or general malaise.*

This stock can be frozen, like Fonds de Volaille *on page 31.*

GLUTEN FREE
MAKES 3½ CUPS

mirepoix *(4 carrots, 1 onion,*
   2 celery stalks)
1 quart cold water
salt
finely ground black pepper
1 bouquet garni
1 small bunch fines herbes,
   finely chopped

TO SERVE AS SOUP
¼ cup vermicelli or wild rice
½ cup cream and/or ¼ cup
   Greek yogurt
fines herbes, *finely chopped*

1   Place the finely chopped *mirepoix* in a saucepan with the water, a little salt and pepper, the *bouquet garni*, and the bunch of *fines herbes*.
2   Bring to the boil slowly, skimming off the impurities as they rise to the surface.
3   Simmer gently over low heat for 20 minutes, then cover and cool before using. Strain the stock when cold.

TO SERVE If serving as a clear soup, strain the stock, bring to the boil and cook the vermicelli or wild rice in it. For a richer soup, purée the strained vegetables and return to the stock with the cream and/or yogurt. The cream or yogurt could also be replaced by milk. Sprinkle with *fines herbes* just before serving.

RIGHT *Fumet de Poisson*

Fumet de Poisson
FISH STOCK

*T*here are several ways of making a traditional fumet *or fish stock. In one method, the vegetables and bones are sweated in butter, then wine and water are added and the mixture is simmered for 20 minutes. This gives a very good stock, but one which is often cloudy. The version which follows does not use any fat at all, therefore the vegetables are not sweated. The flavor is slightly different as a result, but the fumet is not as cloudy — always better when used for a sauce. The proportion of wine used could be increased, up to equal parts water and wine, resulting in a more acid stock, not particularly advisable if the stock has to be reduced for a sauce.*

This stock can be frozen, like Fonds de Volaille *on page 31.*

GLUTEN FREE
MAKES 3½ CUPS

1   Wash the fish bones well, leaving them, if possible, for 20 minutes in a bowl under cold running water.
2   Place the finely chopped *mirepoix* in a saucepan with the bones, the *bouquet garni*, a pinch of salt and a little pepper. Add the white wine and water.
3   Bring to a bare simmer over low heat (this can take up to 15 minutes), skimming off the impurities as they rise to the surface. Simmer slowly for 20 minutes, then remove from the heat and let stand to cool. Strain the stock through a sieve lined with cheesecloth.

2¼ lb. fish bones (sole, flounder, turbot)
mirepoix (1 carrot, 1 onion and 1 celery stalk)
1 bouquet garni
salt
freshly ground black pepper
1 cup white wine
3 cups cold water

Sauce Diable
DEVILED SAUCE

*T*his sauce is an ideal accompaniment for braised vegetables, or for robust main course meats or fish. As it's quite spicy, don't use it with delicately flavored food. If serving with fish, replace the chicken stock used in the tomato sauce with half fish stock, half vegetable stock.

To make a delicious soup, double the quantity of the sauce and thin it with additional stock.

GLUTEN FREE
SERVES 4

1 recipe Sauce à la Tomate *(see page 36)*
1 hot chili pepper, washed and seeded
4 sweet red peppers, washed and seeded
4 shallots, peeled and finely chopped
½ cup white wine
¼ cup cold water
1 tbsp. tarragon vinegar
salt
cayenne pepper
freshly ground black pepper

1   While preparing the tomato sauce, chop the chili pepper and one of the red peppers and add them to sweat with the other ingredients.
2   Place the shallots in a saucepan with the wine, water, vinegar, a pinch each of salt and cayenne, and some pepper. Bring to the boil over low heat and reduce until only about 2 tablespoons of liquid are left.
3   Meanwhile, seed the remaining sweet peppers. Broil until black and blistered and skin them, as described on page 23.
4   Purée two of the peppers. Chop the third one finely and reserve. Add the pepper purée to the reduced shallot mixture and cook slowly without burning for 10 minutes to thicken the purée. Add the chopped pepper.
5   Press the tomato sauce through a conical sieve into the pepper sauce. Bring to the boil and simmer for 5 minutes. Adjust the seasoning if necessary.

Sauce Calypso
CALYPSO SAUCE

A delicious sauce, reminiscent of the commercially famous "Thousand Island" dressing, which is, in fact, a traditional haute cuisine sauce! Prepare it in this way and you will never want to buy a ready-made variety again! It can be used as a salad dressing, with poached eggs or with a shrimp cocktail, for which the sauce was originally designed. It is lighter than a normal mayonnaise sauce because we have replaced some of the oil with Greek yogurt, and we have used only one egg yolk instead of three.

GLUTEN FREE
SERVES 4

1   Let all the ingredients reach room temperature before beginning.

2   In a bowl, mix together the vinegar, a dash each of Tabasco and Worcestershire sauce, ketchup, tomato paste, a pinch of salt and some pepper. Add the egg yolk and garlic and whisk in well.

3   Pour the oil into the mixture very slowly, a few drops at a time at first, whisking continuously. As the sauce starts to thicken, the oil can be poured in a little more quickly.

4   Add the yogurt, by spoonfuls, mixing it in delicately, and flavor with the cognac. Correct the seasoning if necessary.

2 tbsp. tarragon vinegar
Tabasco sauce
Worcestershire sauce
1 tbsp. tomato ketchup
1 tsp. tomato paste
salt
freshly ground black pepper
1 egg yolk
1 garlic clove, peeled and crushed
⅔ cup grapeseed or safflower oil
¼ cup Greek yogurt
1 tbsp. cognac

Sauce Vinaigrette
SALAD DRESSING

T his is the basic salad dressing we always use. Prepared once a week, it keeps well in a large screw-topped jar. All you need to do is shake the bottle well before using, and place a small amount of the dressing in the bottom of the salad bowl. Layer the various ingredients for the salad on top. Toss just before serving.

GLUTEN FREE
MAKES 2 CUPS

1   Place the mustard, salt, a generous amount of pepper and vinegar in the jar. Close and shake to combine the ingredients well.

2   Add the shallots and garlic to the jar. Dry the herbs well, then chop them finely and add to the jar.

3   Pour in all the oil, close the jar again and shake well for 2 minutes. Let stand to marinate for at least 20 minutes before using, and remember to shake again before pouring into the salad bowl.

4   Alternatively, the dressing can be made in a food processor. Process the shallots, garlic and herbs for 30 seconds, then add the vinegar, mustard and seasoning. Process again for 30 seconds. With the machine running, pour in the oil. Process for another minute and store in a jar.

5   For daily use, just shake well before using.

3 tbsp. Dijon mustard
½ tsp. sea salt
freshly ground black pepper
½ cup tarragon vinegar
4 shallots, finely chopped
2 garlic cloves, peeled and crushed
½ cup fines herbes, washed
1¼ cups grapeseed or safflower oil
¼ cup olive oil

LEFT *Sauce Vinaigrette*

Sauce à la Tomate

TOMATO SAUCE

*T*his tomato sauce has not been modified much for Cuisine Santé. The traditional recipe contains a lot more oil and uses flour to thicken it, but we use only the pulp of the tomatoes. If available, add some fresh basil at the end of the cooking.

This tomato sauce can be used to accompany a gratin of vegetables, cooked meats or, more traditionally, serve it with home-made pasta garnished with a little grated Parmesan cheese. This sauce takes longer to make than a simple *coulis*, so make a large amount at a time and freeze or can part of it, ready for last-minute use.

GLUTEN FREE
SERVES 4

1tsp. olive oil
mirepoix (1 onion, 1 carrot and 1 celery stalk)
1 garlic clove, peeled and crushed
1tbsp. tomato paste
1/2 cup white wine
1quart Fonds de Volaille *or* Bouillon de Légumes *(see pages 31 and 32)*
1lb. tomatoes, washed and quartered
salt
freshly ground black pepper
1 bouquet garni
herbes de Provence

1   Heat the oil in a heavy saucepan and sweat the finely chopped *mirepoix* over low heat, covered, stirring occasionally. It should not color. Add the garlic and sweat for 1 minute. Add the tomato paste, stir well and cook it for a minute longer. Then add the white wine and reduce until nearly dry.

2   Add the stock, tomatoes, 2 pinches of salt, some pepper and the *bouquet garni*. Stir well and bring to the boil over medium heat, skimming off the impurities as they rise to the surface. Add a pinch of the *herbes de Provence*, stir and cover. Simmer gently for 20 minutes, then remove the lid and simmer 20 minutes longer, skimming occasionally.

3   Allow the sauce to cool for an hour, then press through a conical sieve. If too thin, reduce over medium heat.

Sauce au Curry

CURRY SAUCE

*T*his sauce is wonderful with simply prepared fish or poultry — steamed, poached or cooked in papillote — or with a baked vegetable. A good stock (fumet *or* court-bouillon *for fish, and* fonds de volaille *for poultry) is essential.*

GLUTEN FREE
SERVES 4

1 onion, peeled and finely sliced
1/2 cup white wine
1/4 cup water
1tsp. butter
salt
freshly ground black pepper
1tsp. Madras curry powder
1 1/3 cups stock (as above, see pages 31-3)
1/2 tsp. rice flour

1   Place the onion slices in a saucepan with the wine, water, butter, a pinch of salt and a little pepper. Cover and place over medium heat. Simmer for 5 minutes, then remove the lid and cook until the liquid has almost completely evaporated, about 5 minutes.

2   Add two-thirds of the curry powder and sweat the mixture for 5 minutes over low heat, stirring well so it does not stick or burn. Add the stock and bring to the boil, stirring frequently. Simmer for 10 minutes, uncovered, skimming off the impurities as they rise.

3   Purée in a food processor or with a food mill, then return to the heat. Bring back to the boil, stirring occasionally.

4   Place the rice flour in a bowl and dilute with half the milk. Stir in a little of the hot sauce, then pour the mixture into the remainder of the sauce. Return to the boil, stirring, and cook for 2 minutes. Add the remaining milk and remove from the heat.

5   Mix the cream, yogurt, and remaining curry powder together, then stir in a little sauce. Pour it back into the sauce, mixing well.

6   Adjust the seasoning if necessary with a little salt and pepper, and serve immediately.

½ cup milk
¼ cup whipping cream
2 tbsp. Greek yogurt

Marinade Café de Paris
MEAT MARINADE

*T*his marinade can be used for many different meat recipes, especially with white meats like veal, chicken, turkey or pork.
   Fermentation develops the unique flavor of the marinade, so it should be left overnight at room temperature. Although the ingredients' list is long, the quantity is enough for only a few slices of meat — four veal cutlets, for instance (see Escalopes de Veau Woronoff, page 123).

1   Place all the ingredients except the oil into a china bowl, and mix well together with a wooden spoon for 3 minutes. Cover with plastic wrap and leave out overnight to marinate at room temperature.

2   The next day, mix with the oil and purée in a food processor. Use to marinate meat or as a basis for a sauce.

GLUTEN FREE

1 tsp. each of tomato ketchup, Dijon mustard, chopped capers, parsley, chives and tarragon, Madeira, Worcestershire sauce and lemon juice
1 pinch each of marjoram, dill, paprika, curry powder and cayenne pepper
1 sprig thyme (leaves only)
1 garlic clove, peeled and crushed
1 shallot, peeled and chopped
1 anchovy fillet, chopped
salt
freshly ground black pepper
grated zest of ½ orange
4 tbsp. grapeseed or safflower oil

LEFT *Marinade Café de Paris*

Coulis de Tomates
TOMATO COULIS

*O*riginally, the vegetables for this sauce were cooked in a lot of olive oil. Here we sweat the vegetables instead, making the sauce much lighter and more digestible.

Being so "santé," we use it often in meat, fish and vegetable dishes. It's also good on top of a poached egg.

GLUTEN FREE
SERVES 4

1 tbsp. olive oil
1 garlic clove, peeled and crushed
1 lb. tomatoes, washed and quartered
1/2 tsp. herbes de Provence
salt
freshly ground black pepper

1   Heat the olive oil in a heavy saucepan and add the garlic. Sweat for 1 minute, then add the tomatoes, herbs, a pinch of salt and a little pepper. Sweat for 3 minutes, tossing over low heat.
2   Cover and simmer for a further 10-15 minutes or until very soft.
3   Push through a sieve and reduce if too liquid.

Sauce Verte
GREEN SAUCE

*T*he traditional recipe uses a rich mayonnaise, but we have cut down on the number of egg yolks used and increased the amount of herbs, adding raw spinach and sorrel to increase the fiber, vitamin and iron content of the sauce. We also replaced some of the oil with Greek yogurt, which gives a creamy taste but is less rich.

This sauce is especially good served with steamed or poached fish, but it can also be a base for salad dressing, a dip for vegetables, or a spread for canapés or sandwiches.

GLUTEN FREE
SERVES 4

2 tbsp. tarragon vinegar
salt
freshly ground black pepper
1 egg yolk
2/3 cup grapeseed or safflower oil
1 shallot, peeled and very finely chopped
1 garlic clove, peeled and crushed
1 cup fines herbes, washed
1/2 cup spinach leaves, washed
2 sorrel leaves, washed
1/4 cup Greek yogurt

1   Let all the ingredients reach room temperature before beginning.
2   Mix the vinegar, a pinch of salt and some pepper in a bowl. Add the egg yolk and whisk in well. Pour the oil into the bowl very slowly, whisking constantly, a few drops at a time at first, then in a thin stream as the sauce thickens.
3   Add the shallot and garlic to the sauce. Drain and dry the herbs, spinach and sorrel, then chop them very finely. Add to the sauce, mix well, and correct the seasoning if necessary.
4   Add the yogurt by spoonfuls, mixing in delicately.
5   Let stand at room temperature for at least 10 minutes before using to allow the herbs to flavor the sauce well.

Sauce Tartare
TARTARE SAUCE

*T*his sauce normally uses two to three egg yolks; we have only used one. The oil is pure and high in polyunsaturated fats, but don't over indulge in the sauce, it still contains a lot of oil! Do not add much salt, as the pickles, tarragon vinegar and parsley provide a good substitute for it.

It is the pickles which give Sauce Tartare the unique taste which goes so well with grilled fish or meat, but the sauce can also be used as a spread for canapés or sandwiches.

GLUTEN FREE
SERVES 4

1   Leave all the ingredients at room temperature for at least 30 minutes before using.

2   Mix the vinegar, a pinch of salt and some pepper in a bowl. Add the egg yolk and whisk well. Pour the oil into the bowl very slowly, whisking constantly, a few drops at a time at first, then in a thin stream as the sauce starts to thicken.

3   Add the shallot and garlic to the sauce. Drain and dry the capers, gherkins and parsley. Chop them very finely, and stir into the sauce. Correct the seasoning if necessary.

4   Leave at room temperature to marinate for at least 20 minutes before using.

2tbsp. tarragon vinegar
salt
freshly ground black pepper
1 egg yolk
2/3 cup grapeseed or safflower oil
1 shallot, peeled and very finely chopped
1 garlic clove, peeled and crushed
1tbsp. capers
4 gherkin pickles
3 or 4 sprigs parsley, washed

Sauce Moutarde/Sauce Cumberland
MUSTARD (CUMBERLAND) SAUCE

*T*he classic recipe for mustard sauce, which had a mayonnaise base, and mustard added at the end, contained about two to three egg yolks. We have eliminated the yolks completely, and use the mustard alone to emulsify the oil.

A spoonful of red currant jelly can be added to the mustard (a recipe given by a British general to a chef during the Napoleonic Wars), and it becomes a Cumberland Sauce — the Cuisine Santé way, of course!

Both sauces are good served with cold meats and fish, and can be used as salad dressings too (but neither will keep well).

GLUTEN FREE
SERVES 4

1   Place the mustard in a bowl with a pinch of salt and a little pepper. For the Cumberland Sauce only, add the red currant jelly and mix gently.

2   Add the oil very slowly, drop by drop at first, then in a thin stream as the sauce thickens, whisking vigorously at the same time.

3   Adjust the seasoning, if necessary, and serve immediately.

2tbsp. Dijon mustard
salt
freshly ground black pepper
1tbsp. red currant jelly (for Cumberland Sauce only)
6tbsp. grapeseed or safflower oil

Sauce Colombo
COLOMBO SAUCE

*T*his sauce is adapted from a very famous dish from the French Caribbean islands of Guadeloupe and Martinique brought to the islands by Sri Lankan settlers during the last century.

The flavor is strong and spicy, so it would be best served with a piece of grilled or poached meat (chicken, pork, or lamb), a baked vegetable, or a poached egg on a bed of wild rice (see Oeufs Pochés Colombo page 55).

GLUTEN FREE
SERVES 4

2 pinches coarse sea salt
10 coriander seeds
½ tsp. mustard seeds
5 each of black peppercorns, white
    peppercorns and caraway seeds
½ tsp. Madras curry powder
1 pinch each of turmeric, ground
    ginger and saffron
½ hot red chili pepper, seeded
    and chopped
2 garlic cloves, peeled and
    crushed
1 onion, peeled and very finely
    chopped
2 tbsp. olive oil
2 oz. eggplant (about ½ small)
juice of 1 lime
1⅓ cups Fonds de Volaille or
    Bouillon de Légumes, as
    appropriate (see pages 31 and
    32)
1 tbsp. coconut cream

1 To prepare the Colombo paste, place the salt, coriander and mustard seeds, black and white peppercorns, caraway seeds, curry powder, turmeric, ginger and saffron into a mortar. Crush them with the pestle. Add the chili pepper and garlic to the mortar and mash to a paste.

2 Sweat the onion in 1 teaspoon of the olive oil.

3 Peel the eggplant, cut into cubes and sprinkle with half the lime juice. Add to the pan with the onion and sweat, covered, until soft.

4 Add two-thirds of the Colombo paste to the vegetables, mix well, and sweat for 3 minutes without coloring. Add the stock, a little at a time, stirring to dissolve the paste well. Bring slowly to the boil, skimming off the impurities as they rise to the surface.

5 Simmer for 30 minutes, then purée in a blender, food processor or food mill. Return to the heat, bring back to the boil, stirring, and simmer 5 minutes longer.

6 Add the coconut to the reserved Colombo paste in the mortar with the remaining lime juice and olive oil, and combine well. Stir a little of the sauce into this mixture, then pour it back into the sauce. Remove from the heat, and stir well to mix the flavors. Pour the sauce over the meat or fish and allow to stand for 5 minutes before serving, so the flavor of the sauce can permeate.

RIGHT *Sauce aux Fines Herbes*

Sauce Beurre Blanc
BUTTER SAUCE

*T*raditionally, this "white butter" sauce is 95 percent butter, with double cream added. Here we reduce the butter by half, include only a little cream, and use Greek yogurt. To finish, season with a drop of lemon juice and a little salt and pepper. Fines herbes or puréed vegetables could also be added.

This sauce can be served with poached eggs or fish, grilled, braised or poached meat, or even a gratin of vegetables.

GLUTEN FREE
SERVES 4

1   Place the shallots in a saucepan with the water, wine and vinegar. Reduce over low heat until only 2 tablespoons of liquid remain, approximately 6 minutes.
2   Add the cream, and reduce again until nearly evaporated.
3   Reduce the heat as much as possible, and add the butter, a few pieces at a time, shaking the pan at the same time. The butter should melt and emulsify, but it must not boil.
4   Off the heat, add the yogurt, by spoonfuls. Adjust the seasoning with lemon juice, salt and pepper. Do not heat again.

4 shallots, peeled and finely
    chopped
2 tbsp. water
1/4 cup dry white wine
1 tbsp. tarragon vinegar
1/4 cup whipping cream
4 oz. softened butter, diced
1/2 cup Greek yogurt
1/2 tsp. lemon juice
salt
freshly ground black pepper

Sauce aux Fines Herbes
HERB SAUCE

*T*his is a very simple sauce, which may be used in various ways: to dress a salad (about 3 tablespoons would be enough for an average salad for four), to accompany hot or cold vegetables, or poached, steamed or grilled fish or poultry. It is also delicious spread on canapés and sandwiches, or as a dip for vegetables.

The fines herbes *give a delightful flavor (and are full of goodness), but any one of these herbs, or others such as dill, thyme or savory could be used instead and give their name to the sauce. If fresh herbs are not available, used dried herbs reconstituted in cold water for a few minutes beforehand; drain, blot well with paper towels, and use as fresh.*

GLUTEN FREE
SERVES 4

1   Beat the yogurt for a minute to make it completely smooth.
2   Place the vinegar with a pinch of salt and some pepper in a bowl. Mix well to dissolve the salt and pepper. Add the oil, whisking well.
3   Add the yogurt, by spoonfuls, whisking constantly.
4   Dry the herbs, and chop them very finely. Add to the sauce, and allow to marinate at room temperature for at least 20 minutes before serving.

3/4 cup Greek yogurt
2 tbsp. tarragon vinegar
salt
freshly ground black pepper
1 tbsp. olive oil
a small bunch fines herbes,
    washed

LEFT *Sauce aux Fines Herbes*

Pâte Feuilletée
PUFF PASTRY

SERVES 4

1½ cups plain flour
½ cup ice cold water
½ tsp. salt
5½ oz. unsalted butter

*I*n the traditional puff pastry recipe, equal amounts of butter and flour are used; here we use one-third less butter. You could substitute hard vegetable fat for the butter, with good results, but do not expect a buttery taste.

1 Sieve the flour into a bowl, and make a well in the center. Place the water, salt and 1 ounce of the butter in the well and into a dough. Wrap in plastic wrap or foil and rest in the refrigerator for at least 20 minutes.

2 Roll the dough in a star shape and place the remaining butter in a lump in the middle of the star. Wrap the dough over the butter and, using the rolling pin, spread the butter out over the dough, flattening the dough into a rectangle 6 inches × 12 inches. Fold in three, then turn so that the opening is to one side. Roll the dough again to the same size. Fold in three again and rest in the refrigerator for at least 20 minutes. The dough now has two "turns."

3 Place the dough with the opening on the same side again, and repeat the rolling and turning so that the dough has four turns. At this stage the dough can be kept in the refrigerator for two or three days or put in the freezer for six to eight months.

4 When you are ready to use the dough, repeat the rolling and turning so that the dough has six turns all together. Roll down to the thickness required.

Pâte à Choux
CHOUX PASTRY

PREHEAT THE OVEN TO 400°F
MAKES 50 PROFITEROLES, 1 GOUGÈRE
OR 4 SWANS

2 eggs
water (for quantity see method)
2 tbsp. butter
salt
⅔ cup flour, sifted on to a
  piece of paper

*T*his pastry uses butter, of course, but when you consider that each recipe — whether for a gougère, swans or for profiteroles — will serve from four to six people, it's not too sinful!

1 Weigh the eggs whole in their shells ("large" eggs weigh about 2 ounces each). Measure out an equivalent weight of water.

2 Place the water, butter and a pinch of salt in a medium pan and heat gently until the butter is melted. Bring to the boil, remove from the heat and add the flour all at once. Stir well to form a dough. Dry this dough over low heat, beating well, for 1 minute.

3 Off the heat, add the eggs, one at a time, beating well between each addition. Make sure that the dough has absorbed one egg before adding the other.

4 Spoon or pipe the dough onto greased baking sheets as required (see pages 78 and 174).

5 Bake in the preheated oven for the recommended time.

TO MAKE PROFITEROLES

1 Put the pastry in a pastry bag and, using a straight ½-inch nozzle, pipe small amounts (about 1 inch in diameter) onto a baking sheet.

2 Brush with a little egg wash.

3 Bake for 15 minutes, then open the oven door a little, and bake for 5 minutes longer.

Pâte à Pissaladière

YEAST DOUGH

*T*he butter has been replaced with olive oil, the egg yolks have been reduced by half, and we use 50 percent whole-wheat flour, which still has a high gluten content to help the flour rise and make the dough lighter.

The recipe makes enough pastry for two pissaladières, *but if you want to make only one, use the leftover dough to make rolls to serve with your next meal.*

FILLS 2 × 10-IN. QUICHE TINS

1 cup white flour (bread flour or
*   all-purpose flour)*
1 cup whole-wheat flour
½ cup lukewarm water
1 cake fresh compressed yeast
*   (2¾ oz.) or 2 tsp. dried yeast*
1 egg yolk
1 tbsp. olive oil
¼ tsp. salt
freshly ground black pepper

1 Sift the white and whole-wheat flours together into a bowl. Sprinkle in the bran left in the sieve. Make a well in the center of the flour.

2 Measure out the lukewarm water (it should be body temperature) and dissolve the yeast in it. Place the egg yolk, olive oil, salt and pepper into the well and add the dissolved yeast. Mix together with a little of the flour to form a wettish paste. Stir in the rest of the flour and knead the dough very well until it becomes elastic. This helps it to rise.

3 Place the dough in a bowl, cover with plastic (a plastic food bag cut at the base and on one side) and leave in a warm room to rise. If in a hurry, heat the oven to the lowest temperature and turn it off. Bring a saucepan of water to the boil and place it in the oven with the dough above it. The damp atmosphere will help it rise, but make sure that the oven door is not opened too frequently. Bring the water back to the boil once or twice during the rising time. The dough should double in size in about 15–20 minutes.

4 A second rising is necessary and it is best to do this after shaping the dough. If you want to make rolls, for instance, the shaping should be done now. (Bake for 15 minutes.) For the *pissaladière*, press half of the dough into a tart pan or pie plate or onto a baking sheet with your hands. Cover with the plastic and place in a warm draft-free area to rise in the same manner as above.

5 Arrange the topping on the dough (see page 76) and bake as soon as possible or the dough will deflate.

Pâte Brisée
SHORT PASTRY DOUGH

The butter content of this pastry has been reduced by 25 percent, which makes the dough less flaky, but it is a good compromise. In many of the recipes, the amount of flour to be used is mentioned. In order to calculate the amount, divide the weight of flour in half to obtain the amount of fat to be used, and then subtract a quarter of it. A whole egg is used in all recipes, and the more (or less) flour, the more (or less) water.

TO LINE A 10-IN. TART PAN

1½ cups (8 oz.) whole-wheat
*   flour*
salt
1 egg
3 tbsp. water
3 oz. butter or polyunsaturated
*   margarine, softened and*
*   cubed*

1   Push the flour into a ring on the work surface, leaving a well in the middle, and place all the remaining ingredients (including ½ teaspoon salt) in the center. Mix the ingredients in the well together roughly, pulling in a little flour at a time, until crumbly. Use a plastic dough scraper or your hand. Bring all the ingredients together and with the palm of your hand push the dough down onto the work surface to blend it all evenly. Do not overwork or it will become tough.

2   Knead lightly, roll into a ball, and wrap (in plastic wrap or foil if the pastry is being prepared a long time in advance or with parchment paper if using within the hour). Always allow the dough to rest for at least 20 minutes in the refrigerator before rolling.

3   If the pastry has been prepared a long time in advance, remember to remove it from the refrigerator at least 20 minutes before use to soften.

4   The pastry freezes very well. Defrost it overnight in the refrigerator or for 1 hour at room temperature.

TO MAKE A *TIMBALE*
This is a marvelous way to present a casserole of meat or fish. Once the pastry would have been for a garnish only, to be thrown away, but now is enjoyed as part of the meal.
Preheat the oven to 350°F.

1   Roll out the pastry and use some to line a straight-sided cake pan about 7 inches in diameter. Prepare a lid separately, slightly larger in diameter. Brush the lid with egg wash (made with egg yolk only for a glossier finish) and decorate it with the remaining dough in the shape of leaves, etc. Brush with egg wash again.

2   Bake the pastry, lined with parchment paper or foil and baking beans for 10–15 minutes, until lightly browned, then remove the paper and beans and brush well with egg wash. Take out of the pan and brush the outside with egg wash. Place on a baking sheet and cook for 2 minutes longer. Repeat this egg washing and baking twice more.

3   Bake the lid on a baking sheet for 10–15 minutes and brush with egg wash similarly.

Pâte à Nouilles
PASTA DOUGH

*T*his is the original Italian pasta dough, except for the type of flour used, the healthier whole-wheat flour. For a lighter texture, some white flour could be substituted for a portion of the whole-wheat flour.

The proportions of the recipe can be increased easily — 1 egg to each ¾ cup flour, 1 pinch of salt and 1 tablespoon olive oil. Do prepare a good amount at a time and freeze the remainder in small quantities to be used on separate occasions.

The dough can also be attractively colored using spinach, beets, or saffron. For this, it would be best to use white flour, and the amount of flour should be increased by about ½ cup to make up for the extra moisture of the coloring or flavoring.

SERVES 4

*1½ cups whole-wheat flour
(plus extra to dust)
2 eggs (large)
2 pinches salt
2 tbsp. olive oil*

1   Put the flour in a large bowl. Make a well in the middle, and place the remaining ingredients in the center (including the coloring or flavoring).

2   Work the wet ingredients thoroughly together first, especially if there are additional ingredients, and gradually pull in a little flour at a time. Continue gradually combining the rest of the flour, until the dough forms a ball. Knead the dough well for 3 minutes, then cover with plastic wrap or foil and place in the refrigerator to rest for at least 30 minutes.

3   Roll the dough into strips 4 inches wide and 24 inches long, either by hand or in a pasta machine. Allow to dry naturally for 20 minutes (a broom handle placed between two tables or two chairs is ideal to hang the strips over). If using any of the colors, be prepared to use a lot more flour for dusting than normal, as there will be more moisture.

4   To cook the pasta, bring a large saucepan of salted water to the boil, then add 1 tablespoon olive oil.

5   Cut the pasta into the shape required (noodles, spaghetti, etc.) and plunge into the rapidly boiling water. Stir well, bring back to the boil and count 3 minutes. Taste the pasta to see if it is done to your liking (*al dente* is the best texture). Stop the cooking by removing from the heat and adding a large glass of ice cold water to the pan. Do not rinse, and leave the pasta in the water until ready to serve.

TO SERVE   Drain the pasta through a sieve without rinsing and transfer to a heated dish. Serve immediately.

❧

SOUPS AND STARTERS

S oups and starters are very important: they are supposed to titillate the appetite, without being too filling, and they should look good enough to arouse delighted expectations for what is to come. They should be delicate, light and sophisticated, and our Cuisine Santé starters and soups are meant to be a combination of all these factors. In addition, they are *santé* because of the reduction of fat and the preponderance of vegetables.

A number of the starters, especially the *tourtes* and quiches, can also be served with a salad as a main course. The soup recipes may be considered as basic formulas with which you can experiment to create your own variations.

Crème Capucine
MUSHROOM CREAM SOUP

T his delicious soup can be prepared ahead of time and reheated. The mushrooms contain protein, and aid digestion due to their fiber content. The usual quantity of cream has been halved and low-fat Greek yogurt added to give the light color and the slightly acid taste of the original crème fraîche.

GLUTEN FREE (EXCEPT FOR THE CROÛTONS)
SERVES 6

13 oz. fresh white button mushrooms, washed
juice of ½ lemon
1 tsp. grapeseed or safflower oil
1 onion, peeled and thinly sliced
1 white of leek, thinly sliced
1 garlic clove, peeled and crushed
4 tbsp. rice flour
1½ quarts Fonds de Volaille (see page 31)
¼ cup whipping cream
¼ cup Greek yogurt
salt
freshly ground black pepper

GARNISH
toasted whole-wheat croûtons (optional)
½ cup parsley, finely chopped

1   Chop the mushrooms and sprinkle with the lemon juice.
2   Heat the oil in a large saucepan, and sweat the onion and leek until soft, covered, about 10 minutes. Add the garlic and cook a minute longer, then add the mushrooms. Raise the heat and sauté them, stirring often. Continue cooking the mushrooms until only 2 tablespoons of liquid remain in the pan.
3   Add the rice flour and mix well, not letting it stick to the bottom of the pan. Add the stock, mix well to dissolve the flour, and bring to the boil, skimming off the impurities that rise to the surface. Cover and simmer for 20 minutes.
4   Strain the soup to separate the solids and purée them, gradually adding some of the liquid. Pass the soup through a conical sieve, then add the cream and bring to the boil again. Simmer 5 minutes longer.
5   Thin the yogurt with a little of the hot soup and stir the mixture back into the remaining soup. Season to taste with salt and pepper.
TO SERVE Serve the croûtons (if using) separately. Add the parsley to the soup just before serving.

Consommé à l'Estragon
TARRAGON CONSOMMÉ

A consommé is usually made with meat that contains a lot of fat. Here we remove all the fat and use very lean meat, which still gives a rich tasting broth. The tarragon lends its own distinctive flavor, and is extremely good for the digestion; it also stimulates the appetite and permits the use of less salt.

You could use the leftover cooked beef and vegetables as the base of a stuffing for vegetables.

SERVES 6

mirepoix *(1 carrot, 1 onion and 1 celery stalk)*
4 oz. sirloin of beef, ground
4 oz. lean round steak, ground
2 tomatoes, washed and quartered
1 green of leek, washed and thinly sliced
1 carrot, washed and finely chopped
2 garlic cloves, peeled and crushed
a large bunch fresh tarragon (1½ oz.)
½ cup Madeira or port
4 black peppercorns, crushed
2 egg whites
2 ice cubes
1½ quarts Fonds de Volaille *(see page 31)*
2 oz. carrots cut into julienne
2 oz. turnips cut into julienne

1   Place the finely chopped *mirepoix* in a large bowl with all the remaining ingredients except the chicken stock, half the tarragon leaves and stems and the Madeira or port. Mix the ingredients well by hand until the ice cubes have melted.

2   Bring the chicken stock to the boil.

3   Add the boiling stock to the contents of the bowl, stir well, then transfer the mixture into the stock pan and return to the heat. Keep stirring slowly so it does not stick to the bottom of the pan. As soon as it boils, turn the heat down and let it simmer, untouched and uncovered, for 30 minutes.

4   Pour carefully into a clean pan through a conical sieve lined with cheesecloth, and let it drip. Do not hurry the process by pressing, or the consommé will become cloudy.

5   Reheat, and add the Madeira or port. Steam the vegetable *julienne* for 3 minutes. Skim the surface of impurities as they rise to the top, then add the remaining tarragon leaves and the vegetable *julienne* and bring just to the boil. Allow to infuse for 5 minutes.

TO SERVE   Spoon from a heated soup tureen into heated soup bowls or consommé cups.

RIGHT *Consommé à l'Éstragon*

Potage Orge Perlé Brunoise
BROWN BARLEY SOUP

*I*nstead of using refined pearl barley, we use the "whole" or "pot" version available in health-food shops, complete with its bran and husk, where all the vital elements lie.

1   Heat the oil in a pan, and sweat the onion *brunoise*, covered, for 5 minutes. Add the leek, carrot and celery. Replace the lid and cook 15 minutes longer.

2   Add the barley and sweat for 5 minutes.

3   Add the stock, a pinch of salt and a little pepper. Bring to the boil and simmer for 30 minutes, skimming impurities off the surface.

TO SERVE Mix the cream and yogurt together in a bowl and stir in a little of the soup, then pour the mixture back into the remaining soup off the heat. Adjust the seasoning.

To serve hot, serve immediately. To serve cold, thin with a little more stock and chill in the refrigerator.

SERVES 6

4 oz. each of onion, leek, carrot and celery brunoise
1 tsp. grapeseed or safflower oil
¼ cup unrefined barley
1½ quarts Fonds de Volaille *(see page 31)*
salt
freshly ground black pepper

TO SERVE
¼ cup light cream
¼ cup Greek yogurt

Potage Crècy
CARROT SOUP

*T*his soup traditionally contains far fewer carrots, with more cream and egg yolks. In our home Mother had already adapted this healthier version, which she made virtually the consistency of a purée when we were too ill for solid food. The addition of yogurt gives it a certain tartness, similar to the flavor of crème fraîche, *but without the richness.*

1   Heat the oil and sweat the onion and leek for 5 minutes in a covered saucepan. Add the carrots, salt and pepper and sweat for 5 minutes longer, covered.

2   Meanwhile, heat the stock, then add it to the vegetables. Simmer slowly for 1 hour.

3   Strain and purée the vegetables in a blender or food processor, gradually adding the liquid. Adjust the seasoning if necessary.

4   Thin the yogurt with milk and pour half into the soup. Heat through briefly without boiling.

TO SERVE Pour the soup into a warmed tureen or into individual bowls, and snip the chives finely with scissors over the top. Pour the rest of the thinned yogurt over the soup in a spiral pattern starting from the center. Draw the blade of a knife over the surface of the soup, from the rim of the bowl to the center alternately to feather the yogurt.

GLUTEN FREE

SERVES 4

1 tbsp. grapeseed or safflower oil
1 onion, peeled and thinly sliced
1 leek, cleaned and thinly sliced
1 lb. carrots, washed and sliced
salt
freshly ground black pepper
1 quart Fonds de Volaille *or* Bouillon de Légumes *(see pages 31 and 32)*
¼ cup Greek yogurt
1 tbsp. milk

GARNISH
a small bunch of fresh chives

LEFT *Potage Crècy*

51

Potage Minestrone
MINESTRONE SOUP

This soup is actually more like a complete meal than a starter! Serve it on a cold winter evening with chunks of crusty garlic bread. You could follow it with a plate of cold meats — perhaps Parma or honey-roast ham or cold poached chicken so you can use the poaching stock for the soup — served with a Cumberland Sauce (see page 39). The pistou, also known as pesto, carries the unmistakable signature of the south of France and can be used in many other dishes. Try it on pasta, salad and ratatouille.

GLUTEN FREE
SERVES 6

¼ cup dried white beans
1 onion, peeled and sliced
1 bouquet garni
freshly ground black pepper
1 tbsp. grapeseed or safflower oil
4 oz. each of onion, leek, carrot and potato paysanne
2 oz. each of cabbage and celery paysanne
3 tbsp. tomato paste
1½ quarts Fonds de Volaille (see page 31)
1 oz. spaghetti
salt

PISTOU
2 garlic cloves, peeled
2 tbsp. parsley, finely chopped
2 tbsp. basil, finely chopped
¼ cup olive oil

1   Soak the beans overnight in cold water. Drain, and place them in a saucepan with fresh water to cover with the onion, *bouquet garni* and pepper. Cover and simmer over low heat for 2 hours until tender.

2   Heat the oil in a large pan, and sweat all the *paysanne* vegetables, except the potatoes, covered, for 15–20 minutes.

3   Add the tomato paste, mix in and cook for 1 minute. Add the stock and bring to the boil. Simmer very gently for 30 minutes, skimming off the impurities as they rise to the surface.

4   Break the spaghetti into pieces by wrapping in a dish towel, holding each end and running the towel down the edge of a table very quickly. Add the potatoes, the cooked beans and short pieces of spaghetti to the soup and simmer for another 10 minutes.

5   Meanwhile, make the *pistou*. Using a pestle and mortar, mash together the garlic and herbs, chopping the herbs at the last moment to retain their flavor. Add the oil, a little at a time, whisking to emulsify the sauce. Alternatively, make the *pistou* in a small food processor.

6   Adjust the seasoning of the soup, and add the *pistou* slowly. Do not boil or the *pistou* will separate.

RIGHT *Potage Minestrone*

Gaspacho Andalous
CHILLED GAZPACHO

*T*his cold soup, Spanish in origin, has been "revamped" by us. It is already awash with vitamins and fiber, but we have cut down on the time it takes to make: a traditional gazpacho could take up to 3 hours to prepare; done our way, it only takes 10 minutes!

SERVES 4-6

1 lb. ripe tomatoes, washed
1 small cucumber, washed
1 green pepper and 1 red pepper, washed
1 onion, peeled
1 quart tomato juice
salt
freshly ground black pepper
cayenne pepper
½ cup fines herbes, washed
1 tbsp. tarragon leaves, washed
2 garlic cloves, peeled
2 tbsp. olive oil
2 tbsp. tarragon vinegar

GARNISH
toasted whole-wheat bread croûtons

1   Trim all the vegetables as necessary and cut into small pieces. Reserve 4 tablespoons of each for garnishing (rinse the chopped onion before use). Place the remainder in a food processor or blender and purée.

2   Add the tomato juice slowly, plus 2 pinches of salt, some black pepper, and the cayenne, half the *fines herbes*, and the tarragon. Place in the refrigerator or freezer to chill well.

3   When ready to serve, using a pestle and mortar, mash the garlic, a pinch of salt, a little pepper and the remaining herbs together to make a thick paste. Add the olive oil slowly, working to blend well.

4   Blend the chilled gazpacho again in the food processor, adding the garlic paste and the vinegar alternately, a little at a time.

TO SERVE   Correct the seasoning if necessary, and serve in a large bowl. Serve immediately — the soup quickly loses its goodness and flavor. Arrange the croûtons, along with the reserved chopped vegetables, in bowls from which the guests can help themselves.

Oeufs Pochés Colombo
POACHED EGGS WITH COLOMBO SAUCE

*T*his poached egg recipe uses a Sauce Colombo *which contains no cream or butter, just a blend of spices, onion, garlic and a little olive oil. Served with a salad, this will make an ideal light meal.*

1   Prepare the poached eggs and keep in a bowl of cold water.
2   Cook the rice.

TO SERVE Trim off the excess egg white and discard. Place the eggs in a bowl of hot water for 3 minutes to reheat then strain off the water and pour the sauce over them. Leave for 2 minutes. Arrange the rice on a large serving dish or individual plates and make a nest for each egg. Lift the eggs from the sauce, with a slotted spoon, and drain for a moment. Place on the rice, and pour a little sauce over the top of each and around the rice. Garnish with parsley or chives and serve immediately. Pass the remaining sauce in a gravy boat.

If you want a smoother sauce, strain it and push through a conical sieve.

SERVES 4

4 poached eggs (see page 15)
5 oz. long grain and wild rice
   (seasoned rice mix)

TO SERVE
1 recipe Sauce Colombo *(see*
   page 40)
4 sprigs parsley or some chives

Oeufs en Cocotte à l'Aveyronaise
BAKED EGGS WITH BLUE CHEESE

*T*his recipe evolved when everyone at home was fighting over the last piece of Roquefort cheese. An oeuf en cocotte *is traditionally an egg covered with cream and baked. Here it is a much lighter preparation, and needs care as there is virtually no means of checking its consistency as it cooks. Do not hesitate to use leftover vegetables in the base if you have any. This dish can also be served cold.*

1   Use the butter to grease four ramekin dishes, then put them in the refrigerator to set.
2   Mix the cheeses together roughly and push through a sieve into a bowl.
3   Break one of the eggs into a cup, beat lightly, and add to the cheese mixture a little at a time, along with the yogurt and seasoning.
4   Spoon a little of the cheese mixture into the greased ramekins, break an egg into each, and cover carefully with the rest of the mixture.
5   Bake in a bain-marie lined with a sheet of parchment or brown paper and half-filled with hot water for approximately 10–15 minutes until set.

TO SERVE Serve immediately in the ramekins on a small plate lined with a doily. Eat with a spoon.

GLUTEN FREE
SERVES 4
PREHEAT THE OVEN TO 350°F

1 tsp. softened butter
4 oz. Roquefort (or other blue
   cheese)
4 oz. Ricotta (or other low-fat
   soft cheese)
5 eggs
1/2 cup Greek yogurt
salt
freshly ground black pepper
paprika

LEFT *Gaspacho Andalous*

55

Rouleau aux Épinards
SPINACH ROLL

*O*nce you have mastered the recipe for home-made pasta, use your imagination and you will be able to serve it in many different shapes and flavors. Rolling the dough is a little difficult (like strudel pastry), but be patient!

In this recipe we combine meat and vegetables (use the leftovers of a previous meal). Alternatively, you could increase the amount of spinach used by about 5 ounces, and omit the meat completely. A fish poacher is ideal for cooking this, as it can take the length.

SERVES 6

Pâte à Nouilles *made with*
    2¼ cups flour (see page 45)
1 onion, peeled and finely
    chopped
1 shallot, peeled and finely
    chopped
1 tbsp. grapeseed or safflower oil
2 garlic cloves, peeled and
    crushed
2¼ lb. spinach or Swiss chard (or
    a mixture), cut into
    chiffonade
5 oz. cooked meat (turkey,
    chicken, pork or lamb),
    ground (about ⅔ cup)
salt
freshly ground black pepper
1 egg
½ cup low-fat cottage cheese
grated nutmeg
egg wash

TO SERVE
1 recipe Coulis de Tomates *(see*
    page 38)
parsley, chervil or watercress
    sprigs
tomato roses (see page 26)

1   Allow the pasta dough to rest in the refrigerator for 20 minutes.

2   Sweat the onion and shallot in the oil for a few minutes in a heavy saucepan, then add the garlic. Sweat for a minute longer, then remove with a slotted spoon and keep to one side.

3   In the same saucepan sauté the spinach *chiffonade* very quickly. Return the onion, shallot, and garlic mixture, to the pan. Increase the heat, add the meat and sauté for 1 minute. Put aside to cool, season and mix well.

4   Beat the egg in a bowl, add the vegetable and meat mixture, cheese and nutmeg, and mix thoroughly.

5   Roll the pasta dough very thinly into a rectangle roughly the size of a dish towel. Place the dough directly on the towel to finish the rolling.

6   Brush the egg wash all over the dough and spread the filling evenly over it. Roll up the dough, with the help of the dish towel, starting on the long side. (If a larger slice is wanted or if your cooking pan is not long enough, start rolling from the narrow end.) Rinse and wring out the moisture from the towel, then wrap it around the roll. Tie the ends with string. It will keep like this overnight if desired.

7   To cook, fill a saucepan or fish poacher with water and bring to the boil. Add salt and put the roll in. Simmer for 30 minutes. When done, add a little cold water to the pan to stop the cooking.

TO SERVE Heat the tomato *coulis.*

Remove the roll from the water only when ready to serve or it will become dry. Remove the dish towel. Cut the roll into slices about ½ inch thick and arrange on individual plates on top of the tomato *coulis.* Garnish with parsley, chervil, watercress sprigs or tomato roses.

RIGHT *Rouleau aux Épinards*

Gâteau d'Herbage à l'Ancienne
VEGETABLE GÂTEAU

*T*his delicious starter or light evening supper can be prepared ahead of time and reheated. It can also be prepared in small ramekin dishes and presented on individual plates.

1 Bring a large saucepan of water with ½ teaspoon salt added to the boil. Blanch the cabbage leaves for 1 minute (count from when the water comes back to the boil). Cool them in a bowl of ice water, drain, and lay flat on a dish towel. Cut out the main stalks.

2 Heat 1 teaspoon of the oil in a large saucepan and sweat the onion and leek, covered. Add the sorrel *chiffonade* and sauté briskly for 1 minute, stirring constantly. Remove to a plate to cool.

3 In the same saucepan heat another teaspoon of the oil and sauté the spinach, seasoned with salt and pepper, over high heat. Cook till soft, about 3 minutes, and stir continuously so that it does not stick. Place on the plate with the other vegetables and mix well.

4 Grease a 1-quart ring mold with the remaining oil, and line it with the cabbage leaves, leaving an overhang of leaves all around to cover the top of the stuffing. Slice the remaining cabbage into *chiffonade* and add to the stuffing vegetables with the herbs. Season well with salt, pepper and nutmeg.

5 In a bowl, whisk together the eggs, the egg white, milk and cream. Add the vegetables and mix well (this should be done at the last minute or too much water will be drawn from the vegetables).

6 Spoon the mixture into the lined mold, fold the overhanging leaves over, and cover with a piece of parchment paper. Bake in a bain-marie in the preheated oven for 50 minutes.

TO SERVE Heat the tomato *coulis.*

Allow the mold to cool for 5 minutes after removing from the oven. Remove the paper covering and any dry leaves. Turn out onto a round serving dish, and clean up any custard which may have seeped through the leaf wrapping. Pour the *coulis* into the middle, and garnish the ring with parsley sprigs.

GLUTEN FREE
SERVES 6
PREHEAT THE OVEN TO 350°F

salt
1 Savoy cabbage, separated into
    leaves
3 tsp. grapeseed or safflower oil
1 onion, peeled and chopped
5 oz. leek, cleaned and chopped
4 oz. sorrel, cut into chiffonade
9 oz. spinach, cut into chiffonade
1 cup fines herbes, finely chopped
freshly ground black pepper
grated nutmeg
2 eggs, separated
1 egg white
¾ cup milk
½ cup whipping cream

TO SERVE
1 recipe Coulis de Tomates (see
    page 38)
parsley sprigs

LEFT *Gâteau d'Herbage à l'Ancienne*

Oignons Farcis 1
STUFFED ONIONS 1

GLUTEN FREE
SERVES 6
PREHEAT THE OVEN TO 350°F

3 large onions, peeled
salt
11 oz. low-fat cottage cheese
4 tbsp. fines herbes, *finely*
*   chopped*
¼ cup Greek yogurt
1 large egg
freshly ground black pepper
½ tsp. grapeseed or safflower oil
¼ cup whipping cream
¼ cup Fonds de Volaille *(see*
*   page 31)*

TO SERVE
4 oz. carrot, cut into julienne
4 oz. broccoli florets
parsley or watercress sprigs
*   (optional)*
chives

*T*hese stuffed onions are delicious as well as healthy and economical. The herbs add to the vitamin and mineral count, and give a wonderful freshness; they also reduce the need for salt. Do not over-blanch the onions; if you do they will be difficult to stuff.

1 Bring a saucepan of salted water to the boil. Cut the onions as described on page 25, and blanch them for 10 minutes.

2 Sieve the cheese into a bowl, and mix in the herbs, yogurt, egg and some pepper.

3 Refresh the onions under cold water and carefully separate the leaves. Chop the hearts, which cannot be stuffed, and add to the cheese stuffing. Stuff each leaf with 1 tablespoon of stuffing, then roll and place in a gratin dish, lightly greased with the oil, keeping the open part down so the stuffing does not escape while cooking.

4 Mix the cream and chicken stock together and pour over the onions. Cover the dish with foil and bake in the preheated oven for 40 minutes, basting every 10 minutes. Uncover and bake 10 minutes longer without basting.

TO SERVE Steam the vegetables until they are *al dente* — no longer than 3 minutes.

You can serve the onions in several ways. To serve from the baking sheet, clean the edges of the gratin dish and place it on a platter lined with a napkin or doily. Arrange a garnish of steamed vegetables and a few sprigs of parsley over the top of the onions. You could also remove the onions from the gratin dish and arrange around the edge of a hot serving platter with the garnish in the middle, or arrange the onions and the garnish alternately, with sprigs of parsley or watercress in the middle. Or, you could prepare large individual plates with the onions arranged in the shape of a flower, each onion leaf being a petal. Arrange the strips of carrots, twisted with chives, to make the stem, with the broccoli as the center of the flower.

Oignons Farcis 2
STUFFED ONIONS 2

*T*his second version of stuffed onions uses meat. It too is delicious, and is very economical as it uses leftovers. Try it with fish as well! If you are on a gluten-free diet, omit the breadcrumbs.

SERVES 4
PREHEAT THE OVEN TO 350°F

4 small onions, peeled
salt
1 small apple
1½tsp. grapeseed or safflower oil
5 oz. cooked lean meat, ground (about ⅔ cup)
¼ cup dry whole-wheat breadcrumbs
¼ cup grated Emmenthal cheese
2 fresh sage leaves, finely chopped, or ½tsp dried sage
freshly ground black pepper
½ cup Fonds de Volaille (see page 31) or ¼ cup Fonds de Volaille and ¼ cup whipping cream

1   Prepare the onions as described in the previous recipe, blanching them and separating the leaves.

2   Chop the onion hearts finely.

3   Peel and core the apple, and cut into very small cubes.

4   Heat 1 teaspoon of the oil in a frying pan and sauté the chopped onion heart briskly. Add the meat, breadcrumbs, apple cubes, cheese and sage. Season well with salt and pepper and remove to a large plate to cool.

5   Stuff the onion leaves with the meat stuffing as described in the previous recipe and arrange in the gratin dish, greased with the remaining oil.

6   Pour the chicken stock over the onions, cover the dish with foil.

7   Bake in the preheated oven for 40 minutes, basting every 10 minutes.

TO SERVE   Serve in one of the ways outlined in the previous recipe.

Oeufs Pochés à la Chantilly

CHANTILLY POACHED EGGS

*T*he *"Chantilly" garnish is traditionally a purée of peas and a* Sauce Beurre Blanc *which contains 95 percent butter and lots of cream. We have kept the peas but replaced half the butter of the sauce with Greek yogurt and reduced the amount of cream. The peas contribute a good amount of vitamin C and fiber too, if the purée contains the skins. However, the texture is more refined if they are strained out.*

1   Allow the pastry to rest for 10 minutes in the refrigerator, then roll out and line four 3-inch tartlet molds. Line with parchment paper or foil and baking beans. Bake blind in the preheated oven until golden brown, about 5 minutes, then remove the baking beans, and bake for another 10 minutes. Keep warm.

2   Reserve the poached eggs in a bowl of cold water.

3   Sweat the onion in the oil in a saucepan, covered, for 5 minutes. Add the lettuce *chiffonade* to the onion with a pinch of salt and a little pepper. Sweat for 5 minutes until tender. Add the peas and toss with the other ingredients for 1 minute. Add the stock, herbs, and another small pinch of salt. Cover the top of the vegetables with a circle of paper, and the pan with a lid. Leave on low heat for 7 minutes. Check to see if the peas are tender enough to be puréed; if not, let them cook for 1–2 minutes longer.

4   Reserve a few whole peas for garnish and purée the remainder of the mixture in a food processor or in a food mill. Bring the milk to the boil and add to the purée. Its consistency should be of a very thick soup.

TO SERVE   Trim the excess white from the eggs when they are cold, and reheat by placing them in a bowl of hot water for 3 minutes.

If serving immediately, place a napkin or doily on a serving plate. Divide the pea purée between the tartlets, place an egg on top and spoon a little of the *Sauce Beurre Blanc* over the egg. Garnish with a pea and/or a parsley or chervil sprig. Place on the serving plate, and serve the remaining sauce in a gravy boat.

If serving on individual plates, pour a little sauce over the base of the plate and place the filled tartlet on the sauce. Garnish the plate with a few peas, and the egg with a parsley or chervil sprig. Serve the remaining sauce separately.

SERVES 4
PREHEAT THE OVEN TO 350°F

Pâte Brisée *made with 1¼ cups (5 oz.) flour (see page 44)*
4 eggs, poached (see page 15)
1 onion, peeled and finely chopped
1 tsp. grapeseed or safflower oil
½ Boston lettuce, cut into chiffonade
salt
freshly ground black pepper
5 oz. frozen tiny peas
¼ cup Fonds de Volaille *or* Court-Bouillon *(see pages 31 and 32)*
1 tbsp. fines herbes, finely chopped
¼ cup milk

TO SERVE
1 recipe Sauce Beurre Blanc *(see page 41)*
parsley or chervil sprigs

LEFT *Oeufs Pochés à la Chantilly*

Terrine de Lapin
RABBIT TERRINE

This terrine was originally wrapped in pork fat and bacon, and also contained pork fat. For the filling we use low-fat pork tenderloin, and the dish is lined with spinach leaves which are non-fatty, protect the meat from drying out, and make the dish look good.

For the best results, prepare over 3 days as advised in the recipe: on the first day, prepare the forcemeat and stock; on the second, cook the terrine; and do not serve it before the third day.

GLUTEN FREE

SERVES 6

2¼lb. rabbit (with liver)
9oz. lean veal
5oz. lean pork tenderloin
salt
freshly ground black pepper
2tbsp. cognac
herbes de Provence
2tsp. grapeseed or safflower oil
2 shallots, peeled and chopped
2 garlic cloves, peeled and
    crushed
4oz. livers (from the rabbit, plus
    chicken livers to make up the
    weight)
¼cup shelled hazelnuts, roasted
¼cup shelled pistachio nuts,
    blanched and skinned
2tbsp. fines herbes, finely
    chopped
mirepoix (1 onion, 1 carrot and
    1 celery stalk)
¼cup white wine
1tbsp. tomato paste
2½cups Fonds de Volaille (see
    page 31)
1 bouquet garni
1 egg
1lb. spinach leaves, washed (or
    lettuce, if not available)

GARNISH
lettuce leaves
gherkins
tomato roses (see page 26)
green onion flowers (see page 25)

TWO DAYS BEFORE SERVING

1   Cut the rabbit as described on page 21, leaving the saddle whole. Remove the meat from the hind and forequarters and the belly, and reserve the bones and sinews for the stock. Cut the meat into cubes and grind with the veal and pork, using a meat grinder or a food processor.

2   Remove the meat from the saddle in two long fillets. Cut off the remaining meat attached to the saddle, grind it, and mix with the rest of the ground meat.

3   Place the rabbit fillets on a plate and sprinkle with salt, pepper, 1 teaspoon of the cognac, and a pinch of *herbes de Provence.*

4   Heat half the oil in a skillet and sweat the shallot and garlic, covered, until soft, about 5 minutes. Add the rabbit and chicken livers and sauté briskly on high heat for 2 minutes. Add half the remaining cognac and flame. Remove to a plate to cool. Grind the livers.

5   Roughly chop half of the hazelnuts and pistachios and mix into the forcemeat with some salt and pepper, half the fresh herbs, the remaining cognac, and the ground livers. Chill in the refrigerator overnight.

6   Heat the remaining oil in a saucepan and sauté the rabbit bones with the roughly chopped *mirepoix.* Deglaze with the wine and then reduce for 2 minutes. Add the tomato paste and mix well over the heat for another 2 minutes, then deglaze again with the stock. Add the *bouquet garni* and leave to simmer for 1½ hours, skimming off the impurities as they rise to the surface. Strain and reduce by simmering until ½cup is left. Allow to cool, and then place in the refrigerator overnight to chill.

ONE DAY BEFORE SERVING

Preheat the oven to 325°F.

1   Mix together the forcemeat, reduced stock and beaten egg, and season with pepper, a little salt and the remaining fresh herbs.

2   Blanch the spinach leaves in boiling salted water, about 1 minute, and refresh under cold water. Line an 8-cup terrine with the leaves, leaving enough overhang to easily cover the top of the forcemeat. Chop up the remaining spinach and add it to the forcemeat. Place half of the forcemeat into the base of the terrine, and arrange the two fillets in the middle, with the remaining whole nuts on either side. Pile high with the remaining forcemeat and spinach leaves.

Terrine de Lapin

3 Cover the terrine with a lid or foil, and place in a bain-marie lined with a sheet of parchment or brown paper and a little hot water. Bake in the preheated oven for 1 hour. Turn the oven off and let the oven cool with the terrine inside. Remove the lid, put weights on top of the meat, and leave in the refrigerator for at least 12 hours.

TO SERVE Dip the base of the terrine into hot water in a bain-marie, and turn out onto a platter lined with lettuce leaves. Cut the first three slices and leave the remainder intact. Garnish with gherkins, tomato roses, and green onion flowers.

For individual plates, place a slice of the terrine on a lettuce leaf and garnish similarly.

Pâté Chaud Paysan
PÂTÉ BAKED IN PASTRY

Pâte Feuilletée *made with*
2¾ cups flour (see below and
page 42)
mirepoix *(1 onion, 1 carrot, and*
1 celery stalk)
2 cups red wine (Côtes du Rhône
type)
1 sprig thyme
1 bay leaf
2 sprigs parsley
1 tbsp. olive oil
5 each of black and white
peppercorns and coriander
seeds, crushed
1 clove
7 oz. each lean beef, veal and
pork, cut into strips
4 oz. lean beef, cut into cubes
5 oz. lean pork, cut into cubes
1 tsp. grapeseed or safflower oil
1 onion, peeled and finely
chopped
2 shallots, peeled and finely
chopped
2 garlic cloves, peeled and
crushed
7 oz. chicken or duck livers, well
trimmed
2 tbsp. cognac
1 egg
½ cup fines herbes, *finely*
chopped
salt
cayenne pepper
freshly ground black pepper
1 tsp. butter
egg wash
1 egg yolk

TO SERVE
1 recipe Sauce Diable *(see*
page 34)
1 recipe Salade de Champignons
de Sabine *(see page 160)*

*T*his is an ideal dish to make use of leftover raw meat. Assorted
pieces of meat, stored in the freezer, can be transformed into this
pâté en croûte. *Although the pâté is wrapped in a rich puff pastry, and
high in calories, the amount consumed by each guest is minimal.*

TWO DAYS BEFORE SERVING

1   Prepare the puff pastry up to the four-turn stage (see page 44),
then allow to rest, well wrapped, in the refrigerator.

2   Place the finely chopped *mirepoix* in a roasting pan with the wine,
thyme, bay leaf, parsley sprigs, olive oil, crushed spices and the
clove. Mix all these ingredients well so that the flavors blend. Place
the meat strips and cubes in this marinade and mix well. Place a piece
of parchment paper directly on top of the meat and cover with foil.

3   Leave to marinate at room temperature for 2 hours, then mix
again and place in the refrigerator overnight.

ONE DAY BEFORE SERVING

1   Heat a skillet, then heat the grapeseed or safflower oil. Sweat the
onion and shallot over low heat until soft, about 5 minutes. Add the
garlic and sweat it for 1 minute. Remove any green portions, nerves
and fat from the livers, then add the livers to the pan. Turn the heat
up and sauté, stirring well, before adding the cognac. Set it alight
then leave to cool.

2   Give the pastry two more turns and return it to the refrigerator.

3   Drain the meat and discard the marinade. Dry the meat well on
paper towels, leave the strips to one side, then grind the cubes using
a meat grinder or food processor. Place in a bowl with the egg,
herbs, 2 pinches each of salt and cayenne, and some pepper, and
work well together by hand.

4   Grind the cooled livers, add to the ground meat, and mix well.

5   Butter a baking sheet lightly and sprinkle with a few drops of
water. Cut the pastry in two, one part slightly bigger than the other,
and roll out both pieces into rectangles, the larger roughly 10 × 14
inches, the smaller 6 × 10 inches. Lay the larger on the baking sheet.

6   Brush with egg wash all over, and then spread a third of the
ground meat over the rectangle on the baking sheet, leaving wide
borders. Arrange half the meat strips over it lengthwise, then cover
with another third of the ground meat. Arrange the remaining strips
over it, and cover finally with the remaining meat. Fold the borders
of the dough up over the meat, and brush with egg wash. Lay the
smaller rectangle on top of this, pressing well to stick the layers
together. Brush with egg wash all over thickly, and let it set for 5
minutes. Add the egg yolk to the remaining egg wash (with a little
water if it is too thick) and brush again. Leave it to set, then cover
loosely with foil.

7   Place in the refrigerator overnight to marinate, along with the
remaining egg wash (covered as well).

THE DAY OF SERVING

Preheat the oven to 450°F.

1   Mix the egg wash with a fork and brush over the pastry. Decorate with leftover dough in a lattice design.

2   Place the sheet in the preheated oven, and turn it down immediately to 350°F. Bake for 1 hour. If the pastry browns too much, cover it with a piece of foil.

TO SERVE   Meanwhile, keep the *Sauce Diable* warm.

Leave the pâté in the turned-off oven for 15 minutes, then transfer to a warm serving dish. Cut into portions with a sharp knife. Serve the sauce separately in a gravy boat with the *Salade de Champignons.*

Pâté Chaud Paysan with *Salade de Champignons de Sabine*

Tourte aux Épinards
SPINACH PIE

The spinach, which is the base of this tourte, *should be washed in three changes of water; it can be very gritty. It also will have traces of nitrates, if not organically grown. Spinach is a healthy vegetable, with a high content of iron, phosphorus, copper, cobalt and vitamins A, B and C. This* tourte *can be served hot or cold.*

**SERVES 6 AS A STARTER,
4 AS A MAIN COURSE
PREHEAT THE OVEN TO 350°F**

Pâte Brisée *made with 2 cups
    (10 oz.) flour (see page 44)*
egg wash
*12 oz. Ricotta (or other
    low-fat soft cheese)*
2 eggs
saffron
*½ cup fines herbes, finely
    chopped*
1 sprig thyme
salt
freshly ground black pepper
grated nutmeg
1 lb. spinach, cut into chiffonade
2 tbsp. skim milk (optional)

TO SERVE
1 recipe Coulis de Tomates *(see
    page 38) or salad greens*
parsley sprigs

1   Allow the pastry to rest in the refrigerator for 20 minutes. Roll out the dough and line an 8-inch tart pan with a removable bottom, leaving a lip all around the edge. Roll out the remaining pastry to make a lid. Brush both parts with egg wash.

2   Heat the oil in a large saucepan. Add the spinach *chiffonade* and toss over high heat for two minutes. Place on a large serving dish, and spread out so that it cools quickly.

3   Push the cheese through a sieve into a bowl. Mix in the eggs, one by one, and a pinch of saffron. Add the herbs, the leaves from the sprig of thyme, a pinch of salt, some pepper and nutmeg.

4   Mix in the spinach *chiffonade*. If the batter is too thick, thin it with the skim milk. Pour the batter into the pastry case and place the pastry lid on top. Press both pieces of pastry together well, using the egg wash to help them stick. Cut off the excess pastry with a knife, and crimp all round the edges with your fingers. Brush with egg wash again, and decorate the top with any leftover pastry. Make a small hole in the center of the top, and keep it open with a chimney made of foil (rolled around the handle of a wooden spoon).

5   Bake in the preheated oven for 40 minutes. After 30 minutes take out of the oven, remove the sides of the tart pan and brush with egg wash. Return to the oven to finish cooking. Repeat the operation twice to obtain a good golden brown color.

TO SERVE Turn the *tourte* out onto a cooling rack, and leave in the oven to cool for 10 minutes or for 5 minutes at room temperature. Serve with tomato *coulis*. Alternatively, leave to cool completely, and serve with the salad greens. Garnish the top with parsley.

RIGHT *Tourte aux Épinards*

Peperonata
PROVENÇAL PEPPER SALAD

*T*his very traditional Provençal dish is usually cooked in olive oil, but we have replaced it with wine and water or chicken stock. If you have already had your quota of eggs for the week, you can omit them from the recipe. The dish is full of vitamins and low in calories; if you leave the pepper skins on, the fiber content will be increased, but they also will be more difficult to digest.

This dish can also be served as a side salad, either tepid or cold, but it must be left to marinate for a few hours to enhance the flavors.

GLUTEN FREE
SERVES 4

1   Cut the flesh of the peppers into strips.

2   Heat half the olive oil in a large pan, and sweat the onion, covered, for 5 minutes. Add the garlic, and sweat for 2 minutes.

3   Sweat the strips of pepper with the onion and garlic for 5 minutes. Add the white wine, water or stock, a pinch of *herbes de Provence*, salt and pepper and simmer, covered, for 5 minutes.

4   Remove the lid and continue simmering until the liquid has reduced by half. Allow to cool for a while.

5   Place the eggs in cold water. Bring to the boil and then boil for 5 minutes. Refresh in cold water to stop the cooking. (If you are preparing well in advance, cut the cooking time for the eggs by 1 minute and do not refresh them.)

6   Add the vinegar to the peppers and adjust the seasoning if necessary. Place in a serving bowl, and mix in the basil.

TO SERVE Shell the eggs, quarter them, and place on top of the *Peperonata*. Serve lukewarm or cold — both are delicious.

2 green peppers and 2 red peppers, skinned (see page 23)
2 tbsp. olive oil
2 onions, peeled and thickly sliced
4 garlic cloves, peeled and crushed
¼ cup white wine
¼ cup water or Fonds de Volaille (see page 31)
herbes de Provence
salt
freshly ground black pepper
4 eggs
2 tbsp. tarragon vinegar
5 fresh basil leaves, chopped, or 1 tsp. dried basil

Paupiettes de Choux
CABBAGE ROLLS

These paupiettes are one of our own creations instead of a modification of an already existing recipe, so they are already healthy. Use them as a cold starter or on toothpicks as amuses-gueules, or hot in the winter months as a garnish for meat…there are endless possibilities.

GLUTEN FREE
SERVES 4

1 small Savoy cabbage
1 Boston lettuce, cut into chiffonade
1 leek, washed
2 green onions, washed
½ cup brown rice
salt
2 sprigs parsley
1 sprig thyme
1 tsp. grapeseed or safflower oil
3 oz. sorrel, cut into chiffonade
1 tomato, peeled, seeded and finely chopped
¼ cup Emmenthal cheese, grated
freshly ground black pepper
¼ cup Greek yogurt
¼ cup Sauce Moutarde (optional, see page 39)

TO SERVE
1 recipe Coulis de Tomates (optional, see page 38)
lemon twists (see page 26)

1   Remove some of the leaves from the cabbage for garnishing. Cut the cabbage into quarters through the stem; remove the center leaves or "hearts" from the cabbage and reserve them. Divide the lettuce into leaves, reserve the heart and cut the leaves into *chiffonade*. Wash the leeks and onions very carefully. Chop the white of the leek and the green onion bulbs finely. Chop the cabbage and lettuce hearts.

2   Cook the rice in plenty of boiling salted water with the green of the leek and green onions, the parsley sprigs and thyme.

3   Cook the cabbage leaves and quarters in a steamer above salted boiling water for 10 minutes with the lid on, and for a further 15 minutes without the lid.

4   Heat the oil in a skillet pan and sweat, one after the other, the green onion, leek, lettuce and cabbage hearts, the *chiffonade* of lettuce and sorrel. Keep them well covered, and allow 2 minutes between each addition. Add the tomato and sweat for a minute longer. Add the cheese, the rice, a pinch of salt and some pepper. Mix well and put on a plate to cool. When it is cold, add the yogurt and adjust the seasoning if necessary. If you want to serve the *paupiettes* cold, add the mustard sauce to the filling and leave to marinate for at least an hour.

5   Divide the cabbage quarters into leaves and lay on a board covered with paper towels to absorb the excess moisture. Divide the stuffing between the leaves, fold in the sides, and roll.

TO SERVE If serving hot, preheat the oven to 350°F. Lay each *paupiette*, opening side down, in a greased 10-inch gratin dish. Cover with foil and place in the oven for 5 minutes to reheat. Serve with a warm tomato *coulis* if you like.

When serving cold, arrange on a platter lined with cabbage leaves, and garnish with the lemon.

RIGHT *Paupiettes de Choux*

Feuilletés aux Champignons
MUSHROOMS IN PASTRY

*T*hese puff pastry feuilletés *are always a huge success. They are simple to make, economical, and taste delicious. You can, if you prefer, prepare one large* feuilleté, *in which case the cooking time should be increased by 5–10 minutes.*

SERVES 4
PREHEAT THE OVEN TO THE MAXIMUM SETTING, NORMALLY 475°F

Pâte Feuilletée *made with 11 oz. flour (see page 42)*
egg wash
2 tbsp. butter
1 lb. button mushrooms, thinly sliced
1 tsp. lemon juice
salt
freshly ground black pepper
⅓ cup white wine
½ cup whipping cream

GARNISH
2 tbsp. parsley, chopped

Feuilletés aux Champignons

1 Prepare the *feuilletés* as shown on page 14.

2 Bake in the preheated oven for 5 minutes, then turn the temperature down to 350°F and bake until the pastry is golden brown, approximately 15–20 minutes. The center part of the pastry cases will rise. When cooked, remove the upper layers with a sharp knife, and use these top parts as a lid. Dry out the bases a little more in the oven.

3 For the filling, melt the butter and sauté the mushrooms over high heat, adding the lemon juice, salt, pepper, and white wine. Cover with a lid as soon as the juices of the mushrooms start to run, turn the heat down to medium and leave them, covered, for 5 minutes. Remove the lid and add the cream. Leave to reduce slowly, for about 10–15 minutes. There must still be a little sauce, or the filling will be too dry.

TO SERVE When the mushrooms are done, mix in half of the parsley. Spoon the mushrooms into each *feuilleté*. Sprinkle with parsley.

If you have prepared one large *feuilleté*, bring it to the table, slice off the ends with a serrated knife, and cut into four portions.

Pudding de Courgettes Soufflé
SOUFFLÉD ZUCCHINI

his delicious starter is halfway between a soufflé and a zucchini terrine "au gratin." Prepared individually in ramekin dishes and served with a tomato coulis, it looks very pretty.

The basic soufflé can be prepared up to a day in advance and reheated in a very hot oven for a few minutes before serving.

If you replace the whole-wheat flour with potato starch the recipe is gluten free.

SERVES 4
PREHEAT THE OVEN TO 350°F

11 oz. zucchini, washed, topped and tailed
salt
1 tsp. butter
1 tbsp. olive oil
2 garlic cloves, peeled and crushed
⅔ cup milk
freshly ground black pepper
cayenne pepper
grated nutmeg
¼ cup Emmenthal or Gruyère cheese, grated
1 heaping tbsp. whole-wheat flour
1 egg, separated
1 tbsp. fines herbes, finely chopped
3 egg whites

TO SERVE
1 recipe Coulis de Tomates (see page 38)
3 tbsp. Parmesan cheese, grated

1   Grate the zucchini finely (by hand or in a food processor) and place in layers in a bowl and sprinkle each layer with a teaspoon of salt. Leave for 20 minutes. Butter four ramekin dishes lightly and refrigerate to set.

2   Rinse the zucchini under cold water to rid them of the salt. Take small amounts at a time in your hand and squeeze well to eliminate as much water as possible. Heat the oil in a skillet, and sauté the zucchini very quickly for 3 minutes to evaporate the remaining moisture, adding the garlic after 2 minutes. Remove to a plate to cool.

3   Place the milk in a saucepan with a pinch of salt, a little black pepper, a pinch of both cayenne and grated nutmeg and bring to the boil. Mix the Emmenthal cheese with the flour in a bowl. Pour a third of the boiling milk into the bowl, mixing well, then return to the rest of the milk in the pan. Bring back to the boil, whisking vigorously, and take off the heat. Add the egg yolk and mix well, then add the zucchini and herbs and mix again. Reserve, covered, in a warm place.

4   Whisk the 4 egg whites until they hold soft peaks (still a little runny). Mix a spoonful into the zucchini batter, and fold the remainder in delicately.

5   Dust the buttered ramekins with white flour, and tap upside-down on the work surface to eliminate the excess. Fill them three-quarters full with the zucchini batter. Line a roasting pan with a sheet of paper (parchment or brown paper) and place the ramekins on it. Pour enough boiling water in the pan to come halfway up the dishes.

6   Bake in the preheated oven for 15 minutes. Remove and leave to cool for 5 minutes. The soufflés will fall. Turn each ramekin out onto a serving plate. If serving more than 1 hour later leave in the ramekins until ready to reheat.

TO SERVE Preheat the oven to 450°F.
Pour some tomato *coulis* over the soufflés and sprinkle with Parmesan. Bake in the hot oven for 5 minutes and serve immediately.

Soufflé au Fromage
CHEESE SOUFFLÉ

*T*his version of a classic cheese soufflé excludes the butter normally used for the roux. The cheese itself contains enough fat.
   This mixture fills a 2-quart soufflé dish, so measure your dish and adjust the quantities accordingly.

SERVES 6
PREHEAT THE OVEN TO 350°F

1²/₃ cups milk
salt
freshly ground black pepper
grated nutmeg
1 tbsp. butter
½ cup flour (plus extra to dust)
²/₃ cup Gruyère cheese, freshly
   grated
5 eggs, separated
2 egg whites
1 tbsp. fines herbes, finely
   chopped

1   Bring the milk, salt, pepper and nutmeg to the boil in a saucepan.
2   Butter a 2-quart soufflé dish and dust it lightly with a little of the flour.
3   In a bowl, mix together the flour and cheese. Pour the boiling milk over this mixture, whisking hard and continuously. Add the egg yolks, one at a time.
4   Beat the egg whites until they form soft peaks, and fold gently into the cheese batter with the herbs.
5   Pour the mixture into the prepared soufflé dish, and bake in the preheated oven for 20–30 minutes.

TO SERVE As with all soufflés, make sure your guests are seated at the table waiting for it. Place the soufflé dish on a plate lined with a folded napkin or a doily and serve *immediately*!

Soufflé au Saumon Fumé
SMOKED SALMON SOUFFLÉ

*T*his soufflé has a major advantage when compared to traditional soufflés — no butter is used, and with a minor change of method, the soufflé works very well.

SERVES 6
PREHEAT THE OVEN TO 350°F

1 tsp. grapeseed or safflower oil
1 medium onion, peeled and
   finely chopped
1¹/₃ cups skim milk
salt
freshly ground black pepper
3 oz. smoked salmon
3 capers, drained and finely
   chopped
¹/₃ cup flour
4 eggs, separated
1 egg white

1   Heat the oil in a skillet, and sweat the onion over low heat, covered, until tender, about 10–15 minutes. Leave to cool briefly.
2   Bring the milk, some salt, and pepper to the boil in a saucepan.
3   Process the smoked salmon in a food processor or purée in a food mill, then mix with the capers in a bowl. Into another bowl containing the flour, pour the boiling milk, whisking hard and continuously. Add the egg yolks one at a time, then season with a pinch of salt and plenty of pepper. Add the salmon mixture and mix well.
4   Beat the egg whites until they form soft peaks, and fold gently into the mixture with the sweated onions.
5   Pour into a 1-quart soufflé dish that has been oiled and lightly floured, and bake in the preheated oven for 30 minutes.

TO SERVE Serve *immediately*, like all the other soufflés.

Quiche aux Oignons
ONION TART

*T*his quiche originated in Alsace where it is called "zewelwai." *Fewer onions were used, and a larger quantity of eggs, cream, ham and butter. Onions cooked this way taste very good.*

1 Allow the pastry to rest in the refrigerator for 20 minutes. Line a 10-inch tart pan with a removable bottom. Prick the base of the pastry with a fork, line with a circle of foil or parchment paper, then cover with baking beans. Bake blind in the oven for 10 minutes then remove the foil or paper and the beans. Brush a little egg wash over the inside, and return to the oven for 2 minutes. Repeat this twice more.

2 While the pastry is cooking prepare the filling. Put the onions in a saucepan with the water, white wine, thyme, bay leaf, salt, pepper and the butter. Cover with a lid and simmer very gently for 10 minutes. Remove the lid and let the juices reduce completely. Be attentive once the juices have evaporated. The onions need to color a little, but stir regularly so they do not stick or burn.

3 While the onions are cooking, heat the oil in a skillet and sauté the ham until golden brown. Drain on paper towels. (If you want to allow yourself a little treat, omit the butter from the filling, and add this fat to the onions while they cook.)

4 When both onions and the pastry base are ready, mix the eggs, cream and milk together in a bowl. Add to the onions off the heat, then add the ham. Remove the bay leaf and thyme, and mix very carefully but thoroughly before transferring to the pastry base. Spread evenly all over and bake for 20–30 minutes in the preheated oven until golden brown on top.

TO SERVE Transfer the pan onto a cooling rack, removing the base and sides and leave to cool for 5–10 minutes before serving. Garnish with a few sprigs of parsley.

SERVES 8 AS A STARTER,
6 AS A MAIN COURSE
PREHEAT THE OVEN TO 350°F

1 recipe Pâte Brisée *(see page 44)*
egg wash
1½ lb. onions, peeled and thickly sliced
¼ cup water
¼ cup white wine
1 sprig thyme
1 bay leaf
salt
freshly ground black pepper
2 tbsp. butter
1 tsp. grapeseed or safflower oil
4 oz. ham or bacon (fat and rind removed), diced
2 eggs
½ cup whipping cream
⅓ cup skim milk

GARNISH
parsley sprigs

Quiche aux Oignons

Pissaladière à la Niçoise
PROVENÇAL ONION TART

A pissaladière *is usually served as a snack in the markets of the south of France, and is the southern version of the onion quiches of Alsace. It can be served as a main course, with an accompanying salad.*

We use oregano in the filling which, like many herbs, is reputed to help digestion and many internal disorders.

SERVES 8
PREHEAT THE OVEN TO 450°F

1 recipe Pâte à Pissaladière *(see page 43)*
1½lb. onions, peeled, halved and thickly sliced
salt
1 bay leaf
1 sprig thyme
1 tbsp. dried oregano or 12 fresh leaves
1 tbsp. olive oil
1 garlic clove, peeled
12 black olives
½ cup white wine
freshly ground black pepper
10 anchovy fillets, drained

1 Let the *pissaladière* dough rise in a warm place. Knock it down and use half of it to line a 10-inch tart pan. Leave in a warm place to rise again. (With the leftover dough, make a few rolls to serve with your next meal.)

2 Meanwhile, place the onion slices in a saucepan with a pinch of salt and the remaining ingredients, except the oregano and anchovies. Simmer over low heat, covered, for 5 minutes, and then cook uncovered until the liquid has evaporated. Continue cooking over the same low heat to brown slightly. Remove the garlic, bay leaf and thyme. Add half of the oregano and mix well.

3 When the dough has risen, cover the top with the onions and arrange the olives evenly around, with the anchovy fillets between them. Sprinkle the remaining oregano over the top.

4 Bake in the preheated oven for 30–40 minutes. Remove from the pan and cool for a few minutes before serving, or serve cold.

Tourte de Courgettes et d'Aubergines

ZUCCHINI AND EGGPLANT PIE

*T*his is a delicious *tourte, or pie, which can be prepared ahead of time and reheated, and it can also be served cold for a buffet or a picnic. It is a very good way to use up the livers that come with chicken and are usually thrown away. We store them in a jar in the freezer and when the jar is full, it is time to make this* tourte.

Seal the vegetables well initially or their moisture will come out while the tourte *is cooking and make the dough soggy.*

1   Allow the puff pastry to rest in the refrigerator for 20 minutes.

2   Slice the eggplant and zucchini, salt well and leave them to drain for 15 minutes. Rinse them to remove the salt, and dry on paper towels. Heat 1 tablespoon oil in a large frying pan and sauté the vegetables briefly over high heat to seal the slices. Be careful not to put too much oil in the pan as both vegetables will absorb as much as you give them. Put aside to cool.

3   Sweat the onions and garlic in a little more olive oil in the same pan, and put aside to cool.

4   Remove any nerves and greenish parts from the chicken livers. Chop them very finely to an almost purée consistency. Place in a bowl, beat the egg into them and season well with salt, pepper and the herbs.

5   Roll out the puff pastry and cut a round shape for the top of the pie. Roll out the rest and use to line an 8-inch tart pan with a removable bottom. Mix the vegetables with the liver and pour onto the pastry base. Brush the edges of the pastry with egg wash and place the lid on top. Crimp the edges with your fingers to stick them together, and make a hole in the center of the top. Keep it open with a chimney of foil (rolled around the handle of a wooden spoon). Brush the top with more egg wash and place in the refrigerator to rest for 10 minutes. Make a decoration on the top with the back of a knife.

6   Place in the preheated oven, and turn it down immediately to 350°F. Bake for 40 minutes.

7   Remove the sides of the tart pan, brush the pastry with egg wash, and leave to brown for a further 5 minutes. Repeat once more.

TO SERVE   Meanwhile, prepare the tomato sauce. Leave the *tourte* to cool for 5 minutes on a cooling rack, base removed, then serve warm with the sauce.

SERVES 6 AS A STARTER,
4 AS A MAIN COURSE
PREHEAT THE OVEN TO 450°F

Pâte Feuilletée *made with 11oz.
    flour (see page 42)*
1½lb. eggplant
5oz. zucchini, *washed, topped
    and tailed*
salt
olive oil
4 green onions, *thinly sliced*
2 garlic cloves, *peeled and
    crushed*
4oz. chicken livers
1 egg
freshly ground black pepper
¾ cup fines herbes, *chopped*
egg wash

TO SERVE
1 recipe Sauce à la Tomate *(see
    page 36)*

LEFT *Pissaladière à la Niçoise*

Gougère
CHOUX PASTRY RING

*A gougère, a choux pastry ring flavored with cheese, is tradition-
ally served during wine tastings in Burgundy — but even if you
don't have such a pleasant task to perform, you can indulge in this
light and tasty confection. If you serve it with a salad as the main part
of a meal with a fruit dessert afterwards, it makes a delicious and
satisfying light lunch or supper.*

SERVES 4
PREHEAT THE OVEN TO 400°F

4 oz. Emmenthal cheese
1 recipe Pâte à Choux *(see page
    42)*
egg wash

TO SERVE
salad greens
1 recipe Sauce Vinaigrette *(see
    page 35)*

ABOVE *Gougère*

1   Cut the cheese in half. Cut one piece into very small cubes (they
need to go through the tip of the pastry bag) and the other into thin
slices with a cheese slicer. Add the cubes to the choux dough and
place in a pastry bag fitted with a ¼-inch plain tip.
2   Pipe four small rings 3 inches in diameter, or one larger ring
about 10 inches in diameter, on a greased baking sheet. Brush with a
little of the egg wash, and place the slices of cheese on top.
3   Bake in the preheated oven for approximately 10 minutes, and
then for 5 minutes longer at 350°F with the door slightly ajar (prop it
open with the handle of a wooden spoon). Increase these times by 5
minutes if you are making the larger ring.

TO SERVE Prepare a few salad greens using different varieties (try lettuce, radicchio, chicory, watercress, etc.) ready to be tossed with the vinaigrette, and placed in the middle of the rings. As soon as the *gougères* are ready, arrange the dressed salad greens and serve immediately. The quantity of salad served with them depends on whether the *gougères* are to be served as a starter or a main course.

Terrine de Foies de Volaille
CHICKEN LIVER PÂTÉ

*D*on't be alarmed by the amount of butter and cream used here, it has already been reduced by half and is shared between 10 people! The stock used should be of the highest quality and should be quite strong before being reduced. The terrine will be at its best 24 hours after cooking, as the flavors will have had time to mingle.

It can also be served warm as a first course. Reheat slowly in a bain-marie, then slice and serve on a bed of Coulis de Tomates *(see page 38), with a few peeled and seeded tomatoes, and chopped parsley.*

If you are on a gluten-free diet, omit the breadcrumbs, and add one more egg instead.

SERVES 10
PREHEAT THE OVEN TO 300°F

1 lb. chicken livers
1 quart Fonds de Volaille *(see page 31)*
3⁄4 cup dry whole-wheat breadcrumbs
4 garlic cloves, peeled and crushed
4 oz. softened butter
3 eggs, beaten
1⁄2 cup whipping cream
2 tbsp. cognac
salt
freshly ground black pepper
cayenne pepper
paprika

GARNISH
aspic
parsley sprigs
tomato rose (see page 26)

1   Wash and drain the livers and lay on a work surface to separate them. Remove the nerves, and any green parts or fat.

2   Reduce the stock by simmering to obtain 1 cup, about 20 minutes, then add the breadcrumbs. Mix well to make a dough or *panade*. Cook over low heat for 2–3 minutes, then add the garlic.

3   Using a food processor or a hand food mill, purée the livers. Add the *panade*, with the butter (reserving about 1 teaspoon), the eggs, cream and cognac and season well to taste. Blend thoroughly and then push through a sieve, to eliminate any nerves still left in the livers.

4   Grease a 6-cup terrine with the remaining butter, and line the bottom with a strip of parchment paper (to facilitate turning out).

5   Pour the liver mixture into the dish, cover with foil and place in a bain-marie. Bake in the preheated oven for 30 minutes, until the pâté sets. Switch off the oven and leave the pâté to cool in the oven. Refrigerate for 24 hours before serving.

TO SERVE Turn out onto a serving dish garnished with chopped aspic and cut two or three slices. Do not slice ahead of time, however, since without coloring and preservative of any sort, oxydization will take place, changing the color of the livers from pink to greenish. Garnish with some parsley sprigs and a tomato rose.

FISH AND SHELLFISH

Cuisine Santé uses a lot more fish than traditional cuisiné because it is lower in fat than meats, and what fat there is, is polyunsaturated. White fish (skate, rainbow trout, sole, haddock, monkfish, turbot and bass) contain less fat than oily ones (salmon and sea trout), and both types are high in protein, vitamins and minerals.

Shellfish, although unfortunately expensive, should be healthy, but they are only worth considering when at their freshest, and when they come from unpolluted waters. They spend their life filtering water for nutrients but, alas, in the process, they also retain the filth we put in that water.

Truites Farcies Grillées
STUFFED GRILLED TROUT

This trout dish has always been a success — ask the television team who came to Clapham House to film A Taste of Health! *The boning can take a long time, but once you have mastered the technique (see page 15) it will become easier and quicker. The combination of prunes and spinach, though unusual, is particularly delicious and nutritious.*

1   For the stuffing, toast the almonds until golden, then allow to cool.
2   Heat the oil in a large pan, and sweat the onion over gentle heat for 1 minute, then add the spinach *chiffonade* and cook over high heat for 2 minutes. Add the mushrooms and cook for a minute longer. Put aside to cool, and then add the almonds and prunes. Season well with salt and pepper.
3   Cut the trout and remove the backbones (see page 15). Remove all the smaller bones with tweezers. Rinse well under cold running water, dry with paper towels, and season with salt and pepper.
4   Stuff the trout with the cooled spinach mixture, packing it in well, and then place the fish on lightly oiled foil on a broiler pan.
5   Broil for 4 minutes on each side, remove and leave for a further 4 minutes to rest before serving.
6   For the sauce, put the yogurt into a bowl and whisk in the olive oil. Season well to taste, then add the chives. Pour into a gravy boat.

TO SERVE   Steam the new potatoes.
Remove the top skin from each trout and arrange them on individual warmed serving plates with the potatoes.

GLUTEN FREE
SERVES 4
PREHEAT THE BROILER TO ITS
MAXIMUM TEMPERATURE

4 trout
salt
freshly ground black pepper
1/3 cup slivered almonds
1/2 tsp. grapeseed or safflower oil
1 onion, peeled and chopped
1 lb. spinach, cut into chiffonade
2 oz. button mushrooms, sliced
2 oz. pitted prunes, chopped

SAUCE
3/4 cup Greek yogurt
2 tbsp. olive oil
a small bunch of chives (1 oz.),
   freshly snipped

TO SERVE
1 lb. new potatoes, scrubbed

Truites Bendor
TROUT BENDOR

*T*hese trout were traditionally accompanied by a very rich sauce made with twice the amount of cream and egg yolks that we have used. The sauce is now much lighter, although it retains the original anise flavor, using dill and Pernod. A little trick is to add a teaspoon of potato starch to the Greek yogurt which allows the sauce to reach boiling point without curdling.

To keep the fish whole, ask the grocer to gut them through the gills.

These trout can be served hot or cold with the sauce. If serving cold, allow them to cool in the stock.

GLUTEN FREE
SERVES 4
PREHEAT THE OVEN TO 350°F

4 coho salmon or rainbow trout (5 oz. each), gutted through the gills and cleaned
salt
freshly ground black pepper
5 tsp. Pernod
5 small sprigs dill
½ lemon, sliced and quartered
1 quart Court-Bouillon *(see page 32)*
5 each of black peppercorns, dill, caraway and fennel seeds, crushed
2 sprigs parsley
1 small bay leaf
1 sprig thyme
5 ice cubes
½ cup milk
¼ cup whipping cream
2 egg yolks
½ cup Greek yogurt
1 tsp. potato starch

TO SERVE
1 lb. vegetables of choice
fresh dill, finely chopped
¼ cup slivered almonds, toasted

1   Cut the tails of the fish into a "V" shape for decorative purposes, then dry the insides using paper towels. Season the interior through the gills with salt and pepper, 1 teaspoon of Pernod per fish, a sprig of dill and lemon slices.

2   Place the fish in an ovenproof dish and cover with the cool *court-bouillon*. Add a pinch of salt and the peppercorns and seeds to the *court-bouillon* along with the parsley sprigs, bay leaf and thyme. Cover with a lid or foil and bake in the preheated oven for approximately 10 minutes, or until the flesh of the fish is firm and the eyes have become opaque.

3   When the fish is done, add the ice cubes to the stock to stop the cooking.

4   For the sauce, combine the milk, cream and ½ cup of the strained fish stock in a saucepan, and bring to the boil. Combine the egg yolks, yogurt and potato starch, then add a little of the boiling liquid and stir well. Pour it back into the saucepan and whisk over very low heat (to get air into it). Let it come to the boil, but immediately remove from the heat, or the yolks will curdle. Add the remaining teaspoon of Pernod. Finely chop the remaining sprig of fresh dill and add it to the sauce. Correct the seasoning if necessary: the sauce should have a fresh taste of anise, rather than tasting of too much salt and pepper.

TO SERVE Steam the vegetables of choice, and sprinkle with the dill. The trout need to be skinned, but this should be done at the last moment as the skin preserves the moisture and tenderness of the flesh. Remove also the brown fat attached to the flesh, being careful not to damage the flesh.

Reheat the stock in the preheated oven while skinning the fish. Warm the fish through by placing in the stock for a minute only.

Arrange the trout on a warm serving dish, cover with some of the sauce and garnish with the slivered almonds. Surround with the steamed vegetables if there is room, or serve them in a separate warmed dish. Pour the remaining sauce into a gravy boat.

RIGHT *Truites Bendor*

Haddock Sauce aux Oeufs

HADDOCK WITH EGG SAUCE

In the classic recipe, the sauce is thickened with a roux of butter and flour, but this is now removed and replaced with a small amount of Greek yogurt plus, of course, the traditional hard-boiled egg. When served with basil, a "natural tranquilizer," the haddock becomes much more digestible.

Start preparing the dish the day before you intend to serve it. Be sure to choose the best quality haddock without coloring or preservatives; it should be pale yellow in color, not deep yellow.

THE DAY BEFORE SERVING

1   Soak the haddock fillet in a mixture of half the milk and half the water overnight at room temperature.

2   Put the egg for the sauce into a pan of cold water, bring to the boil and boil it for 6 minutes exactly. Allow it to cool in the cooking water and keep in the refrigerator overnight.

THE DAY OF SERVING

1   Take the egg out of the refrigerator and bring it to room temperature.

2   Drain the fish on paper towels, and throw away the marinade. Place the fish in a saucepan and cover with the remaining milk and water. Season with white pepper and add the parsley sprigs, thyme and bay leaf. Bring slowly to the boil, cover with a lid and cook for 1 minute, then remove from the heat and let stand 10 minutes longer to infuse and cook.

3   To make the sauce, pour the cooking liquid into another saucepan, leaving ½ cup in the original pan to keep the fish moist. Keep the fish warm. Simmer to reduce the cooking liquid by half, about 15–20 minutes. Mix a little of the liquid with the rice flour in a small cup. Pour it back into the remaining cooking liquid and simmer for 1 minute, stirring. Add the cream and cook a minute longer. Remove the herbs.

4   Shell the hard-boiled egg and separate the yolk from the white. Cut the white into *julienne* strips, and push the yolk through a sieve into the sauce. Add the egg white *julienne*, the yogurt, parsley and basil. Season to taste with salt and white pepper. If necessary, thin the sauce with the liquid remaining in the fish pan.

TO SERVE Steam the vegetables.

Lay the fish on a warmed serving platter and spoon the sauce over it. Surround with the vegetables and lemon slices.

To serve individually, arrange each piece of fish in the middle of a plate, and pour over enough sauce to cover the plate. Garnish with the egg white *julienne*, and arrange the vegetables and lemon slices around the rim of the plate.

GLUTEN FREE
SERVES 4

1 lb. smoked haddock fillet, cut into 4 pieces
1 quart skim milk
1 quart water
freshly ground white pepper
3 sprigs parsley
1 sprig thyme
1 bay leaf
½ tsp. rice flour
1 egg
¼ cup whipping cream
¼ cup Greek yogurt
salt
1 tbsp. parsley, finely chopped
2 tbsp. basil, finely chopped

TO SERVE
turned root vegetables and green vegetables as for Raie à l'Estragon *(see page 99)*
lemon slices

LEFT *Haddock Sauce aux Oeufs*

Sole Farcie Soufflée
SOUFFLÉD STUFFED SOLE

*T*raditionally, this haute cuisine dish has a very rich mousseline of fish as a stuffing, mixed with egg white and a lot of cream. Here we have replaced part of the cream with some Greek yogurt and a little more egg white.

The addition of spices gives it a slightly Oriental taste, but in the summer, you can replace these with a handful of chopped fines herbes for a lighter flavor.

GLUTEN FREE

SERVES 4

PREHEAT THE OVEN TO 350°F

1 Dover sole (2¼ lb.)
1 cup water
⅞ cup dry white wine
mirepoix (1 onion, 1 carrot,
    1 celery stalk)
1 bouquet garni
4 oz. salmon, hake or cod, boned
    and skinned
½ cup whipping cream
½ cup Greek yogurt
1 pinch each of ground allspice,
    cloves and nutmeg
freshly ground black pepper
freshly ground coriander
ice cubes
2 oz. pistachio nuts, shelled
1 egg, separated, and 1 extra egg
    white
2 tsp. grapeseed or safflower oil
1 shallot, peeled and finely
    chopped

TO SERVE
1 lb. broccoli florets
5 oz. each of carrots, turnips and
    rutabaga, cut into julienne
fresh chives

1 Skin the sole on both sides and bone as described on page 16. Reserve the bones.

2 Place the bones in a saucepan, and add the water, half the white wine, the roughly chopped *mirepoix*, and the *bouquet garni*. Bring to a simmer over low heat, skimming off the impurities as they rise to the surface. Simmer gently for 10 minutes and then remove from the heat.

3 Using a pestle and mortar or a food processor, pureé the salmon (or other fish) with one of the egg whites. A little at a time, add half the cream and yogurt, plus the spices, the allspice, cloves, nutmeg, pepper and coriander. To eliminate any bones, nerves or pieces of skin, push the mixture through a sieve into a bowl set on top of another one containing ice cubes. Place in the freezer for 15 minutes, beating well every 5 minutes.

4 Rub the pistachio nuts in a cloth to remove the salt. Alternatively, blanch them for 2 minutes in boiling water, to eliminate the skins and obtain the typical green color. Chop them finely, keeping four whole. Add the chopped nuts to the mixture. Beat the remaining egg white until stiff and fold carefully into the mixture. Place inside a pastry bag with a fluted tip and (following the technique instructions on pages 16–17) pipe the *mousseline* inside the fish. Garnish with the remaining whole pistachios.

5 Drain the fish stock through a conical sieve lined with cheesecloth.

6 Oil a gratin dish with 1 teaspoon of the oil, and place the fish in it. Pour ¼ cup of the remaining white wine and ½ cup of the fish stock over the fish, and cover with foil. Bake in the preheated oven for 10 minutes, then strain most of the juices into a bowl, leaving about 1 tablespoon to prevent the fish from drying up. Return the fish to the turned-off oven, close the door, and leave for another 10 minutes.

7 Meanwhile, heat the remaining oil in a skillet, and sweat the shallot slowly for about 5 minutes. Deglaze with the remaining wine, and reduce until almost completely evaporated. Add the remaining fish stock and cook to reduce by half. Add the remaining cream and reduce for 2 minutes longer. This takes in total about 15–20 minutes.

TO SERVE Steam the vegetables together for 2 minutes with the lid on, and 3 minutes with the lid off (this will keep the broccoli bright green).

Take the sauce off the heat. Mix the remaining yogurt in a bowl with the egg yolk. Combine with a tablespoon of the sauce and pour back into the sauce, a little at a time, stirring well. *Do not reheat.*

Carefully transfer the sole onto a heated serving dish. With a knife, scrape off the bones from around the edges of the sole and discard. Clean the dish well and pour half the sauce over the sole. Pour the remainder into a warm gravy boat. Garnish with some of the vegetables tied into bundles with a blanched chive, and present the remainder in a warm vegetable dish. Serve immediately.

Sole Farcie Soufflée

Darnes de Saumon en Papillote
SALMON STEAKS EN PAPILLOTE

B *y cooking* en papillote *(in paper parcels), these salmon steaks can be flavored to taste with whatever is in season at the market.*
Do experiment with other herbs, fruit or vegetables, as they will add individuality to your cuisine. Here, the combination of asparagus and dill gives a spring-like flavor to the salmon. Any other "hard" vegetable used will need to be steam-blanched, like the asparagus used here, for a few minutes before wrapping in the parcel.

1 Prepare the asparagus for the *papillote* and the garnish at the same time. If they are all large, peel the stems with a potato peeler, starting from the base to about three-quarters of the way up. If you've bought young, thin asparagus, this will not be necessary. Working with the four large spears only, cut the tips off diagonally, about 1¼ inches from the tip, then cut the stems diagonally into ½-inch slices. Bring a steamer to the boil and steam the asparagus tips and slices for 3 minutes.

2 Using a pestle and mortar, mash together half the dill, a pinch of salt, some pepper and the anise liqueur. Rub the paste over the salmon steaks and marinate for at least 10 minutes.

3 Meanwhile, prepare the *papillotes* (see page 28). Place a salmon steak on each sheet of paper with 1 asparagus tip, a quarter of the asparagus slices, ½ tablespoon of white wine and a little of the remaining dill. Close the parcels well and reserve until you are ready to cook. They can be prepared up to 2 hours before serving and kept in the refrigerator, in which case no additional marinating time is necessary.

4 When ready to cook, bake the *papillotes* in the preheated oven for 10 minutes only.

TO SERVE Steam the vegetables for about 10 minutes. Put the potatoes in a warmed dish with the remaining chopped dill, cover well and leave to marinate for 5 minutes before serving. Present the asparagus in a serving dish lined with a napkin.

Bring the *papillotes* to the table unopened on a large serving platter (or on individual plates), and let your guests enjoy the wonderful smell as they open their parcels. Serve the *Sauce Beurre Blanc* separately.

To remove the center bone of the steaks easily, push the tip of a sharp knife deeply into the center bone, and ease it around the bone with a twisting motion to loosen it. Pull the bone out, and remove the side bones in between the fillets on either side of the main bone.

GLUTEN FREE
SERVES 4
PREHEAT THE OVEN TO 450°F

*4 large asparagus spears, about
    8 oz. total weight*
4 sprigs dill
salt
freshly ground black pepper
1 tsp. Pernod, Ricard or Ouzo
4 salmon steaks, 7 oz. each
2 tbsp. dry white wine

TO SERVE
*2¼ lb. baby new potatoes,
    scrubbed*
1¼ lb. asparagus (any size)
1 recipe Sauce Beurre Blanc *(see
    page 41)*

LEFT *Darnes de Saumon en Papillote*

Saumon à la Riga
POACHED SALMON WITH GREEN SAUCE

*T*his is a very traditional buffet dish originated by Pellaprat (author of the famous "bible" of French cuisine of the same name), but instead of using a very rich mayonnaise, we have used our delicious Sauce Verte.

It is best to prepare this dish over 2 days, which leaves enough time for it to marinate in its court-bouillon overnight. Another thick fish, such as a trout, a sea bass, a sea trout or a small hake could be prepared in the same way.

You can baptize a brand-new plant atomizer for this dish — the final aspic needs to be sprayed on!

GLUTEN FREE

SERVES 4

5 quarts Court-Bouillon *(see page 32)*
1 salmon *(4½ lb.)*, with head, gutted
salt
5 each of white and black peppercorns, coriander, dill and caraway seeds, crushed
2 fennel seeds, crushed
1 large sprig dill
5 sprigs parsley
⅞ cup white wine
1 lemon, washed and sliced
1 recipe Sauce Verte *(see page 38)*
1 cucumber, washed
2 tsp. unflavored gelatin

GARNISH
2 tomato roses *(see page 26)*
2 lemons, sliced and halved
1 tsp. cognac
lemon twists *(see page 26)*

THE DAY BEFORE SERVING

1   Leave the prepared *court-bouillon* to cool.

2   If not done by the fishmonger, gut the fish carefully yourself. Clean well under cold running water, and place in a fish poacher. If the fish is too long, cut the head off and cook it separately in water with some lemon juice, and "attach" it when assembling the dish.

3   Strain the cold *court-bouillon* over the fish and add a pinch of salt and the peppercorns and seeds along with the fresh dill, parsley sprigs, white wine and lemon slices. Mix well.

4   Place the fish poacher over medium heat and bring slowly to the boil. At the first bubble, turn the heat off (remove from the heat if using electricity), and place a folded and rinsed dish towel between the poaching pan and lid (see pages 17–18). Allow it to cool completely.

THE DAY OF SERVING

1   Store the *Sauce Verte* in the refrigerator.

2   Slice the cucumber thinly by hand or, for more evenly thin slices, in a food processor. Arrange the slices in layers on a plate with a pinch of salt in between each layer. Cover and leave for 20 minutes.

3   Lift the fish on the tray out of the poacher, and let it drain for a moment. Reserve 1 cup of the stock and filter through cheesecloth or a clean, damp towel. Chill ⅓ cup of it in a small ramekin in the freezer. Sprinkle the gelatin over the cold stock and let it soften, about 5 minutes. Place the ramekin in a shallow pan of simmering water to dissolve the gelatin, stirring constantly. Combine with the remaining ⅔ cup stock. Pour into an atomizer bottle to be used later.

4   Cut a piece of cardboard to the length and shape of the fish and wrap it in foil.

5   Very carefully peel off the entire skin of the fish as well as the brown fatty layer under it to expose the pink flesh. Detach the flesh of the top fillet carefully, one section at a time, and keep to one side, re-assembled to shape. Transfer the bottom part of the fish to the foil-covered board. Remove the bones carefully, and discard.

6   Spread a thick layer of the *Sauce Verte* over the fillet on the board, and lay the top fillets over this, reshaping the fish as accurately as possible. Fix the head back in place.

7 Rinse the cucumber well and dry on paper towels. Starting at the tail end, arrange the slices over the surface of the fish, overlapping, and cover half the head, too.

8 Place the fish in the freezer for 10 minutes to cool quickly (or 20 minutes in the refrigerator), then spray the aspic evenly all over. Return the fish to the freezer for 5 minutes and repeat the operation several times to build up a heavy layer of aspic which will help the fish and cucumber retain their freshness. If the aspic starts to set and block the spray, leave the upper part (the nozzle) of the atomizer submerged in the sink with hot, soapy water for 5 minutes and rinse well; place the bottom part in a bowl of hot water for 1 minute, or until the aspic becomes liquid again. Place the remaining aspic on a shallow plate and set in the refrigerator.

TO SERVE Prepare the serving dish. Using two napkins and some foil, prepare a gondola (see page 29). Lay a third napkin in between the two napkins.

Just before serving, place the fish on its board on the serving dish. Garnish with the tomato roses, lemon twists and half slices of lemon all around. Turn the reserved aspic out on to a towel, chop with a large knife, sprinkle with the cognac and use to garnish the fish.

Huîtres au Gratin
OYSTERS AU GRATIN

This is a delicious way to use oysters, but beware, for oysters, like other shellfish, are very high in cholesterol. With the addition of the egg yolk too this dish is not particularly healthy, so the yolk should be optional (although it gives a richer taste and better color). In their favor, though, oysters are low in carbohydrate and high in protein, iron, and calcium.

GLUTEN FREE
SERVES 4
PREHEAT THE OVEN TO 350°F, AND PREHEAT THE BROILER TO ITS MAXIMUM

24 oysters, washed well
1 tsp. grapeseed or safflower oil
1 shallot, peeled and finely chopped
2 oz. each of leek, carrot, rutabaga and celeriac, cut into julienne
1/2 cup Bouillon de Légumes or Fumet de Poisson (see pages 32 and 33)
1/2 tsp. lemon juice
salt
freshly ground black pepper
1 egg yolk
2 tbsp. Greek yogurt
2 tbsp. whipping cream

1 Put the oysters on a tray in the oven for 2 minutes until they open. Remove from the shell and pour the juices into a bowl. Clean the hollow half shells well and reserve.

2 Heat the oil in a skillet and sweat the shallot until soft, about 5 minutes. Add the vegetable *julienne* and the oyster juice, and leave to simmer very gently for 5 minutes, covered.

3 Add the stock and reduce by half, about 5–10 minutes. Add the lemon juice and season lightly with salt and pepper.

4 Whisk the egg yolk with the yogurt and cream, then pour in the boiling stock reduction and stir well for 1 minute.

TO SERVE Arrange the half shells in a roasting pan or baking sheet the size of the broiler and place a little of the vegetable *julienne* in the shells. Top with the oysters, cover with more vegetable *julienne* and some sauce. Broil for 1 1/2 minutes, then transfer to a serving dish lined with a doily or folded napkin. Serve immediately.

Roulade Bicolore
SOLE AND SALMON ROULADE

*T*hese attractive sole and smoked salmon rolls can be served hot as a main course, as here, hot or cold as a starter, or cold as canapés. If serving as a cold starter, do not make the sauce from the court-bouillon, *but serve the slices of fish on top of the cold cucumber salad. To serve as a canapé, arrange a little cold cucumber salad on a toast round, cover with a slice of fish, and top with a caper flower (see page 25).*

GLUTEN FREE
SERVES 4 AS A MAIN COURSE,
6 AS A STARTER

1 Dover sole (1½ lb.), skinned and filleted
1 cucumber, washed
salt
1 shallot, peeled and chopped
1 green onion, chopped
2 fresh mint leaves, chopped, or ½ tsp. dried mint
½ cup Greek yogurt
freshly ground black pepper
½ lemon
1 tbsp. olive oil
4 slices smoked salmon (about 5 oz.)
1 tbsp. fines herbes, *finely chopped*
2 cups Court-Bouillon (see page 32)
1 sprig thyme
1 bay leaf
parsley sprigs
5 coriander seeds
¼ cup whipping cream
1 egg yolk

TO SERVE
1 lb. broccoli florets
dill sprigs

1   With a sharp knife, slash the shiny side of the sole fillets to prevent shrinkage.
2   Score the cucumber with a decorator, cut it in half lengthwise, and remove the seeds. Slice thinly, sprinkle with a little salt and leave in a glass or earthenware bowl for 15 minutes.
3   Drain and rinse the cucumber, pat dry and return to the rinsed glass bowl with the shallot, green onion, mint and half the yogurt. Season with pepper, the juice of the ½ lemon (cut off and reserve a slice first before squeezing), add olive oil, and leave to marinate for 10 minutes.
4   Place a slice of smoked salmon on a work surface and lay one fillet of sole, shiny side down, on top. Cut away the excess smoked salmon with a knife. Sprinkle with *fines herbes*, salt and pepper. Roll up and secure with a skewer. Prepare three more rolls in the same way.
5   Place the rolls in a steamer filled with the *court-bouillon* and its additional flavoring ingredients – the thyme, bay leaf, parsley sprigs, coriander seeds and the reserved lemon slice. Steam for 5 minutes. Remove from the heat, but keep in the steamer, covered, to stay warm.
6   Strain ½ cup of the *court-bouillon* into a saucepan and bring it to the boil. Mix the remaining yogurt, the cream and egg yolk in a bowl, then stir in a little of the hot *court-bouillon*. Pour this back into the *court-bouillon*.
7   Carefully add the fish rolls and the cucumber slices to the sauce and heat for a few minutes, but do not boil. Remove from the heat and season if necessary.
TO SERVE Steam the broccoli for about 5 minutes.
  To serve traditionally, place a little of the sauce on a heated serving dish, then slice the four rolls and arrange across the middle of the dish, surrounded by the broccoli florets. Serve the remaining sauce in a gravy boat.
  To serve individually, slice each roll and arrange on the warm plate with some broccoli florets and cucumber slices, with the sauce around. Garnish each plate with a sprig of dill.

RIGHT *Roulade Bicolore*

Charlotte de Saumon Verdurette
SALMON TERRINE

*T*his can be cooked in a charlotte or terrine mold or in four small ramekin or terrine dishes, then unmolded and served with a garnish of shrimp and chiffonade of lettuce sautéd very quickly. The salmon used can be fresh or be left from a poached salmon served the day before, an extremely good way to use up leftovers, or any cooked fish can be substituted for the salmon.

1   Blanch the whole lettuce in a saucepan of salted boiling water for 1 minute, then plunge immediately into a bowl of ice-cold water to cool. Lay flat on a towel to drain.

2   Butter a mold or terrines, and line with the blanched lettuce leaves (cut out the stalks if they are thick), leaving an overhang.

3   Cook the peas in a pan of boiling salted water until tender. Purée them in a food processor or with a food mill, reserving a tablespoon whole, for garnishing. Remove to a bowl and mix in one of the eggs beaten with one of the egg whites, a third of the cream, parsley and sorrel. Season well with salt, pepper and a little cayenne.

4   Remove any fat, bones and skin from the salmon and flake the flesh. Purée in a food processor or with a food mill and place in a bowl. Mix in the remaining eggs, egg white and cream and adjust the seasoning.

5   Whichever type of dish you have chosen, first put in a layer of the salmon purée, then a layer of pea purée, and finish with another layer of the salmon. Or you can pour them separately into the dish for a marbled effect. Fold the lettuce leaves over to cover the surface and gently press a circle of buttered foil or wax paper onto the top. Place in a bain-marie and bake in the preheated oven, 10–15 minutes for the individual portions and 30–40 minutes for the large mold.

6   Meanwhile, prepare the sauce. Put the shallots and *court-bouillon* into a pan and reduce by half, about 10–15 minutes. Add the cream and reduce for a further 3 minutes. Allow to cool for 2 minutes and, just before serving, add the yogurt. Reheat if necessary, but do not overheat or it will curdle.

TO SERVE   Steam the carrots until tender. They can be either young — with a little bit of stem left on them — or older, turned, or cut into *julienne*. Reheat the reserved whole peas.

Invert the charlotte onto a round serving dish, surround with a little sauce, and garnish the top with the hot carrots and peas, and a little chervil. Do the same with the ramekins on individual plates.

GLUTEN FREE
SERVES 4
PREHEAT THE OVEN TO 300°F

1 Boston lettuce, washed
salt
butter
9 oz. tiny peas
3 eggs
2 egg whites
½ cup whipping cream
¾ cup parsley, finely chopped
½ cup sorrel, cut into chiffonade
freshly ground black pepper
cayenne pepper
7 oz. fresh or cooked salmon

SAUCE
4 shallots, peeled and finely chopped
2 cups Court-Bouillon (see page 32)
¼ cup whipping cream
½ cup Greek yogurt

TO SERVE
11 oz. carrots, scrubbed
chervil leaves

LEFT *Charlotte de Saumon Verdurette*

Turbotin au Champagne
TURBOT WITH CHAMPAGNE

urbot is a delicious fish, unique in taste and texture, but it is expensive and not always available. Fillets of sole could substitute. The stuffing is made of spinach and sorrel; if sorrel is not available, you can duplicate its acidity by adding a teaspoon of lemon juice to the cooked spinach. Don't waste your most expensive champagne for this, but use a decent inexpensive one and serve your special bottle with the meal. The original sauce was a beurre monté using cream and butter in vast amounts; here we use low-fat Greek yogurt, a little cream and chervil which adds to the delicacy of the sauce.

GLUTEN FREE
SERVES 4
PREHEAT THE OVEN TO 350°F

1 turbot (3¼ lb.), skinned and
    filleted (see page 16), keep
    the head and bones
mirepoix (1 onion, 1 carrot, and
    1 celery stalk)
salt
1 bouquet garni
1 cup cold water
½ bottle champagne
2 tsp. grapeseed or safflower oil
14 oz. spinach, cut into
    chiffonade
4 oz. sorrel, cut into chiffonade
grated nutmeg
1 tbsp. pine nuts, toasted for 5
    minutes in the oven
freshly ground black pepper
½ cup whipping cream
1 egg yolk
1 tbsp. chopped chervil, a few
    whole leaves reserved
¼ cup Greek yogurt

TO SERVE
6 baby carrots, scrubbed and
    trimmed or turned
3 young turnips, washed,
    quartered and turned
12 new potatoes, washed
    (optional)
12 green onions, including 1 in.
    of the green (optional)

1   To make the fish stock, place the rinsed bones and head in a saucepan with the roughly chopped *mirepoix*, a pinch of salt and the *bouquet garni*. Add the water and 1 cup of the champagne, and bring to the boil slowly, skimming off the impurities. Simmer, uncovered, for 20 minutes, then cover and cool before straining.

2   Heat 1 teaspoon oil in a skillet over low heat, then turn the heat up to high and sauté the spinach and sorrel *chiffonade* briskly. Add a pinch of salt and some nutmeg. Cook over high heat, stirring constantly, to eliminate the water. Reserve on a plate to cool. When cold add the pine nuts.

3   Lay the fish fillets on a board, shiny side up. Slash the membrane diagonally along the length with a sharp knife. Season with a pinch of salt and pepper. Arrange a quarter of the spinach/sorrel *chiffonade* in the center of each fillet, and fold the sides over the middle.

4   Use the remaining oil to grease a gratin dish and put in the fillets, open sides down. Pour in enough strained fish stock to cover the fish, then cover the dish with foil and bake in the preheated oven for 10 minutes. Transfer the cooking liquid to a saucepan, leaving a small amount in the dish to keep the fish moist. Leave the fish covered with the foil in the turned-off oven to keep warm.

5   Add all the remaining champagne, except for 1 tablespoon, to the cooking liquid and reduce by half, skimming off the impurities as they rise. Add the cream, and reduce again until it coats the back of a spoon lightly (this can take up to 15 minutes). Take the sauce off the heat and add the remaining champagne. Mix the egg yolk, chopped chervil and the yogurt together in a bowl, stir in a small amount of the sauce, then pour the mixture back into the sauce, stirring well to combine. Do not reheat.

TO SERVE Steam the vegetables and keep warm.
    To serve traditionally, arrange the fillets in the middle of a warm serving dish, and spoon a little sauce over each, pouring the remainder into a warm gravy boat. Surround with the vegetables, and garnish each fillet with a chervil leaf.
    To serve individually, place a fillet to the front of a heated plate, and pour the sauce over it, to cover the base of the plate. Arrange the vegetables at the back of the plate like a crown, alternating the colors. Place a chervil leaf on top of the fillet.

RIGHT *Turbotin au Champagne*

Salade de Lotte aux Poivrons Rouges

MONKFISH WITH RED PEPPERS

*T*his delightful recipe is colorful and delicious and can be served in a variety of ways: as a warm starter, as a salad, as part of a buffet, or as a canapé, stuffed inside a hollowed cucumber. It can also be presented in a feuilleté (see page 14).

GLUTEN FREE
SERVES 4

1lb. monkfish fillet
2 cups Court-Bouillon *(see page 32)*
4 garlic cloves, peeled and crushed
salt
freshly ground black pepper
1/2 tsp. lemon juice
1/3 cup olive oil
2 red peppers, washed, seeded and diced

GARNISH
lettuce leaves
parsley, finely chopped

1 Cut the monkfish fillet into slices and steam for 2 minutes over the *court-bouillon* containing 2 garlic cloves.

2 Place the remaining garlic in a bowl with a pinch of salt, some pepper and the lemon juice. Mix well and beat in the olive oil.

3 Place the monkfish in the dressing to cool.

4 Add the peppers to the monkfish. Stir well, cover, and leave to marinate at room temperature for a few hours.

TO SERVE Serve chilled, in a bowl lined with lettuce leaves and sprinkle with the parsley.

To serve as a warm starter or *salade tiède* (warm salad), reheat very gently in a pan. Arrange the slices of monkfish in a ring on individual plates, surrounded by the peppers. Drizzle some of the dressing over them.

To serve as a canapé, purée the fish salad with 1 tablespoon olive oil in a blender or food processor. Peel a cucumber and hollow out the seeds. Stuff the middle of the cucumber with the fish mixture. Slice and serve.

Raie à l'Estragon
SKATE WITH TARRAGON

*T*his fish is traditionally served in France "au beurre noir," with a butter sauce browned to such an extreme that the butter becomes nearly black. Here the butter has been replaced by a warm vinaigrette flavored with tarragon, which aids in the digestion of this delicious but rich fish.

If skate is unavailable, butterfish fillets could substitute.

GLUTEN FREE
SERVES 4

2½lb. small skate wings (4 wings)
1 onion, peeled and thinly sliced
1 clove
1 sprig thyme
1 bay leaf
parsley sprigs
½ lemon, sliced
1½quarts cool Court-Bouillon (see page 32)
freshly ground black pepper

VINAIGRETTE
salt
2tbsp. tarragon vinegar
2tbsp. fresh tarragon, finely chopped
1tbsp. parsley, finely chopped
4tbsp. grapeseed or safflower oil

TO SERVE
1lb. turned root vegetables (carrots, turnips, rutabaga, celeriac)
1lb. green vegetables (broccoli, spinach, beans) or 8oz. snow peas
8 caper flowers (see page 25)

1   Place the skate wings, dark side up, in a large square roasting pan and add the onion, clove, thyme, bay leaf, parsley sprigs and lemon. Cover with the cool *court-bouillon*. If the fish is not completely covered add water. Sprinkle with pepper and bring slowly to the boil on top of the stove, skimming off the impurities as they rise to the surface.

2   Let it start simmering, then place a damp cloth over the pan, cover with a lid or foil and remove from the heat. Leave for 10–15 minutes.

3   To prepare the vinaigrette, put a little pepper and a pinch of salt into a saucepan, add the vinegar and stir to dissolve. Add the chopped tarragon and parsley, and mix well. (If using dried herbs, use only half the amount; add a tablespoon of water to them, steep for 5 minutes, then drain.) Whisk the oil in gently, then place over low heat to warm through. *Do not* boil.

4   Remove fish from the *court-bouillon* and skin. If you have enough patience, remove the bones too, but work swiftly as the fish will cool rapidly. If it does become too cool, place it in a dish with a little *court-bouillon* and reheat in a low oven.

TO SERVE   While the fish is cooking, steam the root vegetables until tender. Steam the chosen green vegetables as well.

To serve traditionally, lay the fish on a warmed serving platter and spoon the sauce over. Garnish with the caper flowers. Arrange the vegetables around the fish and serve immediately.

To serve individually, bone each wing, and lay on a warmed plate. Pour a little sauce over, and garnish with the vegetables and caper flowers. Serve the remaining sauce separately.

LEFT   *Raie à l'Estragon*

Gigot de Lotte Clouté
MONKFISH IN RED WINE

This delicious dish is very "nouvelle" in the sense that a few years ago, no one would have served fish in a red wine sweet and sour sauce. This is one of the dishes taught to me by Jean Bardet in Châteauroux. He serves it with a braised white cabbage, which makes an original garnish and complements the flavor of the fish and its sauce. If you prefer a more conventional dish, serve it with the vegetables suggested here.

GLUTEN FREE
SERVES 4
PREHEAT THE OVEN TO 350°F

2 large carrots, scrubbed
4 oz. green beans
1 Savoy cabbage (optional)
salt
freshly ground black pepper
4 tsp. grapeseed or safflower oil
mirepoix *(1 onion, carrot trimmings and 1 celery stalk)*
1 garlic clove, peeled and crushed
1¾ cup red wine (such as Beaujolais)
½ cup Bouillon de Légumes *(see page 32)*
1 lb. monkfish fillet
1 shallot, peeled and chopped
1 tbsp. honey
1 tbsp. raspberry vinegar
1 tsp. potato starch

TO SERVE (OPTIONAL)
2 medium turnips, peeled
2 medium carrots, scrubbed
8 oz. snow peas

1 Cut the carrots into *julienne* strips the same size as the beans, keeping the trimmings for the *mirepoix*. Steam the carrots and beans for 3 minutes.

2 If used, cut the cabbage into quarters through the stem and blanch for 5 minutes in boiling salted water.

3 Heat 2 teaspoons oil in a saucepan and sweat the finely chopped *mirepoix* for 5 minutes. Add the garlic and sweat for a minute longer, then deglaze with ½ cup of the red wine and the stock (or water). Place the cabbage in the pan, season with salt and pepper, and braise in the preheated oven for 40 minutes.

4 Remove the skin from the monkfish and cut the flesh into chunks the same length as the beans. Reserve the trimmings for the sauce.

5 Using a larding needle, insert the carrots and beans into the fish. Sprinkle the fish lightly with salt and pepper, place in a heavy ovenproof skillet and drizzle with 1 teaspoon of oil. Bake in the oven for 5–7 minutes. Remove, wrap in foil, and return to the turned-off oven.

6 Heat the remaining teaspoon of oil in the skillet, and sweat the shallot for 5 minutes. Add the monkfish trimmings and sauté. Deglaze with ¼ cup of the red wine, and reduce until a tablespoon is left.

7 Add the honey and let it simmer for 1 minute, then deglaze with the vinegar. Mix the potato starch with the remaining wine and transfer into the sauce. Simmer for 2 minutes.

TO SERVE Cut the monkfish chunks into thick slices. Arrange the cabbage on a heated serving plate and put the monkfish slices on the top. Spoon a little of the sauce over the fish and place the remainder in a gravy boat.

Alternatively, cut the carrots and turnips into *lichettes*, and steam with the snow peas for 3 minutes. Place the fish on a plate, and surround with the sauce and the vegetables.

RIGHT *Gigot de Lotte Clouté*

Bar Farci en Chemise
BASS WRAPPED IN LETTUCE LEAVES

*T*his bass is delicious hot or cold and it's nutritionally rich. To serve hot, follow all the instructions below. If it is to be served cold, omit all the steps for the sauce. Allow the fish to cool in its cooking juices in the foil, and serve with a Sauce Verte (see page 38).

If you are on a gluten-free diet, omit the breadcrumbs and sauté the stuffing for 5 minutes longer.

GLUTEN FREE
SERVES 6

1 sea bass (2 lb.)
salt
freshly ground black pepper
1/2 cup dry vermouth
2 large heads Boston lettuce, washed
3 tsp. grapeseed or safflower oil
9 oz. spinach, cut into chiffonade
2 oz. sorrel, cut into chiffonade
1/2 cup fines herbes, finely chopped
1/4 cup dry breadcrumbs
1/2 cup Greek yogurt
1/4 cup white wine
1/4 cup whipping cream
1 tsp. potato starch

TO SERVE
parsley sprigs
2 lemons
5 oz. each of carrots and potatoes cut into julienne

1 Scale the fish with the back of a knife inside a large garbage can, working from tail to head against the direction of the scales. Remove the insides and gills and wipe well. Bone as described on page 15.

2 Rinse the fish under cold running water, pat dry with paper towels and season the interior with a pinch of salt, a little pepper and 1 teaspoon vermouth.

3 Blanch the whole lettuces for 30 seconds in boiling salted water, then refresh in a bowl of ice water. Arrange the large leaves on a towel. Chop the hearts roughly and reserve.

4 Heat 1 teaspoon of the oil in a large pan and sauté the spinach quickly over high heat. Add the chopped lettuce hearts, stir over the heat for a minute, then add the sorrel and sauté for a minute longer. Add the herbs and breadcrumbs and mix well. Season with a pinch of salt and a little pepper, and leave on a plate to cool. When cold, add half the yogurt.

5 Stuff the fish with the cold stuffing, then wrap it in the lettuce leaves, leaving the head and tail uncovered.

6 Place the fish on a large piece of oiled foil on a baking sheet. Fold the foil up so that it creates an open *papillote*, a package with an opening at the top. Pour in half the white wine and half the remaining vermouth. Drizzle a little oil onto the head and tail so they do not dry out during cooking. Close the package, leaving just a small opening in the foil at the top, and place the baking sheet in the preheated oven. Bake for 15 minutes, then turn the oven off. Remove the fish, and pour the cooking juices into a saucepan. Close the foil tightly and leave the fish in the still warm oven for 15 minutes.

7 Simmer to reduce the cooking juices by half, then add the remaining wine and vermouth, and the cream. Reduce for 5 minutes. Mix the potato starch with the remaining yogurt, stir a little of the sauce into it, and pour it back into the sauce. Allow to come just to the boil, correct the seasoning, and remove from the heat.

TO SERVE Replace the eyes of the fish with parsley sprigs.

Score one of the lemons and then cut into slices. Cut both ends off the other lemon and cut across in half. Carve out a length of the peel around the wider top, and twist it into a knot (see page 26).

Lay the fish on a serving dish, and arrange the lemon slices all around, with the lemon halves at either side of the dish. Pour a little sauce over the fish and serve the remainder in a gravy boat. Garnish the dish with the vegetable *julienne*, steamed until just tender.

Filets de Sole Pochés au Vin Blanc
POACHED SOLE WITH WHITE WINE SAUCE

*T*hese delicious sole fillets are poached in fish stock and white wine in the oven. The sauce, originally a *velouté made with butter, flour and a lot of cream, has become a reduced stock with a small amount of whipping cream and Greek yogurt. The rosemary gives an unusual flavor to the sauce.*

GLUTEN FREE
SERVES 4
PREHEAT THE OVEN TO 350°F

2 Dover soles (1 lb. each)
mirepoix *(1 onion, 1 carrot, 1 celery stalk)*
1 bouquet garni
⅔ cup dry white wine
1 quart cold water
1 tsp. grapeseed or safflower oil
4 shallots, peeled and finely chopped
salt
freshly ground black pepper
⅓ cup whipping cream

TO SERVE
1 recipe Peperonata, *without eggs (see page 69)*
4 large potatoes, quartered and turned
¼ cup Greek yogurt

1   Skin both sides of the sole and fillet them as described on page 16, reserving the bones.

2   Wash the bones well under cold running water and place in a saucepan with the roughly chopped *mirepoix*, the *bouquet garni*, ½ cup of the white wine and the water. Bring slowly to the boil over low heat, skimming off the impurities as they rise to the surface. Simmer for 15 minutes, then leave to cool, covered.

3   Heat the oil in a skillet over low heat, then sweat the shallots, covered, for 2 minutes. Reserve on a plate to cool.

4   Place the fillets shiny side up on a work surface, and slash across the membrane with a sharp knife at 2-inch intervals. Season with a pinch of salt and a little pepper, and scatter the shallots over them evenly. Roll the fillets up along three-quarters of their length.

5   Place the fillets in a gratin dish, with the "tongues" flat at the bottom of the dish. Cover with the stock and the remaining wine, then with a piece of foil, and place in the preheated oven. Poach for 10 minutes.

6   Transfer the cooking liquid to a saucepan to reduce, leaving a little in the fish dish. Put the fish back in the oven, cover well, turn the oven off, and leave the door ajar.

7   Reduce the stock until only 1 cup is left, about 15 minutes. Add the cream, and reduce for 5 minutes longer over low heat.

TO SERVE   Steam the potatoes for 10 minutes.

When ready to serve, reheat the sauce, if necessary, then remove from the heat. Stir the yogurt well, pour 1 tablespoon of the sauce into it and mix well. Add the yogurt mixture to the sauce, stirring thoroughly with a spoon. Do not boil again.

To serve traditionally, arrange the fillets on a warmed serving platter, "tongues" either up or down (both look attractive), and cover with a little sauce. Pour the remainder into a warmed gravy boat. Arrange a green pepper and red pepper slice in a cross over each fillet, then place the remaining peppers all around the dish with the steamed potatoes over the top.

To serve on individual plates, arrange two fillets with "tongues" turned toward the outside of the plate, and cover both fillets and plate with the sauce. Arrange the peppers in crosses all around the plate, twirling a slice of red pepper into a spiral for the top of each fillet. Arrange the potatoes to north, south, east and west of the plate. Serve immediately.

MEAT, POULTRY AND GAME

Meat, especially red meat, contains a lot of saturated fat and a fair amount of cholesterol. In meat's favor, however, it can contain good amounts of protein, vitamins and essential amino acids. Meat is not excluded from Cuisine Santé but we would advise cutting down on red meat in favor of chicken, turkey and rabbit. Use the leanest cuts of all meats, and wherever possible both remove any visible fat before cooking, and discard cooking and rendered fats before preparing the sauce and serving the dish.

Côtes de Porc à l'Auvergnate
PORK CHOPS WITH SAGE

These pork chops are flavored with their classic herb accompaniment, sage. Sage, the "savior," complements pork, giving it goodness and flavor. It also helps digestion of both the pork and the cabbage.

1 Season the chops on both sides, and heat the oil in a skillet. Sear the chops on both sides very quickly (about 2 minutes each side). Put on a plate to cool. When cool, remove the bones and all the fat.

2 Put the onion and shallot into the same pan and sweat for 5 minutes. Add the garlic and sweat for another minute. Deglaze with the wine and let it simmer for 1 minute before adding the cream, the stock and sage. Simmer this sauce for another minute.

3 Bring a steamer containing salted water to the boil. Trim off any damaged outer cabbage leaves, and quarter the head, cutting through the stem to obtain sections which will hold together. Steam each quarter for 5 minutes, then plunge into a bowl of ice water to fix the color. Drain thoroughly, and remove the cores carefully.

4 Oil a gratin dish lightly and pour in half the sauce. Arrange the four pork chops on top. Place a cabbage quarter on top of each chop, and grate the cheese over all. Bake in the preheated oven for 25 minutes, basting with the sauce every 5 minutes after 10 minutes.

5 Tilt the gratin dish and spoon the sauce, onion and shallots into a saucepan. Add the remaining sauce and simmer for 5 minutes, then purée. Meanwhile, keep the chops warm in the turned-off oven.

TO SERVE Arrange the chops, each with its cabbage topping, on a warmed serving dish or individual plates. Serve the sauce in a warm gravy boat, and the carrots in a warmed vegetable dish. Garnish the dish with the sage leaves.

GLUTEN FREE
SERVES 4
PREHEAT THE OVEN TO 400°F

4 pork loin chops
salt
freshly ground black pepper
1 tsp. grapeseed or safflower oil
1 onion, peeled and finely
    chopped
1 shallot, peeled and finely
    chopped
2 garlic cloves, peeled and
    crushed
2/3 cup dry white wine
1/3 cup whipping cream
1/2 cup Fonds de Volaille (see
    page 31)
8 fresh sage leaves, chopped, or
    2 tsp. dried sage
1 Savoy cabbage
1 oz. Emmenthal cheese

TO SERVE
1 recipe Carottes Vichy (see page
    160)
4 fresh sage leaves, blanched

Médaillons de Porc à l'Aigre-Doux
PORK MEDALLIONS WITH GINGER

These little pieces of pork fillet are sautéd very quickly to retain all their juices, and later coated with a sweet and sour sauce. We use a little honey, instead of sugar, to sweeten the sauce, and instead of a traditional demi-glace *thickened with flour, we use a simple reduction to thicken. This preparation is a perfect adaptation of a traditional dish to a nouvelle cuisine look and a Cuisine Santé taste!*
If you omit the tartlets, the dish is gluten free.

SERVES 4
PREHEAT THE OVEN TO 375°F

Pâte Brisée *made with 1¼ cups (5 oz.) flour (see page 44)*
1 pork tenderloin (1 lb.)
salt
freshly ground black pepper
2 tsp. grapeseed or safflower oil
mirepoix (1 onion, 1 carrot and 1 celery stalk)
1 tbsp. tomato paste
½ cup white wine
2 cups Fonds de Volaille *(see page 31)*
1 sprig thyme
1 bay leaf
2 sprigs parsley
1 oz. fresh ginger root, peeled and cut into tiny julienne
1 lime, peeled and cut into tiny julienne
½ cup water
2 tbsp. light brown sugar
1 large pear, peeled
1 large apple, peeled
⅔ cup red wine
1 pinch ground cinnamon
1 clove
1 tbsp. dark brown sugar
1 tbsp. honey
2 tbsp. vinegar

TO SERVE
8 pieces each of turned carrots and zucchini

1   Allow the pastry to rest for 20 minutes in the refrigerator. Use it to line four small tartlet molds. Line with parchment paper or foil and baking beans and bake blind in the oven until golden brown, about 12 minutes.

2   Trim the fat and sinew from the tenderloin, and cut the meat into 1-inch slices. Pound the slices to flatten them. Salt and pepper lightly and set aside.

3   Heat half the oil in a skillet and sauté the meat trimmings until well browned. Add the roughly chopped *mirepoix* and sweat until soft. Add the tomato paste and cook for 1 minute. Add the white wine and allow to reduce, about 5 minutes. Add the chicken stock, herbs, a little salt and pepper, and simmer for a minimum of 30 minutes. Skim off the impurities as they rise to the surface. Strain the sauce through a conical sieve and replace in the cleaned pan to reduce further until it coats the back of a spoon lightly.

4   Put the *julienne* of ginger and lime in a saucepan with the water and light brown sugar. Simmer gently for 5 minutes, then reserve on one side.

5   Using a melon baller, carve the pear and the apple into balls. Place the balls in a saucepan with the red wine, cinnamon, clove and the dark brown sugar. Bring slowly to a simmer and poach until the fruit is tender. Remove the fruit balls and leave the juice to reduce slowly so it forms a shiny glaze (for the fruit later).

6   In another saucepan, heat the honey and let it brown slightly (it will be ready when it exudes a marvelous smell of honey). Add half the vinegar, leave to reduce for 1 minute, then add the sauce and the ginger and lime *julienne* with their juices. Simmer very gently for 3–5 minutes.

7   Heat a heavy skillet, and rub the remaining oil and some salt and pepper on the pieces of pork. Sauté for 1 minute on each side, then reserve in a warm place. Deglaze the skillet with the remaining vinegar and the sauce. Adjust the seasoning, remove from the heat, and place the meat in the sauce to marinate.

TO SERVE   Steam the carrots and zucchini, and arrange them on a heated serving platter or individual plates. Arrange the slices of pork on top, and garnish with the warm tartlets filled with the fruit balls reheated in their juices, and coated with the juice. Pour the sauce over the meat and around the plate, and serve the remainder in a gravy boat. Garnish with the lime and ginger *julienne*.

RIGHT *Médaillons de Porc à l'Aigre-Doux*

Rôti de Porc aux Pommes
STEAM-ROAST LOIN OF PORK WITH APPLES

GLUTEN FREE

SERVES 4

½ tsp. lapsang souchong tea
    leaves
½ tsp. Indian tea leaves
½ quart boiling water
4 oz. dried prunes, washed
2¼ lb. pork loin roast (4 chops),
    boned
salt
freshly ground black pepper
2 Golden Delicious apples,
    washed
½ lemon
1 tbsp. red currant or apple jelly
1 cup white wine
mirepoix (1 onion, 1 carrot and
    1 celery stalk)
1⅓ cups Fonds de Volaille (see
    page 31)
1 tbsp. grapeseed or safflower oil
tarragon wine vinegar

TO SERVE

7 oz. each of carrots, celeriac,
    turnips and parsnips, cut into
    julienne
14 oz. broccoli
1 cauliflower, cut into florets
parsley sprigs

*T*o prepare the pork, the meat is first steamed, then roasted. The steaming dissolves the fat, which runs into the steaming water, and the roasting completes the cooking and gives an attractive color. This method of cooking may seem a little strange, but the result is tender and very delicious.

The addition of prunes brings a little sweetness to the flavor of the pork, and fruit helps to dissolve fat, thereby helping digestion.

THE DAY BEFORE SERVING

1   Prepare a pot of tea with the leaves and boiling water, let it infuse, then strain. Soak the prunes in the tea overnight in the refrigerator. The next day, pit the prunes and chop the flesh roughly. Reserve the tea.

THE DAY OF SERVING

1   Ask the butcher to bone the meat before you bring it home, or prepare it yourself, removing the skin, fat and each bone, one after the other.

2   Push a needle through the center of the loin to make a hole, then enlarge this with your finger. Insert half of the prunes, pushing them well in. Salt and pepper the meat and tie it up with string into a roll. Rub with the remaining prunes (reserving 1 tablespoon for the sauce later). Allow to marinate for at least 2 hours at room temperature (or overnight in the refrigerator).

3   Preheat the oven to 450°F. Weigh the roast and allow 10 minutes roasting time per pound plus 15 minutes resting with the oven turned off (this does not include the steaming).

4   Bring some water and ½ cup of the prune tea to the boil in the base of a steamer. Put the meat in the top, cover and leave over the heat for 2 minutes. Then, without uncovering, take off the heat, and leave for 10 minutes. Turn the meat over, replace the lid, and put back on the heat for 2 minutes. Remove from the heat, still covered, and leave for another 10 minutes. This slow steaming method will let the fat run out without toughening the meat.

5   Prick the apples all over with the tip of a knife to prevent the skin from bursting, then cut in half across their "equators." Remove the core carefully, leaving a base, and sprinkle each half with a few drops of lemon juice. Spoon the red currant or apple jelly into the core holes of each half.

6   Put the pork into a roasting pan and place in the preheated oven. Turn it over every 5 minutes to give an even color. After 10 minutes, turn the oven down to 350°F and add the *mirepoix*, the apples and half the wine. Cook for the remaining time, then allow the meat to rest on a plate with the apples.

7   Add the stock to the wine and *mirepoix*, and push through a conical sieve into a fat-separator. Discard the *mirepoix* left in the sieve. Transfer the sauce to a saucepan and simmer to reduce by half, about 10 minutes.

8 Heat the oil in a small skillet and slowly sweat the remaining prunes to "caramelize" them, about 5 minutes. Deglaze the pan with a dash of vinegar and the remaining wine. Reduce for 2 minutes, then add the reduced stock. Purée the sauce then simmer for 5 minutes, removing the impurities as they rise to the surface, until the sauce coats the back of a spoon. Correct the seasoning if necessary, then, just before serving, add 2 tablespoons of the prune tea.

TO SERVE Prepare the vegetables. Steam the *julienne* of root vegetables, the broccoli and cauliflower florets for about 5 minutes.

Remove the strings from the roast and carve it. If carving in the kitchen, arrange the chops and the vegetables on a warmed platter and garnish with the apples and a few parsley sprigs. (Pour the carving juices on the root vegetables to season them.)

If the meat is to be carved at the table, arrange the vegetables in warmed serving bowls ready to be served at the table. Serve the apples on a separate plate with some parsley sprigs in the middle. Pour a little sauce over the *julienne* and serve the remainder in a gravy boat.

Rôti de Porc aux Pommes

Carré de Porc Glacé

GLAZED RACK OF PORK

*T*his is a slightly different way to serve pork loin, on the bone in a rack, and here again sage helps to make the meat more digestible. The sweet-sour sauce is made with apple or red currant jelly, but do buy the kind now available which contains much less sugar, and make sure it contains no artificial flavoring or preservatives. The best kind, of course, is the one you made yourself in the summer.

GLUTEN FREE
SERVES 4
PREHEAT THE OVEN TO 450°F

1 rack of pork (4 chops)
salt
freshly ground black pepper
1 tbsp. grapeseed or safflower oil
mirepoix (1 onion, 1 carrot and
    1 celery stalk)
1 cup dry white wine
1/3 cup red currant or apple jelly
2 tbsp. cognac
1 1/3 cups Fonds de Volaille (see
    page 31)

TO SERVE
2 apples
1 orange
8 pieces of each of the following
    turned vegetables: carrots,
    turnips, celeriac, and
    rutabagas
4 chop frills (see page 28)

1   Remove the rind from the pork rack and chine the bones (your butcher can do this for you when you buy the meat), so that the joint carves more easily. Remove as much fat as possible, and weigh the meat. Calculate the cooking time, allowing 40 minutes per pound. Season the meat with salt and pepper.

2   Heat the oil in a roasting pan in the preheated oven. Add the rack, skin side down, then turn over after 5 minutes. After 10 minutes, pour the fat out of the pan, and add the *mirepoix* and half the white wine. Turn the oven down to 350°F.

3   Put the red currant or apple jelly into a saucepan with most of the cognac (reserving 2 teaspoons for later) and heat gently. Brush this glaze over the top of the meat, and return to the oven. Repeat this operation at least three times to obtain a good glaze. Reserve 1 tablespoon of jelly for later. Make sure, too, that the *mirepoix* does not burn; add some water as soon as the moisture evaporates.

4   Cut the apples in half through their "equators." Remove the cores carefully so that the apple halves are not pierced at the bottom, and prick the skin all over with a sharp knife to prevent the apple from exploding while cooking. Put a teaspoon of jelly inside each hole, and place the apple halves in the roasting pan with the meat until tender, about 10 minutes. Peel the orange (see page 27), and slice across into 4 slices. Drizzle the remaining cognac over and set aside, covered.

5   When the meat is cooked, put it on a plate to rest in the turned-off oven for at least 10 minutes. Add the rest of the white wine to the *mirepoix* as well as half the remaining jelly, and reduce for 3 minutes on top of the stove. Add 1 cup of the chicken stock and reduce for 3 minutes longer. Strain into a fat-separator. Pour the fat-free sauce into a saucepan, add the remaining stock and another teaspoon of jelly, and reduce again for 3 minutes. Pour into a gravy boat.

TO SERVE Meanwhile, steam the vegetables for 5–10 minutes, depending on size.

Garnish the meat with chop frills and place in the center of a warmed serving dish. Place the slices of orange in the steamer for a minute to heat, and arrange around the meat. Place the baked apple halves on top of the orange slices, and arrange the carrots in between. Serve the remaining vegetables separately.

Traditionally, the whole roast is brought to the table to be carved, but it can be carved in the kitchen, if that is easier.

LEFT *Carré de Porc Glacé*

Filets Mignons de Porc à la Normande

PORK FILLET WITH APPLE

GLUTEN FREE
SERVES 4
PREHEAT THE OVEN TO 450°F

1 pork tenderloin (1½lb.)
salt
freshly ground black pepper
grapeseed or safflower oil
7oz. each of carrots, turnips,
    leeks and celery, cut into
    julienne
1 cooking apple, chopped
1 shallot, peeled and chopped
2tbsp. Calvados
⅔cup hard cider
2cups Fonds de Volaille (see
    page 31)
½cup whipping cream

*Filets Mignons de Porc
à la Normande*

This recipe is a combination of cuisine bourgeoise and cuisine nouvelle. In the bourgeoise, the meat would have been a chop or cutlet and the sauce thickened with a butter and flour roux or beurre manié; in the nouvelle, the sauce would have been a reduction of cream. Our Cuisine Santé version does not use any flour and only a little cream — the trick is the apple purée added at the end!

1   Season the pork with a little salt and pepper. Heat 1 teaspoon of the oil in an ovenproof skillet or casserole and sauté the pork quickly on all sides to seal in the juices. Place in the preheated oven for 15 minutes, then turn the oven off. Transfer the pork to a plate and rest in the oven.

2   Meanwhile, steam the vegetable *julienne* until *al dente*, about 3 minutes. Cook the apple to a purée with 2 tablespoons water, then strain and discard skin and cores.

3   Put the skillet back over the heat, but discard the fat and clean the pan with paper towels. Add 1 tablespoon oil and gently sweat the shallot and the vegetable *julienne*, covered, for 5 minutes. Deglaze the pan with the Calvados and flame it. Add the cider and boil to reduce by half. Add the chicken stock and the cream and again reduce by half. Add any juices that have run out of the pork. Remove the vegetables from the sauce and reserve with the pork.

4   Add the apple purée, and simmer for another minute. Season well.

TO SERVE   Slice the meat and arrange it on a bed of the vegetable *julienne*. Strain some of the sauce through a conical sieve over the meat, and strain the rest into a gravy boat. Serve immediately.

Gasconnade d'Agneau
LAMB WITH GARLIC

*T*his recipe is definitely for garlic lovers. Garlic is one of the best vegetables to ward off all sorts of illnesses; it lowers cholesterol, and helps digestion. Remember to remove the green germ inside each clove as it is this part that is hard to digest and responsible for garlicky breath.

You could ask your butcher to take out the hip-bone when you buy the meat. This makes both the cooking and the carving easier.

1   Remove the excess fat from the leg and take out the hip-bone at the thick fillet end. Weigh the roast, and calculate the cooking time, allowing 15 minutes per pound for pink lamb, and 20–25 minutes for well done. Allow 10 minutes resting time in the turned-off oven, which will make carving easier.

2   Using a pestle and mortar, work together 4 garlic cloves, the anchovies, salt, pepper and 1 teaspoon of olive oil. Make a few slits in the flesh of the leg with a knife, and push in some of the garlic purée. Rub the rest of it all over the outside of the leg, and allow to marinate at room temperature for 20 minutes.

3   Meanwhile, blanch the remaining garlic cloves in a saucepan of boiling water for 2 minutes. Drain and reserve.

4   When the meat has marinated, sear it in 1 tablespoon of olive oil in a heavy roasting pan on top of the stove, turning to brown it all over. Place the pan in the preheated oven. After 5 minutes turn the meat over, and add the *mirepoix*, ½ cup of the wine and the blanched cloves of garlic.

5   Turn the oven down to 400°F, and cook for the calculated time. Add a little water from time to time throughout the cooking to keep the vegetables moist. This will also ensure that the fat runs out of the meat.

6   When the meat is cooked, turn the oven off and leave the roast in the oven, wrapped in foil, on a platter to rest for 10 minutes. Pick out and reserve the garlic for the sauce. Add the stock and scrape the bottom of the pan, then strain into a fat-separator. Let it stand for the fat to rise.

7   Purée the fat-free stock with the garlic, and pour into a saucepan. Add the remaining white wine, and reduce the sauce to obtain the right consistency; it should coat the back of a spoon. This will take about 5 minutes.

TO SERVE   Steam the beans, broccoli and carrot *julienne* for 5–7 minutes, depending on size.

Carve the meat, putting the juices into the sauce, and present on a warmed serving dish or individual plates, surrounded by the vegetables. Serve the sauce separately in a warm gravy boat.

GLUTEN FREE
SERVES 6
PREHEAT THE OVEN TO 450°F

1 leg of lamb (4½ lb.)
8 oz. garlic cloves, peeled
2 anchovy fillets
salt
freshly ground black pepper
olive oil
¾ cup white wine
mirepoix (1 onion, 1 carrot and
    1 celery stalk)
1 cup Fonds de Volaille (see
    page 31)

TO SERVE
11 oz. green beans
11 oz. broccoli florets
1 lb. carrots, cut into julienne

Filet d'Agneau en Papillote
LAMB FILLET EN PAPILLOTE

GLUTEN FREE
SERVES 4
PREHEAT THE OVEN TO 450°F

1¼ lb. lamb loin roast
    (tenderloin)
2 sprigs rosemary, about 4-in.
    long
salt
freshly ground black pepper
2 tsbp. grapeseed or safflower oil
4 oz. dried apricots, washed
½ cup dry white wine
1 white of leek, washed, halved
    lengthwise and sliced across
    thinly
1 tbsp. flour mixed with 3 tbsp.
    water

TO SERVE
1 recipe Sauce à la Tomate or
    Coulis de Tomates (see pages
    36 and 38)
1 lb. spinach, cut into chiffonade
11 oz. each of carrots, turnips and
    rutabagas, cut into julienne

This dish combines the sweet flavors of lamb, dried apricots and rosemary; and by using a paper bag, one can help to retain the savor of all these ingredients. The papillote *can be prepared ahead of time and needs only be put in the oven 10–15 minutes before serving. This lamb is best served pink.*

1   Trim the lamb well. Using a pestle and mortar, crush together the leaves of a sprig of rosemary, 2 pinches of salt, some pepper and 1 tablespoon oil. Rub the lamb with this and allow to marinate for 20 minutes.

2   Place the dried apricots and wine in a saucepan, bring to the boil and simmer for 2 minutes, then remove from the heat and soak for 20 minutes. Drain the apricots, reserving the marinade, and chop them roughly.

3   Heat a skillet well, and sauté the lamb very quickly all over, without adding any oil; this should take no longer than 2 minutes. Place the lamb on a plate to cool.

4   Add 1 teaspoon oil to the pan, and sweat the leek for 5 minutes, covered.

5   To prepare the paper parcel, have ready a piece of parchment paper of about 15 inches square. It should be at least 4 inches larger all around than the piece of lamb. Shape into a *papillote* as described on page 28. Lay the paper flat on the work surface, the fold lying horizontally. Near the fold, on the half nearest you, place half the apricots, half the leeks and half the remaining sprig of rosemary. Place the lamb on top, and cover with the remaining rosemary, leek and apricots. Pour over the reserved wine marinade.

6   Rub a little flour paste on the side of the paper nearest you, and fold the other part over it. Rub a little more flour paste on this seam and fold over again by about ½ inch to seal. The paste will set and seal the *papillote* completely.

7   Lay the paper package on a baking sheet and place in the preheated oven. Bake for 10 minutes for pink lamb, 15 minutes for medium, and 20 minutes for well done. Rest in the turned-off oven or in a warm place for 5 minutes before serving.

TO SERVE   Steam the carrot, turnip and rutabaga *julienne* for 4–5 minutes. (The *julienne* could also be added to the *papillote*, but expect them to taste of rosemary! Another alternative is to cook them in a separate *papillote* with a tablespoon of white wine or water.) Sauté the spinach *chiffonade* briskly in 1 tablespoon oil, and season with salt and pepper.

Pour the *coulis* or tomato sauce into a gravy boat. Place the spinach on a warmed serving platter and arrange the vegetable *julienne* around the edges. Bring to the table along with the *papillote* on a carving board, a knife and hot plates. Open the *papillote* at the last moment and discard the sprigs of rosemary. Carve the meat and serve it along with the vegetables and sauce.

RIGHT *Filet d'Agneau en Papillote*

Côtelettes d'Agneau en Cuirasse
LAMB CHOPS

This is an haute cuisine classic. Prepare it well in advance, which will give you more time to attend to the rest of the dinner. It keeps very well overnight in the refrigerator, or for up to 3 months in the freezer.

SERVES 4
PREHEAT THE OVEN TO 450°F

Pâte Brisée *made with 2¼ cups
    (11 oz.) flour (see page 11)*
4 lamb chops (rib chops)
1 tbsp. grapeseed or safflower oil
salt
freshly ground black pepper
1 egg, beaten
4 large thin ham slices, halved
7 oz. duxelle of mushrooms (see
    page 23)

SAUCE AU PORTO
2 tbsp. butter
3 shallots, peeled and finely
    chopped
½ cup port
2½ cups Fonds de Volaille (see
    page 31)

TO SERVE
6 oz. snow peas
7 oz. broccoli
6 oz. carrot, cut into julienne

1   Rest the pastry for 20 minutes in the refrigerator.

2   Trim the chops well, then heat the oil in a skillet. Season the chops on both sides, then sauté them quickly for 1 minute on each side. Reserve on a cooling rack. Later bone them and remove all traces of fat.

3   Roll the pastry into a rectangle about 10 × 16 inches and brush with the beaten egg. Cut the pastry into eight rectangles; cut the shorter side in half and then divide the longer side into four rectangles just over 3 inches wide, leaving a strip at the end for garnishing. On four of the rectangles layer a half slice of ham, some *duxelle*, a chop followed by some *duxelle* and another half slice of ham to finish. Fold the pastry around the sides of the chop, and brush with beaten egg. Place another pastry rectangle on top, tucking the excess underneath. Brush all over with beaten egg and garnish with strips of the reserved pastry, so that each looks like a little parcel. Brush again with beaten egg, and place in the refrigerator to rest for a few minutes (these can be prepared a long time in advance).

4   Brush again with egg just before baking, and put on a baking sheet. Place in the preheated oven, turn the heat down to 350°F, and bake for 20 minutes.

5   Meanwhile, make the sauce. Melt the butter in a saucepan and sweat the shallots over low heat for 5 minutes. Add most of the port and reduce by half. Add the stock and simmer very gently for 15 minutes. Add the remaining port, then strain the sauce (or leave the shallots in), and pour into a gravy boat.

TO SERVE   Steam the vegetables together for 5–10 minutes, depending on size.

If serving traditionally, present the parcels on a doily-lined serving platter, with the vegetables to the side. Pass the sauce separately.

If serving individually, place a meat parcel on a warmed plate, surround with vegetables, and pour the sauce around at the last moment.

LEFT   *Côtelettes d'Agneau en Cuirasse*

Pot au Feu
BEEF CASSEROLE

*A*nother very traditional French country dish, this is wonderful when prepared in large quantities for informal family affairs. Half of it can be frozen for another occasion, any leftover meat can be made into a Boeuf en Gelée (see page 122) and the juices are usually served as a soup.

SERVES 8

4 leeks
6 lb. beef, using a combination of
    chuck roast, cross-cut shank,
    short ribs, oxtail kept whole
    and tied like a roast, and
    lower rib bones
3 onions, unpeeled and washed
1 clove
4 carrots, peeled
4 small turnips, peeled
4 small parsnips, peeled
2 bouquets garnis
1 quart strong Fonds de
    Volaille (see page 31)
coarse sea salt
5 each of white peppercorns and
    coriander seeds, crushed
½ cup white wine
2 tbsp. butter
freshly ground black pepper

TO SERVE

1 recipe Choux Rouge Braisé,
    using a Savoy cabbage with
    the leaves whole, not chopped
    (see page 163)
1 lb. small new potatoes, washed

TWO DAYS BEFORE SERVING

1   Soak the leeks in a large bowl of cold water for 30 minutes. Shake dry, bend in two, and tie together with string.

2   Rinse the meats well and dry on paper towels. Place in a large saucepan with one of the onions, studded with a clove, the remaining whole vegetables and the leeks. Add the *bouquets garnis*.

3   Pour in the stock and add as much water as necessary to cover the meat and vegetables completely. Add ½ teaspoon salt, the peppercorns and coriander seeds, and bring slowly to the boil over medium heat, skimming off the impurities as they rise to the surface. Simmer gently for 2 hours, adding water as it reduces, so that the meat and vegetables are always covered. Allow to cool and reserve in the refrigerator overnight.

THE DAY BEFORE SERVING

1   Remove all the fat congealed on top of the stock and bring slowly to the boil over medium heat.

2   Meanwhile, peel the remaining onions, cut them in half through the root, and slice across thickly. Place in another saucepan with the white wine, 1 cup of the stock, the butter, a pinch of salt and a little pepper. Simmer gently, letting the liquid evaporate (it may take up to 40 minutes) completely to allow the onions to brown. Add to the meat and vegetables in the other pan, and leave to simmer for 1½ hours. Cool, and reserve again in the refrigerator overnight.

THE DAY OF SERVING

Preheat the oven to 350°F.

1   The stock should be firmly set. (If not, and you want to use it to make *Boeuf en Gelée*, see page 122.) Remove the layer of fat congealed on the surface. Bring slowly to the boil over medium heat. Detach the meat from the bones and replace in the stock. Cut the vegetables up into smaller pieces (although they do look good left whole), and return them in the stock as well. When it has heated through, the *Pot au Feu* is ready to serve.

TO SERVE   Steam the potatoes over stock instead of water for 10 minutes (or longer if they are large). Reheat the cabbage.

Strain the stock through cheesecloth to remove the impurities and serve with some cut-up vegetables as a soup. For the main course, arrange the meat on a serving dish or individual plates with the vegetables all around. Offer mustard, chutneys, horseradish sauce and pickles to accompany the meat.

If there are meat and stock left over, you can use them to prepare *Boeuf en Gelée*.

RIGHT *Pot au Feu*

Sauté de Boeuf Minute
SAUTÉD STEAK WITH TOMATO SAUCE

True to its name, this dish is prepared at the last minute. It uses rump rather than fillet steak to make a stronger sauce. It is an ideal dish to prepare when steak is on the menu and unexpected guests turn up! Steak for two can be cut into strips which are cooked very quickly, then served with a sauce which combines a traditional cream sauce and a Coulis de Tomates. Try it, as below, with fresh noodles tossed into the sauce, or simply with vegetables for a gluten-free dish.

SERVES 4
PREHEAT THE OVEN TO ITS LOWEST TEMPERATURE

1 recipe Pâte à Nouilles *(see page 45)*
1 lb. lean rump or round steak
pepper
cayenne pepper
grapeseed or safflower oil
3 shallots, peeled and finely chopped
1 garlic clove, peeled and crushed
¼ cup Madeira
¼ cup white or red wine
¼ cup whipping cream (optional)
1 recipe Coulis de Tomates *(see page 38)*
salt

TO SERVE
1 lb. broccoli or green beans
1 tbsp. fines herbes, finely chopped

1   Allow the pasta dough to rest in the refrigerator for 10 minutes. Cut into noodles, and dry on a floured tray lined with a towel.
2   Cut the meat into little-finger-sized strips and season with pepper and a pinch of cayenne (do not salt).
3   Heat a skillet well. This is very important as the end result of both meat and sauce depends on the heat of the pan, and on the way in which the meat will be cooked. Add 1 teaspoon oil to the pan and toss the strips of meat over high heat for 2 minutes only. Reserve, covered on a plate, in the warm oven.
4   Let the skillet cool for a moment, then add the shallots with a drop more oil. Sweat slowly over medium heat until soft, about 5 minutes. Add the garlic and sweat for 1 minute. Deglaze with the Madeira, wine and the juices that have run from the meat. Reduce almost completely, then add the cream (if using), and reduce by half. Add the tomato sauce and simmer for 2 minutes.
5   Remove from the heat and add the meat with a pinch of salt. Do not boil again but allow to marinate for 2 minutes before serving.
TO SERVE   Steam the vegetables until tender. Boil the fresh noodles until *al dente*, about 2 minutes, then pour a little cold water over them to stop the cooking. Drain and place on a warmed serving dish or individual plates, and pour a little of the sauce over them. Using a slotted spoon, place the meat on the bed of noodles, and sprinkle with the fresh herbs. Serve immediately with the vegetables. Serve the remaining sauce in a gravy boat.

Boeuf Bourguignon
BEEF STEW

*T*his is a very traditional cuisine bourgeoise dish. Start preparing it 2 or even 3 days in advance; the meat will be more flavorful and the sauce free of fat. Present it in pastry timbales (see page 44) to impress your guests even more (but the dish will no longer be gluten-free).

TWO DAYS BEFORE SERVING
Marinate the beef overnight with half the wine, the roughly chopped *mirepoix*, a pinch of salt, some pepper, the herbs and a pinch of allspice.

THE DAY BEFORE SERVING
1   Drain the meat and dry it on paper towels. Discard the *mirepoix* and marinade.
2   Heat half the oil in a skillet and sweat the bacon to render the fat. Remove the bacon, drain off the fat, and add the remaining oil to the skillet.
3   Sauté the beef over very high heat in two batches, so that it browns well.
4   Return the bacon to the skillet, add the cognac and flame. Add the tomato paste, stir well, and add enough of the remaining red wine to cover well.
5   Add the turned vegetables, the pearl onions (one of them studded with the clove), the muslin "spice bag," *bouquet garni* and a little nutmeg.
6   Cover and bring to the boil, skimming off the impurities as they rise to the surface. Simmer very gently for 15 minutes. The vegetables should now be tender, so lift them out and reserve on a plate.
7   Continue cooking the meat for another 20 minutes until done. Return the vegetables to the stew, cook and allow to cool. Refrigerate overnight.

THE DAY OF SERVING
1   Remove the layer of congealed fat on the surface, bring back to the boil, and simmer for 5–10 minutes.
2   Cook the peas in salted boiling water and add to the casserole.
TO SERVE Steam the broccoli.
    Remove the "spice bag" and *bouquet garni*. Reduce the sauce if necessary, adjust the seasoning and serve in the *timbale* or *timbales*, topped with the parsley.

SERVES 4

1 lb. chuck steak, cubed
1 bottle red wine (Côtes du Rhône)
mirepoix (1 onion, 1 carrot and 1 celery stalk)
salt
freshly ground black pepper
1 bay leaf
1 sprig thyme
ground allspice
2 tbsp. grapeseed or safflower oil
7 oz. smoked slab bacon, trimmed and diced
3 tbsp. cognac
1½ tbsp. tomato paste
4 each of the following vegetables, turned: carrot, turnip, potato and zucchini
12 pearl onions, peeled
1 clove
1 muslin "spice bag" containing 1 allspice berry, ¼ cinnamon stick, 1 slice fresh root ginger and a strip each of lemon, orange and lime peel
1 bouquet garni
grated nutmeg
5 oz. frozen tiny peas

TO SERVE
1 lb. broccoli
1 large or 4 small pastry timbales (see page 44)
1 tbsp. parsley, finely chopped

Boeuf en Gelée

BEEF IN ASPIC

*T*his delicious cold buffet dish is a very good way of using the leftover meat from a Pot au Feu.

The vegetables can be leftover from the Pot au Feu, *or fresh and either steamed until tender, or boiled in the stock while it is reducing.*

SERVES 4

1 lb. leftover Pot au Feu *meat (see page 118)*

1½ quarts leftover Pot au Feu *stock*

2 medium carrots, peeled, scored and sliced

2 turnips, peeled, scored and sliced

2 parsnips, peeled, scored and sliced

1 white of leek, washed, sliced and leaves reserved

2 tsp. unflavored gelatin (optional)

1 Lift the meat from the stock and cube it.

2 Strain the stock well and cook the sliced vegetables and the leaves from the leek in it until just tender. Reserve them on a plate to cool, then reduce the stock until there is about 1½ cups left.

3 If the stock did not contain enough natural gelatin to set it firmly after refrigeration (see the recipe for *Pot au Feu*), soften the gelatin and add to the hot stock after it has been reduced. Stir well to dissolve. (If the stock had set, omit the gelatin.) Reserve ½ cup of this aspic.

4 Mix the meat cubes with the remaining aspic or gelatinous stock.

5 Pour half the reserved aspic into the bottom of a loaf pan or terrine, and allow it to set in the refrigerator. When set, garnish with some vegetable slices and leek leaves dipped in the remaining aspic. Place in the refrigerator to set the garnish. Pour the remaining aspic into the terrine through a strainer, and refrigerate to set.

6 When the meat and its aspic start to set, arrange it in layers in the terrine, interspersed with vegetable slices and leek leaves.

7 Leave it overnight in the refrigerator to set. Serve with a salad.

Boeuf en Gelée

Escalope de Veau Woronoff
VEAL WORONOFF

*T*he traditional Beurre Café de Paris *uses a lot of butter and is finished with sweet cream and soured cream. In this version we eliminate the butter and marinate the meat in the* Marinade Café de Paris, *which gives it an exceptional taste. Pork, chicken, turkey and even fish — strips of monkfish, for instance — could be prepared in the same way as the veal.*

An ideal accompaniment is fresh noodles (see page 45), but if you use these, the dish is no longer gluten free.

SERVES 4

1 recipe Marinade Café de Paris
  (see page 37)
4 veal cutlets (4 oz. each)
2 tbsp. grapeseed or safflower oil
1/2 tsp. potato starch
1/2 cup Greek yogurt
1/4 cup whipping cream
1/4 cup milk

TO SERVE

1 cucumber
12 oz. Pâte à Nouilles *made with
  2 1/4 cups flour (see page 45)*
1 tbsp. parsley, finely chopped

THE DAY BEFORE SERVING
Prepare the ingredients for the marinade. Place in a bowl, cover, and leave overnight (or 12 hours at least) at room temperature.

THE DAY OF SERVING
1   Trim the cutlets well. Mix the oil into the marinade and purée it in the blender or food processor. Marinate the cutlets in it for 30 minutes at room temperature.

2   Scrape the marinade off the meat and put into a skillet.

3   Mix the potato starch with the yogurt, cream, and milk, add the marinade and heat gently. Do not boil.

4   Place the meat into this mixture and gently poach for 3 minutes on either side.

TO SERVE Prepare the cucumber garnish. Peel, halve and seed the cucumber and cut into chunks. Blanch in lightly salted boiling water for 2 minutes. Drain and refresh immediately under the cold tap. Cook the noodles. Remove the meat from the sauce and keep in a warm place. Reheat the cucumber in the sauce gently, remembering not to let it boil.

On a heated serving dish make a bed of noodles, and place the cutlets on top. Arrange the pieces of cucumber around the plate and spoon the sauce over the meat. Sprinkle the parsley over the top.

Escalope de Veau Jurassienne en Croûte

VEAL EN CROÛTE

SERVES 4

PREHEAT THE OVEN TO 350°F

Pâte Feuilletée *made with*
  2¼ cups flour (see page 42)
4 thin veal cutlets (4 oz. each)
salt
freshly ground black pepper
2 tsp. grapeseed or safflower oil
4 red peppers, skinned (see page
  23) and diced
8 slices Emmenthal cheese
  (½ oz. each)
11 oz. duxelle of mushrooms (see
  page 23)

SAUCE
2 cups Fonds de Volaille *(see*
  page 31)
2 shallots, peeled and finely
  chopped
1 garlic clove, peeled and
  crushed
2 tbsp. white wine vinegar
2 tbsp. water
¼ cup white wine
1 tomato, peeled, seeded and
  diced
1 sprig thyme
1 bay leaf
parsley sprigs

TO SERVE
1 recipe Ratatouille Provençale
  (see page 156)

These little pastry parcels can be made the day before you wish to serve them. The original recipe used double the amount of cheese, a slice of ham, and a béchamel *made with flour and butter. The red pepper addition, tasty and colorful, is a new idea!*

1   Allow the pastry to rest in the refrigerator for 20 minutes.

2   Season the cutlets lightly with salt and pepper. Heat 1 teaspoon oil in a skillet and quickly sear the cutlets on both sides. Reserve to cool.

3   To make the sauce, simmer to reduce the stock by half. Sweat the shallots in 1 teaspoon of the oil for 5 minutes, then add the garlic and sweat for 1 minute longer. Add the vinegar, water and white wine and reduce until nearly dry. Add the reduced stock, half the red peppers and the tomato. Season with a little salt and pepper, add the thyme, bay leaf and parsley sprigs, and simmer for 30 minutes, skimming off the impurities as they rise to the surface.

4   Meanwhile, roll the dough out and cut into eight 4½-inch squares. Have ready the cheese slices, the veal, the *duxelle* and the remaining red peppers. Divide the *duxelle* and peppers into four parts, one for each pastry "parcel."

5   On each of four pastry squares lay a slice of cheese, then half the alloted amount of *duxelle* and red pepper, the slice of veal, the remaining red peppers and *duxelle*, and top finally with another slice of cheese. Brush the edges of the dough with egg wash then fold the excess dough up around the layers. Brush the edges of the remaining squares of dough with egg wash and place over the top, making sure the first layer of dough is completely covered. Press to seal. Brush the tops with egg wash and make a criss-cross pattern with a blunt knife. The pastry parcels may be chilled for 20 minutes or overnight if you like, well brushed with egg wash.

6   Bake in the preheated oven for 20 minutes. Brush with egg wash again half way through the cooking time to obtain a shiny finish.

7   Reduce the sauce until it lightly coats the back of a spoon. Remove the thyme, bay leaf and parsley sprigs, and purée the sauce. Return to the heat and adjust the seasoning.

TO SERVE Pour the sauce into a warm gravy boat, and arrange the little veal parcels on a heated serving dish lined with doilies or a folded napkin.

Serve with the ratatouille.

RIGHT *Escalope de Veau Jurassienne en Croûte*
with *Ratatouille Provençale*

Blanquette de Veau (ou Lapin)
BLANQUETTE *OF VEAL (OR RABBIT)*

A blanquette *of veal is one of the most traditional of French dishes. It can also be made with rabbit. Here, it has been adapted to make it healthier by eliminating the flour and butter* roux, *most of the cream, and the fat.*

Preparation should cover 2 days, but each day requires only a few minutes of actual work, and the flavor is considerably enhanced by the overnight marination.

The blanquette *could be further garnished by a green vegetable such as steamed broccoli, by some croûtons or by a timbale (see page 44). (The latter two, however, contain gluten.)*

GLUTEN FREE

SERVES 4

1½ lb. veal shoulder, trimmed
   or 1 rabbit (2¼ lb.) and
   mirepoix *(1 onion, 1 carrot
   and celery stalk)*
½ tsp. salt
2 quarts water
mirepoix *(1 onion, 1 carrot and
   1 celery stalk)*
1 bouquet garni
4 sprigs parsley
1 quart Fonds de Volaille *(see
   page 31)*
8 pieces each of the following
   turned vegetables: carrots,
   turnips, rutabagas and
   potatoes
4 pearl onions
1 tbsp. potato starch
¼ cup whipping cream
5 oz. small, white, closed button
   mushrooms
3 tsp. lemon juice
1 tsp. grapeseed or safflower oil
freshly ground black pepper
½ cup white wine
4 oz. frozen tiny peas

TO SERVE

3 tbsp. fines herbes, *finely
   chopped*
2 oz. Greek yogurt

TWO DAYS BEFORE SERVING
This applies to a rabbit *blanquette* only. Cut the rabbit as described on page 21, place the pieces in a large saucepan, and add the salt, the water and *mirepoix*. Bring to the boil, turn the heat off and allow to marinate overnight in the refrigerator.

ONE DAY BEFORE SERVING
1   For the veal *blanquette*, bring the salt and water to a boil. Cut the veal into 1-inch cubes, and wash in cold running water to remove any impurities. Put the cubes in the boiling water, bring back to the boil, and blanch for 2 minutes.

2   From now on the instructions are the same for veal and rabbit. Drain the meat, rinse under cold running water, and drain again. Put into a large, clean saucepan or heatproof casserole with the roughly chopped *mirepoix, bouquet garni* and parsley sprigs. Add the cold stock, and bring to the boil slowly, skimming off the impurities as they rise to the surface.

3   Add the carrots, turnips and rutabagas (the potatoes will go in later), along with the pearl onions, and cover. Simmer until the vegetables are done (about 5–10 minutes for the turned vegetables, a little longer for the onions). Turn the heat off, cover, and allow to cool. When cold, place in the refrigerator overnight.

THE DAY OF SERVING
1   Remove the fat which has congealed on the surface, and place the pan over low heat. Remove the turned vegetables and onions and reserve in a bowl with a little stock so that they do not become dry. Bring the stock in the pan back to the boil, adding the potatoes. When the potatoes are tender, remove and reserve with the other vegetables. When the meat is done (about 10–15 minutes), remove it and reserve in a warm place with a little stock, well covered.

2   For the sauce, strain the stock and discard the *mirepoix, bouquet garni* and parsley sprigs. Place the stock in a large, clean saucepan and reduce by simmering until 1¼ cups remain. Mix the potato starch and cream in a bowl, and pour in a little of the hot stock. Mix well, then pour back into the stock. Stir while it returns to the boil, then simmer very gently for about 5 minutes, or until it lightly coats the back of a spoon.

Blanquette de Veau

3 Wash the mushrooms carefully, then leave them for 1 minute in a bowl of water with 1 teaspoon of the lemon juice. Heat the oil in a skillet, and add the mushrooms, some salt and pepper, and another teaspoon of lemon juice. Sauté briskly over medium heat for about 2–3 minutes until the juices start to run. Add the white wine, cover, and simmer until the mushrooms are done, about 5 minutes. Remove the lid and reduce the juice by half (about 2 minutes).

4 Pour the mushrooms and their juices into the pan holding the *blanquette* sauce. Add the meats and all the reserved vegetables, including the peas. (If you wish to freeze the *blanquette*, now is the time to do so.)

5 Reheat the *blanquette* slowly over low heat, and simmer for 3–4 minutes.

TO SERVE Reserve a tablespoon of herbs for garnish, mix the rest with the yogurt, and stir into the warm sauce. Add the remaining lemon juice and taste the sauce. Adjust the seasoning if necessary.

Serve the meat and sauce on a large, warm platter, arrange the vegetables around it, and sprinkle the center with the remaining herbs.

Timbale de Veau aux Petits Pois
VEAL TIMBALE WITH PEAS

This recipe originally used lamb or another red meat, but when searching for ways to cut down on red meat, this veal alternative proved delicious. No flour is used in the sauce; its body comes from the onions, tomato paste, and reduction. The addition of the peas gives an attractive color to the stew as well as providing vitamins and fiber. Use frozen pearl onions if you can't find fresh — they're just as good. If you are on a gluten-free diet, do not serve the pastry timbale.

SERVES 4

Pâte Brisée *made with 2¼ cups (11 oz.) flour (see page 44)*
1 onion, peeled and finely *chopped*
salt
freshly ground black pepper
1¼ lb. lean veal (leg or *shoulder), trimmed and cubed*
1 tbsp. grapeseed or safflower oil
½ cup white wine
2 tbsp. tomato paste
1 cup Fonds de Volaille (see page *31)*
12 pearl onions, topped, tailed, *blanched and peeled*
1 bouquet garni
2 sprigs parsley
10 coriander seeds
1 lb. frozen tiny peas, blanched
1 lb. turnips, cut into julienne, *blanched*

1 Allow the pastry to rest in the refrigerator for 20 minutes. Roll out and make a *timbale* (see page 44). Bake it.

2 Sweat the onion in a heavy casserole, covered, over low heat for 10 minutes.

3 Salt and pepper the meat, then push aside the onions and the oil in the casserole, and sauté the meat quickly over high heat. Remove the meat and onions from the pan and leave on a plate to cool.

4 Remove the fat from the casserole, deglaze with the white wine, and reduce until nearly dry. Add the tomato paste and let it cook and stick to the pan without burning. Return the meat and onions, add the chicken stock and pearl onions, and bring to the boil slowly, removing the impurities as they rise to the surface. Simmer, covered, for 15 minutes.

5 Add the *bouquet garni*, parsley sprigs and coriander seeds, then simmer for 20 minutes longer.

6 Add the peas and turnip *julienne*. Simmer for 5 minutes, uncovered.

7 Test the meat to see if it is cooked; it should be soft. When done, remove it with the vegetables, except for the onion. Reserve with a little of the stock to moisten.

8 Reduce the juices left in the casserole by half. Purée with the onion in a blender or food processor, then pour back into the casserole with the meat and vegetables. Let it return just to the boil, and check the seasoning. (At this stage the meat and vegetables could be left to cool to be served the next day, or to be frozen.)

TO SERVE Warm the *timbale* and its lid in a low oven. Pour the stew into it and cover with the lid. Present on a serving dish lined with a doily or napkin.

RIGHT *Timbale de Veau aux Petits Pois*

Poulet Farci Fendu au Four

BAKED CHICKEN WITH ZUCCHINI STUFFING

*T*his dish is a challenge for any cook. See pages 18–19 for full details on how to bone the chicken. Roasting is the favored method here as it drains off all the fat, which is later discarded. The stuffing contains more vegetables, and less fat, than the original. Serve with an assortment of vegetable purées.

1   Bone the chicken as described on pages 18–19, then sprinkle with salt and pepper.

2   For the stuffing, grate the zucchini, or cut them into thin *julienne* strips, sprinkle with a little salt and leave for 10–15 minutes. Rinse well, then squeeze dry by handfuls to eliminate the salt and juices. Heat the oil and sweat the onion and garlic until soft, then add the zucchini. Sweat for 2 minutes. Remove and spread out on a large serving dish and leave to cool.

3   In a bowl, soften the Ricotta, and add the cooled vegetable mixture, the fresh herbs and a pinch of *herbes de Provence*. Mix well, then add the Parmesan, egg white, and the breadcrumbs. Season well.

4   Lay the chicken flat, skin side up and, with your fingers, separate the skin from the flesh. Lay the stuffing between the flesh and the skin of the leg, then the breast, one side at a time, making sure not to break the skin between the two breasts.

5   Rub the whole chicken with a little oil and some salt and pepper. Roast in the preheated oven in a roasting pan lined with foil for 10 minutes, then turn the oven down to 350°F and roast for a further 40–50 minutes until golden brown.

TO SERVE Lift the chicken out delicately, on the foil, and allow the fat and juices to run back into the pan. Strain the juices through a conical sieve into a fat-separator, discard the fat carefully and mix the remaining juices with the *coulis*. Heat through quickly, carve the chicken as described on page 134, and serve immediately with the vegetable purées and salad greens.

SERVES 6
PREHEAT THE OVEN TO 450°C

1 chicken (3½ lb.)
salt
freshly ground black pepper

STUFFING
1 lb. zucchini, washed, topped
*   and tailed*
½ tsp. olive oil
1 onion, peeled and chopped
1 garlic clove, peeled and crushed
4 oz. Ricotta (or other low-fat
*   soft cheese)*
1 tsp. fines herbes, finely chopped
herbes de Provence
¼ cup grated Parmesan cheese
1 egg white
¼ cup dry whole-wheat
*   breadcrumbs*

TO SERVE
Coulis de Tomates *(see page 38)*
Purées de Légumes *(see page*
*   151)*
green onion flowers (see page
*   25)*
salad greens

LEFT *Poulet Farci Fendu au Four*

Chaud-Froid de Volaille
CHICKEN CHAUD-FROID

A traditional chaud-froid *is not very popular in France, but now that we all recognize the healthiness of plainly boiled poultry, it should become more popular. The classic recipe had a butter and flour* roux *to thicken the white sauce, to which was added a lot of cream, with more cream plus tomato paste in the pink sauce, and yet more cream and a purée of spinach in the green sauce. As usual, we have substituted Greek yogurt for the cream, but a fat-free soft cheese would be even better. The base of the sauces is the stock in which the chicken cooks, but no* roux *is added, and it is reduced to concentrate the natural gelatin it contains.*

If you select brands of curry powder and paprika which contain no gluten, this dish is gluten-free.

Plan to prepare this dish over 2 days.

SERVES 6

1 chicken (3¼ lb.)
1 sprig thyme
1 bay leaf
salt
15 peppercorns, crushed
juice of ½ lemon
1 extra chicken carcass
mirepoix *(3 carrots, 2 onions and 2 celery stalks)*
1 bouquet garni *plus remainder of the leek*
3 garlic cloves, peeled

SAUCES
7 oz. carrots, peeled and sliced
7 oz. spinach, cut into chiffonade
1 garlic clove, peeled
1 tsp. mild curry powder
5 pinches each of paprika and cayenne pepper
¼ cup Greek yogurt
2 oz. Ricotta (or other low-fat soft cheese)

GARNISH
parsley sprigs

THE DAY BEFORE SERVING

1 Clean the chicken and rinse it. Dry it well, inside and out, and place the sprig of thyme, bay leaf, ¼ teaspoon salt, a third of the peppercorns and half the lemon juice in the cavity. Put in a large saucepan with the chicken carcass, the *mirepoix, bouquet garni* and leek, garlic, ½ teaspoon salt and the remaining peppercorns.

2 Cover with water and place over medium heat. Bring to the boil, skimming off the impurities as they rise to the surface. This can take up to 20 minutes. Then turn the heat down and simmer for 1 hour; the liquid should barely move. Turn off the heat and allow to cool at room temperature, then place the saucepan in the refrigerator overnight.

THE DAY OF SERVING

1 Start by removing all the fat congealed on the surface of the cooking liquid. Remove the chicken and strain the stock first through a sieve and then through cheesecloth into another pan. Carve the chicken, keeping the skin and smaller bits to put into the stock for extra gelatin. Remove the fillet from the breast and cut the breast in half. Separate the thighs from the drumsticks and cut the thighs in half lengthwise, to remove the bones. You should obtain twelve pieces. Lay the pieces on a tray to cool in the refrigerator. Keep all meat trimmings from the carcass for later use.

2 Put the bones and skin into the stock and bring to the boil. Remove the pieces of skin and the bones immediately, as the natural gelatin will have been extracted. Reduce the stock to obtain 2½ cups, which will take approximately 30–40 minutes.

3 Steam the carrots until soft. Purée them later with ¾ cup of the reduced stock and a little salt and pepper if necessary. Sauté the spinach with a little water, salt and pepper, then purée it. Drain well in a fine sieve, and blot with paper towels to remove the excess moisture. Add ¾ cup reduced stock to this purée as well. Put both purées in the freezer to thicken, stirring occasionally until they are of a good coating consistency.

4   For the third sauce, which has a Colombo flavor, mash the garlic clove, curry powder, paprika and cayenne pepper together using a pestle and mortar. Add the yogurt and soft cheese a little at a time. Thin the mixture with the remaining reduced stock. Adjust the seasoning if necessary, and place in the freezer to thicken, as with the other two sauces.

5   When all three sauces can coat the back of a spoon, bring the chicken out of the refrigerator on its cooling tray and place over a baking sheet (so that sauce falling through can be retained). Spoon the carrot sauce over four of the chicken pieces, the spinach sauce over another four, and the Colombo-type sauce over the final four. Coat each piece well about three times. Reserve what remains of each sauce.

6   Mix the remaining carrot sauce with the remaining Colombo-type sauce. Pour onto a large, flat serving platter, at least 16 inches in diameter. Make a pastry bag from a triangle of paper and pour into it 2 tablespoons of the remaining green sauce. Pipe small dots of green sauce all around the sauce-lined platter at about ½-inch intervals. Run a sharp knife from the center of these dots in toward the center of the dish in a "comma" shaped movement (see the photograph). Place the platter in the refrigerator to set. Pour the remaining green sauce onto a dinner plate to line the bottom. Refrigerate to set.

7   Chop the small bits of chicken left over from the carving and attached to the carcass, and mix with the sauces left on the sheet from the coating process. Pack into one ramekin dish, and place in the refrigerator. (This will make a delicious terrine, which can be served the next day.)

TO SERVE   Take everything out of the refrigerator. Arrange the chicken pieces on the platter, combining the colors well, and garnish with parsley. Cut the jellied green sauce from the plate into shapes to garnish the chicken pieces. Serve immediately.

Chaud-Froid de Volaille

Poulet Grillé au Citron Vert

GRILLED CHICKEN WITH LIME

*S*tart preparing this dish the day before you want to serve it so that it can marinate overnight in the refrigerator. The lime dissolves the fat completely, and gives the chicken a wonderfully exotic taste. It's a perfect dish for a barbecue.

GLUTEN FREE
SERVES 4

1 chicken (2¼ lb.)
salt
freshly ground black pepper
½ tsp. ground ginger (preferably fresh)
1 small bunch green onions, washed
2 limes, washed
½ tsp. light brown sugar
⅓ cup water

TO SERVE
1 recipe Riz Complet aux Poireaux (see page 162)
2 chop frills (see page 28)
Coulis de Tomates (see page 38)
parsley sprigs

THE DAY BEFORE SERVING

1   Bone the chicken as described on pages 18–19, reserving the carcass for chicken stock. Salt the chicken lightly and sprinkle pepper generously all over it, along with the ginger.

2   Remove most of the green from the green onions, chop them finely and spread on a plate large enough to fit the flattened chicken. Lay the chicken over the onions, skin side down, pressing down well. Using a zester, cut the lime rind into *julienne*. Sprinkle over the chicken. Squeeze the lime juice over the chicken and rub it in well. Cover with plastic wrap and keep in the refrigerator overnight. (If you really do not have time to leave overnight, leave for 2 hours at room temperature.)

THE DAY OF SERVING

1   Drain the chicken of all its juices and dry it well with paper towels. Remove the onion.

2   Meanwhile, recuperate all the lime zest and blanch it for 1 minute in boiling water. Strain, then put in a saucepan with the sugar and water and leave to simmer until only about 2 tablespoons of liquid are left in the pan.

3   Heat the broiler to maximum, lay the chicken on a rack flesh side up, and place under the heat. After 2 minutes, turn the temperature down (if there is no control, leave the chicken for 2 minutes directly under the broiler, then place it on a lower shelf). Broil for 12 minutes on each side. Turn the broiler off and leave for 5 minutes longer.

TO SERVE Carve the chicken. Cut the bird in half lengthwise through the skin that holds the breasts together. Cut each breast in half again on the diagonal (to make four pieces) and cut the legs in half through the joints.

Make a bed of rice on a warm serving platter, and re-assemble the chicken in its original shape. Put chop frills on the drumsticks. Pour the tomato *coulis* all around and serve any remaining in a gravy boat. Garnish with parsley and the drained *julienne* of lime zest.

Poulet Sauté à l'Estragon
CHICKEN WITH TARRAGON

*T*he traditional recipe roasts chicken pieces in their own fat plus some butter, but the method here is more of a braise, with the chicken fat running into the braising liquid, which will be separated later. The vast amount of cream normally used is reduced drastically, although a little is still used along with Greek yogurt, in order to preserve the original creamy taste of the tarragon sauce. Do not chop the tarragon ahead of time as it will lose its aromatic qualities.

GLUTEN FREE

SERVES 4

PREHEAT THE OVEN TO 375°F

1 chicken (2¼ lb.)
salt
freshly ground black pepper
3 tsp. grapeseed or safflower oil
2 shallots, peeled and crushed
2 garlic cloves, peeled and crushed
mirepoix (1 onion, 1 carrot and 1 celery stalk)
fresh tarragon
½ cup dry white wine
2¼ cups Fonds de Volaille (see page 31)
½ cup whipping cream

TO SERVE
brown rice
Lichettes de Légumes *(see page 24)*
2 tbsp. Greek yogurt

1   Cut the chicken into 10 pieces (see page 20). Remove the fillets and cut the wings in half. Separate the thighs and drumsticks.

2   Remove the wing tips and the ends of the drumsticks and use with the carcass (discarding the tail, fat and skin) to make stock, or freeze the carcass to use another time.

3   Remove the excess skin and fat from the chicken pieces. Salt them lightly and pepper generously. Heat 2 teaspoons of the oil in a heavy skillet or cast-iron casserole and, when hot, sauté the chicken pieces very quickly to sear them. Reserve on a plate.

4   Dab the pan with paper towels to remove the oil, taking care not to take any of the pan juices. Replace over low heat, add the remaining oil and sweat the shallots and garlic until soft, about 2–3 minutes. Add the finely chopped *mirepoix* and sweat for about 5 minutes or until soft. Add the chicken thighs and drumsticks, putting a tiny sprig of tarragon underneath each piece, plus the white wine, bring to the boil, and place in the preheated oven.

5   After 7 minutes, turn the oven down to 350°F and add the breast pieces with bone. After 7 more minutes, add the other pieces of white meat and check that there is still enough moisture. If not, add a little water. Tuck a tiny sprig of tarragon underneath each chicken piece as you put it into the pan.

6   After another 7 minutes, remove the boneless breast pieces and reserve on a plate. Continue cooking 7 minutes longer, then remove all the pieces and reserve with the others in a warm place. Place the pan over high heat.

7   Add the chicken stock and let it simmer for 5 minutes. Push it through a conical sieve into a fat-separator, extracting as much flavor as possible from the *mirepoix*. Rinse the pan of all its fat and impurities and pour the fat-free stock back into it. Add the cream and 2 tablespoons of chopped tarragon, and reduce the sauce by three-quarters until it becomes syrupy, about 10 minutes.

TO SERVE Prepare the brown rice.

Remove the sauce from the heat to cool it a little, and arrange the rice on a heated platter. Place the chicken on top and surround with the vegetables. Add a quarter of the sauce to a bowl containing the yogurt. Stir well and pour back into the remaining sauce, mixing thoroughly. *Do not heat again.* Spoon a little of the sauce over the chicken and place the rest in a gravy boat. Just before serving, sprinkle about 1 teaspoon of chopped tarragon over the chicken.

Fricassée de Volaille au Concombre

CHICKEN FRICASSEE WITH CUCUMBER

As with many of our recipes, no flour is used here to thicken the sauce — that is done by reducing. And again we use just a small amount of whipping cream, in place of the traditional larger amount of double cream. This makes this dish ideal for those on a gluten-free diet.

GLUTEN FREE

SERVES 4

PREHEAT THE OVEN TO 375°F

1 chicken (2¼ lb.)
salt
freshly ground black pepper
3 tsp. grapeseed or safflower oil
1 leek, halved lengthwise, washed and cut into 1-in. julienne *slices*
2 shallots, peeled, halved and thinly sliced
½ cup Madeira
mirepoix (1 onion, 1 carrot and 1 celery stalk)
½ cup white wine
1⅓ cups Fonds de Volaille *(see page 31)*
½ cup whipping cream
2 tomatoes, peeled, seeded and cut into thin strips

TO SERVE
1 cucumber
14 oz. potatoes, peeled and turned
parsley or chervil sprigs

1   Cut the chicken into 10 pieces as described on page 20. Keep the carcass for a future chicken stock (store it directly in the freezer after removing the fat, skin and tail). Season the chicken pieces with salt and pepper.

2   Heat 2 teaspoons oil in a skillet or heavy cast-iron casserole and sauté the pieces of chicken very quickly, starting with the skin side. Reserve on a plate.

3   Dab the pan with a paper towel to blot the oil, taking care not to remove the pan juices. Sweat the leek and shallot, covered, in the pan juices. After 5 minutes, when the vegetables are soft, deglaze the pan with half the Madeira. Reduce for 5 minutes, and reserve.

4   Heat the remaining oil in the same pan and add the *mirepoix*. Cover and sweat for 5 minutes. Place the chicken pieces on top of the *mirepoix* and add the wine. Bring to the boil on top of the stove, then place in the preheated oven.

5   After 7 minutes, remove the chicken wings and breasts and reserve in a warm place. Add more water to the casserole if necessary, so that the vegetables do not burn. After a further 7 minutes, remove the remaining chicken, but check first to see that it is thoroughly cooked; when a skewer is inserted into the thickest part of the thigh, the juices should be clear. If the juice is pink, leave the chicken for 3 minutes longer. Turn off the oven and put all the chicken pieces into a covered dish in the still warm oven.

6   To make the sauce, add the chicken stock to the casserole. Bring to the boil, then pour through a conical sieve into a fat-separator. Meanwhile, reheat the leek, shallot and Madeira mixture in the skillet, covered. Deglaze with the remaining Madeira, reduce for a minute longer, then add the fat-free stock and juices. Reduce for 5 minutes over low heat then add the cream. Leave to reduce for 2 minutes more, by which time it should coat the back of a spoon lightly. Add the tomato strips and heat through gently for 1 minute.

TO SERVE   Score the cucumber, keeping the trimmings for garnish. Cut the cucumber in half lengthwise, seed and drain, then cut each half into thick slices. Alternatively, you could cut the cucumber halves into 1-inch sections and turn them like the carrots and potatoes. Steam the cucumber pieces and peel for 5 minutes and reserve. Steam the potatoes until tender (about 5 minutes).

Meanwhile, skin the chicken pieces, lay on a heated serving dish or individual plates and spoon over the sauce. Arrange the potatoes all around the dish or plates. Garnish with parsley or chervil.

LEFT *Fricassée de Volaille au Concombre*

Poulet Sauté Stanley
CHICKEN STANLEY

his very traditional recipe has a mild curry taste. Instead of the usual roux of flour and butter, we have used onions to thicken the sauce.

If you select a curry powder which contains no gluten, this dish is gluten-free.

SERVES 4
PREHEAT THE OVEN TO 375°F

1 chicken (2¼ lb.)
salt
freshly ground black pepper
3 tsp. grapeseed or safflower oil
2 medium onions, peeled, cut in half through the root and thinly sliced
2 garlic cloves, peeled and crushed
1 tbsp. mild Madras curry powder
½ cup dry white wine
1⅓ cups Fonds de Volaille (see page 31)
7 oz. button mushrooms, washed and rinsed with 1 tsp. lemon juice
¼ cup whipping cream
¼ cup Greek yogurt

TO SERVE
Purées de Légumes (rutabaga or potato, see page 151)
parsley or chervil sprigs

1 Cut the chicken into 10 pieces as described on page 20. Lightly salt and generously pepper the pieces.

2 Heat a heavy cast-iron casserole, add the oil, and sear the chicken pieces on all sides very quickly over high heat. Remove from the pan and reserve. Dab the pan with a paper towel to blot the oil, taking care not to remove any of the pan juices. Add the onions to the pan, cover, and sweat over low heat for about 10 minutes, stirring occasionally so that they do not burn. Add the garlic and sweat for 1 minute. Add the curry powder, and cook for another minute, stirring well.

3 Add the white wine and reduce for 3 minutes, then add the stock. Bring to the boil and put in the chicken thighs and the drumsticks. Cover, and place in the oven for a total cooking time of 30 minutes. After 10 minutes, add the wings and turn the oven down to 350°F. After 15 minutes, add the breasts. With every addition, turn all the other chicken pieces in the liquid. After 20 minutes, add the mushrooms, and cook for a final 10 minutes.

4 Remove the pieces of chicken and keep warm, wrapped in foil. Remove the mushrooms and keep warm. Strain the juices through a conical sieve into a fat-separator. Put the fat-free juices in a saucepan with the cream to reduce for 5 minutes over low heat, stirring often so that it does not stick.

5 Place half the onion left in the sieve into a blender, food processor or food mill, and purée with the reduced sauce. Mix the yogurt with a little of the hot sauce, then pour back into the remaining sauce and add the remaining onions. Adjust the seasoning if necessary. Reserve in a warm place.

TO SERVE Warm the vegetable purée. Skin all the chicken pieces and reserve, well covered, in a warm place.

To serve traditionally, arrange the chicken pieces along the middle of a warmed serving dish, cover with a little sauce, and place a small parsley or chervil sprig on each piece of chicken. Arrange the mushrooms around the dish, and serve the purée in a vegetable bowl, the remaining sauce in a gravy boat.

To serve individually, arrange a piece of chicken on the front of the plate, and cover it and the plate with the sauce. Arrange vegetable purée *quenelles* (see page 26) toward the back of the plate, along with the mushrooms. Serve immediately.

Ballotine de Faisan
BALLOTINE OF PHEASANT

This recipe requires a modicum of boning skill, use the technique for boning chicken (see pages 18–19). Choose a pheasant which has not been hung for too long — 2 days maximum. Rather than the usual rich foie gras *and pork, this stuffing uses a little pork and veal, more of the latter as it is leaner. The mushrooms will moisten the mixture in the same way as the fat from the* foie gras *would have done — but with no fat at all. And another moistening tip is to add cream cheese to the stuffing; it contains slightly more fat than Greek yogurt, but makes the stuffing a little more succulent.*

GLUTEN FREE
SERVES 4

1 pheasant (about 1½lb.)
salt
freshly ground black pepper
1½tsp. grapeseed or safflower oil
1 cup Madeira
mirepoix (½ onion, 1 carrot and 1 celery stalk)
1 sprig thyme
1 bay leaf
parsley sprigs
1 cup Fonds de Volaille (see page 31)

STUFFING
2 shallots, peeled and chopped
pheasant or chicken livers (see method), roughly chopped
4 oz. mushrooms, chopped
5 oz. lean veal, ground
4 oz. pork tenderloin, ground
1 egg
¼ cup Greek yogurt
ground allspice
pheasant fillets (see method)

TO SERVE
1 lb. turned vegetables

1   Clean the pheasant, reserving the liver. Cut down the backbone and bone completely, including the legs and wings. Remove the breast fillets, taking care not to split the skin, and season the bird well with salt and pepper.

2   For the stuffing, heat ½ teaspoon oil in a skillet and sweat half the shallot for a minute or so before adding the pheasant liver. Flame with ¼ cup of the Madeira, then reserve on a plate. Sweat the remaining shallot gently in the same pan with a further ½ teaspoon oil, then add the mushrooms. Season with salt and pepper immediately and cook over high heat until the juices have evaporated. Add another ¼ cup of the Madeira, and boil to reduce. Mix in the reserved shallot and liver, and put the mixture on a dish to cool.

3   Mix the ground veal and pork with the egg. Add the yogurt and season with salt, pepper and a pinch of allspice.

4   Lay the pheasant on a work surface, skin side down, and place the meat stuffing over the pheasant flesh. Cover this with a layer of the mushroom and the liver mixture, and place the reserved pheasant fillets in the middle, one along the other.

5   Roll the pheasant up carefully, making sure the filling is completely enclosed, and sew the edges together with string and a trussing needle. Tie with string at intervals along the bird to keep the oblong shape.

6   Sweat the *mirepoix* gently in a large pan with the remaining oil until the vegetables exude their liquids, then add the ballotine. Increase the heat slightly and brown the outside of the ballotine.

7   Add the remaining Madeira and other ingredients and bring to the boil. Simmer, covered with a tight-fitting lid, for 40 minutes. Take the pan off the heat and leave for 10 minutes longer to rest.

8   Remove the ballotine from the cooking liquid and keep warm. Strain the sauce and remove the fat. If the sauce is too thin, reduce until it coats the back of a spoon. Taste, and correct the seasoning if necessary.

TO SERVE   Steam the vegetables for about 5 minutes.
    Carve the ballotine, place the slices in the middle of a warmed serving dish, and surround with the vegetables. Pass the sauce separately in a gravy boat.

Perdreaux Vignerons
BRAISED PARTRIDGES

Some people cannot eat game because they find it hard to digest, but the use of sage, a digestive herb, will help.

Beginners might find it a little tricky to bone these partridges, in which case leave the bones in to be tackled by your guests. This is quite usual, but you will then need to use chicken bones with the partridge giblets to make the stock.

Use fresh vine leaves if you are lucky enough to have a nearby grape vine — as we do, growing in our conservatory at the School — but if not, omit them. Never use the ones preserved in brine, they are full of additives and give a bitter taste to the partridge.

If you are on a gluten-free diet omit the breadcrumbs and toast, and use the chopped liver mixture to replace the breadcrumbs in the stuffing.

SERVES 4

PREHEAT THE OVEN TO 450°F

2 partridges, with giblets
salt
freshly ground black pepper
5 tsp. grapeseed or safflower oil
mirepoix (2 onions, 2 carrots and 2 celery stalks)
4 oz. red grapes, halved and seeded
4 oz. dry whole-wheat breadcrumbs
3 fresh sage leaves, or 1/2 tsp. dried sage
1/4 cup Greek yogurt
1 tsp. tomato paste
1 cup dry white wine
7 oz. fresh tomatoes, halved and seeded
3 cups cold Fonds de Volaille (see page 31)
1 bouquet garni
2 fresh vine leaves
2 slices bacon
2 shallots, peeled and sliced
2 tbsp. cognac
2 tbsp. Madeira
4 slices whole-wheat bread

TO SERVE

Purées de Légumes (celeriac, apple, and rutabaga, see page 151)
grapes, seeded and halved, or 4 small bunches
4 chop frills (see page 28)

1   Bone the partridges as described on pages 18–19 (but leave the thigh bones and drumsticks to give shape to the bird). Season well on all sides. Divide the finely chopped *mirepoix* between three bowls.

2   To prepare the stuffing, heat 1 teaspoon of the oil over low heat, and add the contents of one bowl of *mirepoix*. Sweat for 5 minutes, covered with a lid. Add the halved grapes and sauté for 1 minute over medium heat. Add the breadcrumbs and 2 chopped sage leaves. Stir well so that the bread absorbs the juices and the sage flavor. Reserve on a plate to cool. When cold, add the yogurt and mix well.

3   Heat 1 teaspoon of the oil in a saucepan and briskly brown the bones and giblets (excluding the liver, which is reserved for later). Lower the heat, add the second bowl of *mirepoix*, and sweat for 3–5 minutes or until soft. Add the tomato paste, let it sweat for 1 minute, and then deglaze with half the white wine. Reduce for 1 minute, then add the tomatoes and sweat, covered, for 5 minutes. Add the cold chicken stock, the *bouquet garni* and the remaining sage leaf. Add a pinch of salt and bring to the boil slowly, skimming off the impurities as they rise to the surface. Allow to simmer, and reduce, uncovered, for at least 1 hour.

4   Rub the partridges with paper towels inside and out, and season again. Divide the stuffing in half, and stuff the inside of each bird. Using string and a trussing needle, re-shape the partridges as if they were whole. Place a vine leaf on each breast and a slice of bacon on top. Secure with string.

5   Heat 2 teaspoons of the oil in a skillet large enough to hold both birds, and sear on all sides. Add the remaining *mirepoix* and white wine, and bring to the boil. Place the partridges on top of the *mirepoix*, one leg side down, and place in the preheated oven. Braise for 5 minutes, then for another 5 minutes on the other leg side. Remove the vine leaves and the bacon, and braise the birds breast up for a final 10 minutes, adding a little water if necessary, and basting frequently to brown. Turn the oven off and leave the birds, wrapped in foil, to rest for at least 15 minutes.

6 Pour the stock into the braising juices, and strain through a conical sieve into a fat-separator. Pour the fat-free liquid back into the skillet. Continue reducing if too thin; it should lightly coat the back of a spoon. Taste and adjust the seasoning.

7 Remove the strings and cut the partridges in half through the breast, making sure you divide the stuffing equally. Place a chop frill around each drumstick.

8 Just before serving, sweat the shallots in the remaining teaspoon of heated oil. Add the partridge livers and sauté for 1 minute. Add the cognac and flame it. Add the Madeira and remove the pan from the heat. Leave covered for 5 minutes for the flavors to blend and, in the meantime, toast the 4 slices of bread. Trim them to the size of a half partridge. Chop the livers and shallots and spread over the toast. Arrange the four half partridges on the four slices of toast.

TO SERVE Warm the vegetable and apple purées.

To serve traditionally, arrange the partridge toasts around a warm serving dish and serve the purées separately. Garnish with the extra grapes, arranged in a bunch. Serve the sauce in a gravy boat.

To serve individually, place the partridge on its toast at the bottom of the plate and, using two spoons, shape the different purées into *quenelles* (see page 26) and arrange them at the top of the plate. Garnish with a small bunch of grapes. Pour a little sauce over the partridge just before serving, and the remainder into a gravy boat.

Perdreaux Vignerons

Gigot de Dinde Farcie
STUFFED TURKEY THIGH

*T*his recipe requires some considerable skill as the boning is delicate. (This is a case when a good relationship with your butcher could be an advantage!) Once again, a predominantly vegetable stuffing is healthier and less fatty than a more traditional meat one. The gigot can be prepared ahead of time and reheated. It can also be served cold, sliced more thinly, on a bed of shredded lettuce or young spinach leaves — but if you choose to do this, you must prepare it at least 24 hours before serving.

If you are on a gluten-free diet, omit the breadcrumbs, double the amount of cheese and sauté the zucchini for 5 minutes longer.

SERVES 4
PREHEAT THE OVEN TO 450°F

1 large turkey leg quarter (about 2½ lb.)
grapeseed or safflower oil
mirepoix (1 onion, 1 carrot and 1 celery stalk)
¼ cup white wine
1 garlic clove, peeled and crushed
1 sprig thyme
2 cups Fonds de Volaille (see page 31)

STUFFING
3 oz. zucchini, washed, topped and tailed
salt
1 small onion, peeled and finely chopped
1 garlic clove, peeled and crushed
freshly ground black pepper
3 tbsp. low-fat cottage cheese
1 egg, beaten
½ cup fines herbes, finely chopped
¼ cup fresh whole-wheat breadcrumbs
⅓ cup each of Parmesan and Emmenthal cheese, grated
herbes de Provence

TO SERVE
1 lb. spinach, washed, chopped and sautéd in a little oil
Carottes Vichy (see page 160)

1 For the stuffing, grate the zucchini and sprinkle with a little salt. Drain in a colander for 30 minutes, then rinse and squeeze dry.

2 Bone the turkey leg quarter (see page 20) and carefully remove enough meat from around the bone cavity to leave a flat piece of meat ready to be stuffed. Grind the meat from around the bone cavity or chop finely in a food processor; there should be about 9–10 ounces.

3 Heat ½ teaspoon of oil and sweat the onion in it for 5 minutes. Add the garlic, sweat for a minute longer and add the zucchini to sweat for another 5 minutes. Leave on a plate to cool.

4 In a bowl, work together the cottage cheese and three-quarters of the beaten egg. Add the fresh herbs, the ground turkey meat, the onion and garlic and mix well by hand. Season well with salt and pepper. Add the zucchini along with the breadcrumbs, cheeses and *herbes de Provence*, to the meat mixture. Mix well to obtain a firm stuffing.

5 Brush the remainder of the egg over the meat, season it well, and place the stuffing in the middle. Bring the two ends together and seal tightly, tying with string or sewing with string and a trussing needle. (If there is too much stuffing, pack it into small ramekins and bake in a bain-marie in the moderate oven for 30 minutes later. Allow to cool in the oven, then weight them down and refrigerate overnight; the result will be lovely little pâtés!) Weigh the turkey and calculate the total braising time by allowing 15 minutes per pound, plus 15 minutes resting before carving.

6 Heat about 1 tablespoon of the oil in a heavy casserole or ovenproof skillet, and sear the turkey on all sides. Add the finely chopped *mirepoix* and sweat until just softened. This can take up to 20 minutes.

7 Add the white wine and bring to the boil. Add the garlic and the thyme. Place in the preheated oven, and cook for the calculated time.

8 Reduce the temperature to 350°F after about 15 minutes, and keep adding a little water to prevent the vegetables from burning as the liquid evaporates.

9 When the turkey is cooked (the juices should run clear when it is pierced with a skewer), place it on a plate. Put it back in the turned-off oven to rest for another 15 minutes.

10   Put the roasting pan along with the vegetables and juices from the meat, on the top of the stove, add the stock and boil to reduce to a good sauce consistency, about 10 minutes. Push the mixture through a conical sieve into a fat-separator, and discard the remaining *mirepoix*. Pour the fat-free sauce into a gravy boat.

TO SERVE   Remove the strings from the turkey and carve. Arrange the slices on a bed of the spinach and surround with the carrots. Pour a little of the sauce over the meat so that it does not dry up. Serve the remaining sauce separately.

Gigot de Dinde Farcie

Paupiettes de Dinde Verveine Menthe
BRAISED TURKEY ROLLS WITH MINT

*T*his is a wonderful dish, and looks like the best of nouvelle cuisine. Once again, the mirepoix vegetables and the shallots are sieved to give the sauce its smooth consistency and, to make the sauce lighter, we add a little Greek yogurt at the last moment, instead of the large amount of cream in the original recipe.

1 Flatten each cutlet with a meat cleaver. Rub the verbena and mint well together to mix the flavors, then sprinkle each cutlet lightly with salt and pepper and the mixed herbs, pressing well into the meat.

2 Brush the cutlets with the beaten egg. Place two pieces of bacon on top of each cutlet and brush with more egg. Roll them up and secure loosely with string.

3 Heat the oil in a casserole or large skillet, and sear the *paupiettes* quickly. Remove them, discard any fat, then sweat the *mirepoix* and the shallots until soft, about 2 minutes. Add half of the chicken stock and the *paupiettes*, bring to the boil, then braise in the preheated oven for 10 minutes.

4 Keep the *paupiettes* warm in between two plates in the turned-off oven, and return the casserole or skillet to the heat on top of the stove. Deglaze with the Madeira, then add the wine and remaining stock. Bring to the boil and allow to simmer for 1 minute.

5 Push the sauce through a conical sieve into a fat-separator, allow the fat to come to the surface and discard. In the meantime, rinse the pan quickly. Return the fat-free sauce to the pan, add the cream and reduce for 2 minutes. Off the heat, add the yogurt. Keep in a warm place.

TO SERVE Steam the carrots, turnips and parsnips and the broccoli florets. Glaze in a little butter just before arranging on the platter or plates.

Remove the string from the *paupiettes* and slice them thinly.

If serving traditionally, place the slices in the middle of a warm serving platter and surround with the vegetables. Pour the sauce into a gravy boat.

If serving individually, pour a little sauce on to each plate and arrange the sliced *paupiettes* among the vegetables.

GLUTEN FREE
SERVES 4
PREHEAT THE OVEN TO 350°F

3 large turkey breast cutlets
¼ tsp. dried lemon verbena
¼ tsp. dried mint
salt
freshly ground black pepper
1 egg, beaten
6 slices Canadian bacon, rind
    and fat removed
1 tsp. grapeseed or safflower oil
mirepoix (½ onion, 1 small
    carrot, and ½ celery stalk)
2 shallots, peeled and finely
    chopped
1⅓ cups Fonds de Volaille *(see*
    page 31)
2 tbsp. Madeira
½ cup white wine
¼ cup whipping cream
¼ cup Greek yogurt

TO SERVE
1 lb. turned carrots, parsnips and
    turnips
1 lb. broccoli
butter

LEFT *Paupiettes de Dinde Verveine Menthe*

Ballotine de Lapin au Thym
POACHED STUFFED SADDLE OF RABBIT WITH THYME

*T*he dish can be prepared ahead of time and reheated. It can also be served cold on a buffet table; set the sauce with a little gelatin dissolved in Madeira, added when the sauce was hot. Carve at the last moment so that the meat stays as moist as possible.

The eggplant chunks puréed into the stock thicken it as effectively as flour, and also add vitamins and fiber. The braising makes the dish very moist, but do not overcook or the meat will become tough.

GLUTEN FREE

SERVES 4

PREHEAT THE OVEN TO ITS LOWEST TEMPERATURE

1 rabbit (2¼ lb.), fresh or frozen
4 sprigs thyme
herbes de Provence
salt
freshly ground black pepper
¼ cup cognac
4 tbsp. grapeseed or safflower oil
7 oz. duxelle of mushrooms (see page 23)
mirepoix (1 onion, 1 carrot and 1 celery stalk)
1 tbsp. tomato paste
½ cup dry white wine
2 cups Fonds de Volaille (see page 31)
1 lb. tomatoes, washed and quartered
1 bouquet garni
3 oz. chicken breast, skinned
4 oz. lean veal shoulder or leg meat
1 egg
¼ cup Greek yogurt
1 pinch each of ground cloves, allspice and nutmeg
1 tbsp. fines herbes, finely chopped
1 small eggplant
juice of ½ lemon
2 shallots, peeled and finely chopped
¼ cup Madeira

TO SERVE

Purées de Légumes (rutabaga and/or celeriac, see page 151)
1 lb. green beans, topped and tailed

1   Cut the rabbit into pieces, but keep the saddle whole and then bone it (see page 21) being sure not to pierce the skin or the presentation will be less spectacular. Bone the remaining pieces, reserving the bones for the stock. The meat will be ground later.

2   Using a pestle and mortar, mash together 2 sprigs of thyme, a pinch of *herbes de Provence*, a pinch of salt and a little pepper, and 1 teaspoon each of the cognac and oil. Spread this paste over the saddle and leave to marinate while the forcemeat is being prepared.

3   To start the stock, crush the bones into small pieces along with any meat left on them, and brown in a saucepan with 1 teaspoon of the oil, about 10–15 minutes.

4   Meanwhile, prepare the *duxelle* of mushrooms, retaining the stalks for later use. Reserve on a plate to cool.

5   Add the roughly chopped *mirepoix* to the bones in the saucepan. Cover and sweat for 5 minutes until soft. Add the tomato paste and sweat, uncovered, for 2 minutes, stirring well. Add the wine and simmer to reduce until nearly dry. Add the remaining cognac and flame, stirring well until the flames die down. Pour in the chicken stock, and add the tomatoes, the mushroom stalks, one sprig of thyme, a pinch of *herbes de Provence* and the *bouquet garni*. Bring slowly to the boil, skimming off the impurities as they rise to the surface, and simmer for at least 30 minutes.

6   Meanwhile, prepare the stuffing. Grind the reserved rabbit meat except for the fillets and saddle using a meat grinder or in small amounts in a food processor, along with the chicken and veal. Mix all the meats together well by hand to remove the sinews. Beat the egg with the yogurt in a bowl, and add it gradually to the meat, working well in between each addition. Add the mushroom *duxelle*, spices and fresh herbs and remaining sprig of thyme, and mix well. Alternatively, roll the meat mixture into a sausage, divide in two, put the *duxelle* in the middle, and re-form.

7   Cut a sheet of foil which is 2 inches larger all around than the saddle, and rub with 1 teaspoon of the oil. Lay the saddle on it, fillet sides up. Put the stuffing in a sausage shape in the middle of the saddle and fold the sides over to overlap each other. (If the two sides do not overlap, leave some of the stuffing out. Bake this separately in a well-covered dish in a bain-marie in an oven preheated to 350°F for 30 minutes.) Close the foil carefully over the stuffed saddle, and twist the ends closed.

8 Strain the stock through a conical sieve and return to the same saucepan. Peel, seed and cube the eggplant, rub it with the half lemon, and add the cubes to the stock. Lower the foil-wrapped saddle into the pan, add a little water if necessary to cover the saddle, then cover with a lid and bring to the boil over low heat. Leave to barely simmer for 40 minutes, turning it around halfway through, then turn the heat off and leave to rest for 10 minutes. Remove the foil package and keep in a warm oven. Purée the eggplant with the stock in a food processor or blender to form the sauce.

9 Heat the remaining oil in a skillet over low heat, add the shallot and sweat, covered, for 5 minutes until soft. Deglaze with the Madeira, flame, and toss the pan until the flames die down. Add half of the eggplant sauce, mix well and pour the contents of the skillet back into the sauce, then reduce for 5 minutes over low heat. Reduce the sauce, if necessary, to coat the back of a spoon.

TO SERVE Prepare the purée(s) and steam the beans (3 minutes with a lid, then 3 minutes without).

Unwrap the ballotine. Using a very sharp knife, delicately cut four ½-inch slices from one end.

To serve traditionally, arrange the beans on both sides of a warm serving platter, and lay the ballotine in the center. Place the slices next to the cut side, as if they had been sliced on the platter. Serve the sauce in a gravy boat and the purées in vegetable dishes.

To serve individually, pour some sauce over the base of the warm plates, lay two slices of meat on each plate, and arrange the beans all around. Shape *quenelles* of purée (see page 26) and arrange toward the back of the plates. Serve the remaining sauce in a gravy boat.

Ballotine de Lapin au Thym

Lapin aux Pruneaux
BRAISED RABBIT WITH PRUNES

Another traditional French country dish, prepared over 2 days, this combines poaching and braising. The only difference between the original recipe and this one is the reduction of the sauce instead of thickening it with flour.

The prunes give fiber and a certain sweetness to the sauce. Served with the vegetables and rice indicated below, there is a high proportion of vitamins, protein and fiber, with very little fat.

GLUTEN FREE

SERVES 4

1 rabbit (2¼lb.), fresh or frozen
7oz. prunes
mirepoix (2 onions, 2 carrots, and 2 celery stalks)
2 garlic cloves, peeled and crushed
1⅓ cups red wine (Côtes du Rhône type)
1⅓ cups Fonds de Volaille (see page 31)
1 bouquet garni
ground allspice
salt
freshly ground black pepper
1 tbsp. red currant jelly
2 tsp. grapeseed or safflower oil
4oz. slab bacon
4oz. pearl onions, blanched and peeled
2 tbsp. cognac
1 tbsp. tomato paste
1 strip each of orange and lemon peel (removed with a potato peeler)
4oz. tomatoes, washed and quartered

TO SERVE

4oz. each of carrot and celeriac julienne
1lb. small green beans, topped and tailed
brown rice
2 chop frills (see page 28)
parsley or chervil sprigs

ONE DAY BEFORE SERVING

1   Cut the rabbit into pieces as described on page 21.

2   Wash the prunes well. Soak them in warm water for 2 minutes to eliminate the chemicals in their skins, then rinse well in two changes of water.

3   Place the rabbit in a large saucepan with the prunes, half the roughly chopped *mirepoix*, one of the garlic cloves, the red wine, chicken stock, *bouquet garni* and a pinch of allspice. Add a pinch of salt, some pepper and the red currant jelly. The meat should be covered with liquid; if not, add a little more stock. Bring slowly to the boil over medium heat, skimming off the impurities as they rise.

4   Let it simmer for 1 minute, stirring occasionally, then remove from the heat. Cover the surface of the liquid with a circle of parchment paper, and the pan with a lid. Leave to cool at room temperature, and when cold store in the refrigerator overnight.

THE DAY OF SERVING

1   Take the pan out of the refrigerator, remove the congealed fat on the top, and lift out the meat, prunes and *bouquet garni*. Leave the meat on a cooling rack to drain, and keep the *bouquet garni* and prunes to one side. Reheat the stock and strain through a conical sieve. Discard the *mirepoix*.

2   Heat a large skillet over medium heat, then add half the oil. Cut the slab bacon into small rectangles across the width, then sauté slowly so that the fat melts, and the meat browns.

3   Add the onions to the bacon to brown lightly.

4   When all the fat is rendered and the bacon and onions are golden brown, remove from the pan with a slotted spoon and reserve them both on a plate on paper towels. Discard the fat in the pan and wipe clean with paper towels. Add the remaining oil, sauté the pieces of rabbit over medium-high heat very quickly, letting them brown well. Pour the cognac over the rabbit, and flame. Let the flames die down, and reserve the rabbit pieces on a plate.

5   Add the remaining *mirepoix* and ¼ cup of the rabbit stock to the pan. Sweat over low heat, covered with a lid. Stir occasionally and cook until soft, about 5 minutes. Add the remaining clove of garlic and let it sweat for 1 minute, then add the tomato paste, and continue cooking a minute longer. Add ½ cup of the stock, mix well and leave to reduce until nearly dry. Add the remaining stock, a little at a time, to dissolve the tomato paste.

Lapin aux Pruneaux

6 Add the pieces of meat, bacon cubes, whole onions, prunes, *bouquet garni*, the orange and lemon peel and the tomatoes. Bring to the boil slowly, skimming off the impurities as they rise, and simmer, covered, for 1 hour. Check to see if the rabbit is done; the meat should be very tender when pressed with a finger, and it should detach easily from the bones.

7 Remove the rabbit, prunes, bacon and onions from the rest of the ingredients. Cut the meat carefully off the forequarters and the saddle. Reserve them all together, wrapped in foil to keep warm and moist.

8 Strain the stock through a conical sieve (discarding everything in the sieve) into another saucepan and reduce on medium heat for about 10 minutes to obtain the right flavor and consistency; it should coat the back of a spoon. Replace the reserved ingredients in the sauce and keep warm.

TO SERVE Steam the carrot and celeriac *julienne*, and the green beans, and cook the rice. Add the *julienne* to the rabbit. Prepare two chop frills for the rabbit thighs.

To serve traditionally, arrange a mound of rice in the center of a large, warmed serving dish, with the rabbit pieces on top and down the sides. Arrange some of the vegetables around the meat and pour some sauce over the top. Serve the remaining sauce and vegetables separately.

To serve individually, pour on enough sauce to cover the base of a warmed plate. Lay a piece of rabbit in the center, and garnish it with one or two pieces of vegetable *julienne*. Surround the meat with a few beans and place *quenelles* of rice (see page 26) on the top part of the plate. Place a parsley or chervil sprig on top of the rice. Serve the remaining vegetables and sauce separately.

VEGETABLES AND SALADS

Vegetables are important in Cuisine Santé, but we have not included a lot of specific recipes as the best way to serve them is generally as fresh and as close to uncooked as possible (see Ingredients). There are, however, serving suggestions throughout the book, most of which are based on a quick steaming. Steam vegetables only until *al dente*, or leave them still crunchy. This method keeps in all their nutritional value. Vegetables can also be eaten raw in salads. Try to have a salad at least once a day, as the French do, either before dessert, or before the main course, as a starter.

Purées de Légumes

VEGETABLE PURÉES

The following recipe can be adapted to most root vegetables, to potato, celeriac, carrot, parsnip, turnip or rutabaga. For vegetables like spinach, broccoli, cauliflower and Brussels sprouts, which already contain a lot of water, omit the milk but keep the Greek yogurt to give the creamy texture and slightly acid taste, reminiscent of the traditional crème fraîche. *If you use a food processor to make the purées, be careful, as the machine tends to over-develop gluten, in potatoes especially, making them gluey.*

These purées can be prepared a few hours in advance and reheated in a bain-marie (stir occasionally).

SERVES 4

1 lb. prepared vegetables
½ lemon (for celeriac only)
salt
⅔ cup milk
freshly ground black pepper
grated nutmeg
¼ cup Greek yogurt

1   Trim and peel the vegetable as appropriate. After peeling the celeriac, rub it with lemon juice to prevent discoloration. Cut the vegetables into large pieces, put into a saucepan of lightly salted, boiling water and cook until tender, about 10–15 minutes. Alternatively, steam them until very tender.

2   Drain, keeping the water to make a soup or consommé, and place the vegetable chunks into the saucepan back over the heat to dry.

3   Put the milk into a saucepan and bring to the boil. Season with pepper and nutmeg.

4   Purée the vegetable in a food processor, food mill, or with a potato masher, adding the hot milk. Mix well, then add the yogurt and keep warm, covered.

TO SERVE   Season the purée with a little more pepper and salt, beat well to obtain a smooth consistency, and serve in a heated vegetable dish, or shape into *quenelles* (see page 26) and serve on individual plates.

Salade Niçoise

*L*ike many of our salads, this one is almost a meal in itself, containing protein, carbohydrate, fat, vitamins, minerals and fiber. It differs from the traditional recipe only in that it uses a much lighter dressing, and very much less dressing. It can be served in small quantities as a starter, but is best as a main course in the summer, or as part of a buffet presentation. It's also very pleasant in the winter when it will remind you of those distant hot, summer days.

The decorative arrangement of the different vegetables in the bowl is very important. Arrange them basically as I describe, but use your own creativity and imagination as well — this is one of the major pleasures of cooking!

GLUTEN FREE
SERVES 4

¼ *head Boston lettuce*
2 oz. *thin green beans or snow peas, topped and tailed*
4 oz. *tuna fish in olive oil*
2 *large anchovy fillets*
1 *egg*
1 *celery stalk, trimmed*
1 *red pepper, washed, halved and seeded*
2 *tomatoes, washed*
1 *head of Belgian endive*
juice of ½ *lemon*
⅓ cup *Sauce Moutarde (see page 39) made with half olive oil, half grapeseed or safflower oil*
4–8 *black olives marinated in olive oil and herbes de Provence*

1   Separate the lettuce into leaves and wash carefully. Spin them dry, then break the largest leaves in half.

2   Steam the beans or snow peas for 3 minutes, then rinse under cold water. Cut the beans into ½-inch lengths.

3   Drain the tuna fish and anchovies well, and leave on paper towels to soak up the remaining oil. Break the tuna into large chunks and halve the anchovies lengthwise.

4   Put the egg in a pan of cold water, bring to the boil, and continue cooking for 5 minutes.

5   Remove as many strings as possible from the celery. Cut it into tiny *julienne*. Cut the pepper into thin *julienne*, skin side down. Remove the stalk end of the tomatoes, and cut each into six wedges.

6   When ready to assemble the salad, cut the endive in half lengthwise, then across thinly. Sprinkle with the lemon juice to prevent discoloration.

7   Place the dressing at the bottom of a large salad bowl, and cover with the lettuce leaves. Arrange the tomato wedges around the sides of the bowl, then a ring of beans or snow peas inside, followed by rings of the celery *julienne*, red pepper, tuna and endive. Push the hard-boiled egg through a sieve into the remaining circle, and arrange the anchovies in a star shape on top. Place the olives in the middle.

TO SERVE   Show your guests the beauty of your salad before you toss it, mixing carefully but thoroughly.

RIGHT *Salade Niçoise*

Fenouil à la Provençale

BRAISED FENNEL

Considered medicinal in the ancient civilizations of the Mediterranean, fennel was used in infusions and concoctions for all sorts of ailments. It is still a characteristically Mediterranean vegetable. Although low in vitamins and minerals, fennel is high in fiber and low in calories. An initial steaming, therefore (instead of blanching in water), followed by braising, keeps in all the goodness. Both vegetable and juices should be served.

GLUTEN FREE
SERVES 4
PREHEAT THE OVEN TO 350°F

4 small fennel bulbs, washed and quartered
salt
2 tbsp. olive oil
mirepoix (1 onion, 1 carrot, 1 celery stalk)
1 recipe Coulis de Tomates (see page 38)
1 cup Fonds de Volaille (see page 31)
1 sprig thyme
1 bay leaf
2 sprigs parsley
herbes de Provence
freshly ground black pepper

1 Steam the fennel quarters for 10 minutes over boiling salted water. Reserve on a cooling rack.

2 Heat half the olive oil and sweat the roughly chopped *mirepoix*, covered, until tender, about 5 minutes. Add the tomato *coulis*, chicken stock, thyme, bay leaf, parsley sprigs and a pinch of *herbes de Provence*. Season with a pinch of salt and a little pepper. Simmer for 10 minutes, covered. Remove the lid and reduce for 5 minutes, removing the impurities and the fat as they rise.

3 Scoop out the *mirepoix* vegetables with a slotted spoon and place in the bottom of a gratin dish. Arrange the fennel on top and coat with the tomato sauce. Sprinkle with the remaining olive oil and bake in the preheated oven for 20 minutes, covered with foil. Remove the foil and allow to brown lightly, approximately 10 minutes.

TO SERVE Take the fennel out of the gratin dish. Arrange the vegetables as a base in a hot serving dish, and spoon over a little of the sauce. Arrange the fennel quarters on top in a star shape, topped with more sauce. More traditionally, serve straight from the gratin dish, set on a plate with a doily or napkin in between.

Salade d'Endives
ENDIVE SALAD

GLUTEN FREE
SERVES 4

3 heads Belgian endive, washed
lemon juice
1 red apple, washed
2 oz. Emmenthal cheese, cut into
   small cubes
¼ cup walnuts
4 tbsp. Sauce Vinaigrette (see
   page 35)

*H*ere is a delicious way to enjoy Belgian endive. It is naturally high in fiber, but the addition of walnuts and apple gives a lot more goodness.

1   Cut the endives in half lengthwise and slice across thickly (reserving a few whole leaves for garnish). Sprinkle with lemon juice to prevent discoloration, and place in a mixing bowl.
2   Core the apple and cut into cubes. Add to the endive.
3   Add the Emmenthal to the endive and apple.
4   Chop half the walnuts coarsely and add to the salad.
5   Pour the vinaigrette over the salad, toss well, then place in a salad bowl lined with the whole endive leaves. Garnish with the remaining walnuts and marinate for at least 10 minutes before serving.

Poireaux Vinaigrette
LEEKS VINAIGRETTE

GLUTEN FREE
SERVES 4

4 large leeks
½ cup Sauce Vinaigrette (see
   page 35)
½ cup fines herbes, *finely
   chopped*
1 tbsp. capers, drained and finely
   chopped
2 cocktail gherkins, drained and
   finely chopped

GARNISH
½ hard-boiled egg

RIGHT *Salade d'Endives* and
Poireaux Vinaigrette

*N*ot long ago every corner café in France used to serve food at lunchtime for their regulars; now the regulars grab fast food and hurry back to the office. These leeks were part of the standard menu offered by the patron, *along with something like* Côte de Porc Charcutière, Cervelas Vinaigrette *and an* Hors d'Oeuvre Garni.

   The leeks can be prepared a few hours ahead of time and the important stage is the cooling down in the vinaigrette, so that they absorb its flavor. The dish is best served either tepid or ice cold, when it makes a very refreshing summer evening starter.

1   Remove the green of the leeks, reserving the pale green and white parts. Cut through the center, leaving the root attached, and clean very carefully to remove any sand or grit. Soak in cold water for 5–10 minutes.
2   Cut the leeks to fit inside a steamer, and steam for approximately 10 minutes until tender but still crunchy. Take the upper part of the steamer off and leave to cool for 2 minutes. Take the leeks out and cut in half across the width. Place on a flat dish and cover with vinaigrette. Leave to marinate and cool.
3   Drain the leeks and arrange on a serving dish. Mix the vinaigrette with the herbs, capers and gherkins. If too thick, add a little more vinaigrette. Spoon the dressing over the leeks. Chop the yolk and white of the egg separately and push through a sieve. Sprinkle over the top.

Ratatouille Provençale
BRAISED RATATOUILLE

Traditionally, all the vegetables in ratatouille are first fried in olive oil, resulting in a very rich and heavy stew. Our version is much lighter, because we sweat the vegetables, then reduce, rather than fry.

At the last moment, if available, add a few chopped basil leaves to the ratatouille. Serve it as a garnish for a meat or fish dish, or with scrambled eggs as a main course for a brunch or evening meal.

GLUTEN FREE
SERVES 4

2 tbsp. olive oil
1 onion, peeled and thickly sliced
2 garlic cloves, peeled and crushed
1 green pepper and 1 red pepper, washed, halved and seeded
1 small eggplant, washed
juice of ½ lemon
salt
freshly ground black pepper
2 zucchini, washed, topped and tailed
11 oz. tomatoes, peeled and seeded
1 sprig thyme
1 bay leaf
herbes de Provence

1 Heat half the olive oil in a large saucepan and sweat the onion, covered, for 5 minutes. Add the garlic and sweat for a minute more.

2 Slice the peppers, add to the onion and garlic, and sweat for 5 minutes, covered.

3 Cut the eggplant into quarters, and sprinkle them with lemon juice. Cut across into small chunks, and sprinkle with lemon juice again. Add to the saucepan, sprinkle lightly with salt and pepper, and sweat, covered, for a further 10 minutes.

4 Cut the zucchini in half lengthwise and slice thickly. Add to the saucepan, sprinkle lightly with salt and pepper, and sweat, covered, for 10 minutes.

5 Remove the lid and continue cooking to let the juices evaporate and the vegetables brown slightly.

6 Add the tomatoes, the thyme, bay leaf and a pinch of *herbes de Provence*. Simmer, covered, for a further 15 minutes.

7 Remove the lid and let the juices reduce well, but make sure the vegetables do not burn. Try not to stir too often, or the vegetables will break up.

TO SERVE Remove the thyme sprig and bay leaf, let the mixture cool slightly, then add the remaining olive oil. Serve either as a garnish with a meat or fish dish (see page 125) or in a heated vegetable dish.

Navets Glacés
GLAZED TURNIPS

A classic French cuisine garnish, this is revamped here with honey instead of sugar, to give a very special taste to the turnips.

In spring, use the baby new turnips with their flavorful skin; in the winter, use the old ones turned, or cut into the various shapes (julienne, lichette, etc.) mentioned throughout the book.

GLUTEN FREE
SERVES 4

3 lb. turnips
1 tbsp. grapeseed or safflower oil

1 Place the turnips in a saucepan and barely cover with water. Add the oil, honey, a pinch of salt and pepper.

2 Cover with a lid and bring to the boil on high heat. Simmer for 2 minutes, then remove the lid and boil, again over high heat, so that the water evaporates, a maximum of 10 minutes (the timing will depend on how the turnips are cut).

3 Just before serving add the herbs and toss lightly.

1 tbsp. honey
salt
freshly ground black pepper
1 tbsp. fines herbes, finely
    chopped

Salade de Choux aux Lardons
CABBAGE AND BACON SALAD

*T*his salad, normally prepared with a vast amount of fatty bacon, has been rendered a little healthier by the use of Canadian bacon which is slowly cooked so that all the fat is removed. In the traditional recipe, both the bacon and fat are added to the salad. Here, we throw away the fat. To make the croûtons without oil, follow the method on page 25. Omit them for a gluten-free dish.

SERVES 4

1 Quarter the cabbage and shred it. Let it marinate in cold water and 1 tablespoon of vinegar for 15–20 minutes to tenderize it a little.

2 To prepare the dressing, crush 1 garlic clove into a bowl, and add 2 pinches salt, a little pepper, and 1 tablespoon of the vinegar. Mix thoroughly and whisk in 5 tablespoons of the oil. Keep to one side.

3 To prepare the croutons, heat ½ tablespoon oil, crush the remaining garlic into it, and sweat for 2 minutes. Place on one side to cool. Add 3½ tablespoons oil and the herbs. Mix well and brush this herbed oil onto the slices of bread. Stack the slices on top of each other and put aside to marinate for 10 minutes. Cut into 1 × ½-inch rectangles, arrange on a baking sheet, and toast in the preheated oven until golden brown. Keep in a warm place.

4 To prepare the bacon, blanch the slices for 1 minute in boiling water, putting them in one at a time so they do not stick together. Rinse well, place onto paper towels to dry, then cut up into small pieces. Heat the remaining oil in a skillet over medium heat, add the bacon and sweat over low heat, to render the fat, for approximately 7–10 minutes.

5 Drain off all the fat, leaving the bacon in the pan, and increase the heat (to make the essential pan juices needed to finish the dressing).

6 Drain and dry the cabbage, toss in a salad bowl with the dressing, and leave for 5 minutes to marinate. Toss again.

7 Just before serving, drain the bacon on paper towels. Add the bacon to the salad, and toss again.

8 Deglaze the pan with the remaining vinegar, and pour over the salad. Toss, and serve immediately.

1 small white cabbage
4 tbsp. white wine or tarragon
    vinegar
3 garlic cloves, peeled
salt
freshly ground black pepper
10 tbsp. grapeseed or safflower
    oil
3 tbsp. fines herbes, finely
    chopped
4 thick slices whole-wheat bread
4 slices Canadian bacon, fat
    and rind removed

Salade Gribiche
MIXED SALAD

*T*his salad, full of vitamins, protein and fiber, is quite filling and nourishing, and can therefore be served as a meal. Be careful when blanching the green vegetables; it should be done in a steamer over very high heat so that none of the goodness is lost.

The gribiche *dressing can also be used on a simple lettuce salad, giving it a fuller flavor.*

GLUTEN FREE
SERVES 4

½ head Boston lettuce
salt
4 oz. broccoli florets, washed
2 oz. snow peas, washed, topped and tailed
1 egg
1 celery stalk, washed and trimmed
2 tomatoes, washed
1 cucumber, washed
2 oz. Gruyère or Emmenthal cheese
1 shallot, peeled and finely chopped
1 tbsp. capers, drained and finely chopped, and a few cut into flowers (see page 25)
1 gherkin pickle, drained and finely chopped
⅓ cup Sauce Moutarde (see page 39) made with 1 extra tsp. Dijon mustard

1   Separate the lettuce leaves and wash them. Spin dry, then break the largest leaves in half.

2   Prepare a steamer with 1 quart water and 1 teaspoon salt, and bring to the boil. Steam the broccoli and snow peas for 3 minutes each, then rinse in cold water to stop the cooking and fix the color. Drain in a colander and set aside to cool.

3   Put the egg in a pan of cold water, bring to the boil, and simmer for 6 minutes. Cool under cold running water.

4   Peel all the strings from the celery. Cut into thin *julienne* strips. Remove the stalk end of the tomatoes and cut each into six wedges.

5   If the cucumber is large, cut it in half and remove the seeds before slicing thinly. If it is small, simply halve lengthwise and cut across in thin slices.

6   Cut the cheese into small cubes.

7   Add the shallot, capers and gherkins to the mustard sauce. Shell the egg, and push through a sieve into the dressing. Mix well, and adjust the seasoning if necessary.

8   Place the dressing at the bottom of a large salad bowl and cover with the lettuce leaves. Arrange the cucumber slices around the side of the bowl, in a ring. Arrange a ring of tomatoes inside the cucumber ring, and a ring of cheese cubes inside that. Arrange the snow peas in a star shape in the middle with the celery *julienne* between each point. To finish, place the broccoli florets in the middle of the snow peas star.

TO SERVE   Bring the bowl to the table and let your guests enjoy your artistry before, alas, you ruin it all by tossing the salad!

Alternatively, arrange all the ingredients separately around the edge of a plate and spoon the dressing into the center. Garnish with caper flowers.

Salade de Champignons de Sabine
MUSHROOM SALAD

This is a very quick and simple salad, which Mme. Brassart prepares for us for a quick working lunch. It is always well appreciated, as it is nourishing — full of vitamins, minerals and fiber — as well as refreshing and light.

In the summer, basil adds its distinctive flavor, in the winter, parsley and chervil.

GLUTEN FREE
SERVES 4

7 oz. button mushrooms, washed
1 lemon
7 oz. ripe tomatoes, washed
salt
freshly ground black pepper
4 tbsp. olive oil
2 tbsp. basil and/or fines herbes, finely chopped

1 Leave the mushrooms to soak for 3 minutes in cold water with the juice of half the lemon.

2 Cut the tomatoes into thin slices, and place in overlapping circles in the center of a round serving dish.

3 To prepare the dressing, place a pinch of salt, a little pepper and the remaining lemon juice into a bowl. Mix well, then whisk in the olive oil. Drizzle 2 tablespoons of this over the tomatoes.

4 Drain the mushrooms well, then slice them thinly and arrange all around the tomatoes. Spoon the remaining dressing over them.

5 Sprinkle the herbs all over the tomato and mushrooms, and marinate for 5 minutes before serving.

Carottes Vichy
VICHY CARROTS

Originally, this recipe contained half a stick of butter and 2 tablespoons of sugar, and it used Vichy water which has a very high salt content. We have omitted all three of these ingredients.

These carrots can be served as a garnish for a meat or fish dish, or with, perhaps, a poached egg for the main course of a light supper.

GLUTEN FREE
SERVES 4

1 lb. carrots, scrubbed
1 cup Fonds de Volaille (see page 31)
salt
freshly ground black pepper
½ tbsp. honey
1 small slice fresh ginger root, peeled
1 tsp. parsley, finely chopped

1 Score the carrots along their length using a decorator or scorer, then slice them thickly.

2 Place the carrot slices in a saucepan, barely cover with chicken stock, and add some salt and pepper, the honey and ginger. Cover, bring to the boil, and leave to simmer for 1 minute. Remove the lid and continue simmering until the saucepan is nearly dry. Discard the ginger or chop up and mix in with the carrots.

TO SERVE Toss the carrots well in the remaining juice, and sprinkle with the parsley. Place in a heated vegetable dish, or use as a garnish.

Salade Waldorf

WALDORF SALAD

*T*his salad, made famous by a French chef at the Waldorf-Astoria in New York, was dressed originally with a Sauce Rémoulade. This sauce contained a minimum of three egg yolks and a lot of mustard. Although we keep the mustard, we use no egg, thus reducing the amount of cholesterol, and the traditional raw ingredients are packed with vitamins, minerals and fiber.

1   Peel the celeriac, and rub with the lemon. Cut into pieces small enough to pass through the funnel of a food processor (fitted with a thin *julienne* or grating blade). Rub these with lemon juice as well, then grate in the machine. Sprinkle with more lemon juice.

2   Core the apple, and cut it in half. Grate in the machine and mix in with the celeriac. Mix in enough mustard sauce to bind the celeriac and apple together, about 3 tablespoons.

3   Cut half the mushrooms into slices and the remainder into dice, and sprinkle both with lemon juice. Mix the diced mushrooms with the celeriac and apple. Wrap the slices in plastic wrap, and reserve for later.

4   Chop half the walnuts, reserving the best ones for garnishing later. Mix the chopped nuts into the salad.

5   Press the salad mixture into four ramekins, cover, and refrigerate to set for at least 20 minutes before serving.

TO SERVE   Lay mushroom slices and parsley sprigs around the edge of a serving dish or individual plates, and turn the salads out into the middle. Spoon any remaining sauce over the top. Lay the walnut halves on top. Garnish with tomato roses, and serve immediately.

GLUTEN FREE
SERVES 4

1 small celeriac, washed
1 lemon, cut in half
1 Granny Smith apple, washed
½ recipe Sauce Moutarde *(see page 39) made with double the amount of mustard*
4 oz. button mushrooms, washed
½ cup walnut halves

GARNISH
parsley sprigs
4 small tomato roses (see page 26)

Riz Complet aux Poireaux
BROWN RICE WITH LEEKS

*T*his *delicious dish, combining brown rice and leeks, is packed full of vitamins, minerals and fiber. It can be served on its own, served in a* feuilleté *or butterfly case (see page 14) with vegetable* julienne *(see page 23) or as a garnish for a main course dish.*

GLUTEN FREE
SERVES 4
PREHEAT THE OVEN TO 350°F

1¼ *cups brown* Basmati *rice*
2¼ *cups* Fonds de Volaille *or*
    Bouillon de Légumes *or*
    water (see pages 31 and 32)
1 bouquet garni
salt
freshly ground black pepper
1 *tbsp. grapeseed or safflower oil*
1 *lb. leeks, cut in half lengthwise,*
    washed and sliced

TO SERVE
1 *tbsp. olive oil*
2 *tbsp.* fines herbes, *finely*
    chopped

1   Wash the rice well in a strainer to remove the impurities and some of the starch.

2   Bring the stock to the boil with the *bouquet garni* and seasoning. Allow it to brew, covered, for 5 minutes.

3   Heat the oil in a heavy ovenproof casserole. Sweat the leek, covered, for 10 minutes, until soft.

4   Add the rice, well drained, and sweat with the leek for 5 minutes, without coloring, over low heat.

5   Remove ¼ cup of the stock and put aside to cool; add the remainder, with the *bouquet garni*, to the casserole. Stir well, and cover with a piece of parchment paper and a lid. Place in the preheated oven for 50–70 minutes. Take out of the oven, pour in the reserved cold stock, and keep warm.

TO SERVE Drizzle on the olive oil and add the herbs. Mix well and taste for seasoning. Transfer to a heated dish and serve.

Choux Rouge Braisé

BRAISED RED CABBAGE

*C*abbage is rich in vitamins, minerals, calcium, magnesium and sulphur; it is also low in calories and high in fiber. The only trouble is that it has been so misused over the years that no one now dares to produce it at a dinner table, because of its unkind and unworthy reputation. This very traditional sweet and sour recipe is perfect as an accompaniment for a chicken or fish dish.

You could also braise a Savoy cabbage in the same way, keeping the leaves whole, which is very good with Pot au Feu (see page 118).

GLUTEN FREE
SERVES 4
PREHEAT THE OVEN TO 350°F

1lb. red cabbage, quartered
⅔ cup golden raisins
⅔ cup lager beer
salt
freshly ground black pepper
1 bay leaf
1 tbsp. grapeseed or safflower oil
2 onions, peeled and sliced
2 Golden Delicious apples,
    washed and cored
1 tbsp. honey
1 tsp. tarragon vinegar
1 garlic clove, peeled

1   Shred each cabbage quarter. Place in the top of a steamer and steam for 5 minutes, turning occasionally.

2   Wash the golden raisins very carefully. Place them in a small saucepan with the beer, salt, pepper and the bay leaf. Bring to the boil and leave on one side to cool.

3   Heat the oil in a large ovenproof skillet or cast-iron casserole, and sweat the onion, covered, for 5 minutes. Uncover, and let the onions color slightly. Add the cabbage and toss for 5 minutes over low heat.

4   Cut the apples in small cubes and toss in with the cabbage.

5   Add the vinegar and honey to the beer and golden raisin mixture and pour into the apples and cabbage. Mix well. Add the whole garlic clove. Lay a sheet of parchment paper on top of the cabbage, cover, and braise in the preheated oven for 40 minutes or until tender, tossing every 15 minutes.

TO SERVE Remove the bay leaf and garlic. Using a slotted spoon carefully transfer the cabbage and golden raisins to a warmed vegetable dish, or if serving with a meat, arrange around the prepared meat. If serving individually, arrange a nest of cabbage surrounded by the golden raisins, with the meat or fish on top.

LEFT *Riz Complet aux Poireaux* and *Choux Rouge Braisé*

DESSERTS AND CAKES

The French, probably even more than other people, love to eat a sweet dish before leaving the table, in spite of all the warnings about sugar. In our dessert recipes, however, sugar is either partially (in some cases entirely) eliminated, or it is replaced by another ingredient which will bring out the natural sweetness of the dish's principal element. Most fruits, in fact, are quite high in natural sugars.

In addition, the sorbets here are much less sweet than traditional ones, and are therefore far more refreshing. They can even be served as a middle course (*entremet*) on formal occasions, to cleanse the palate. The soufflés, made without butter, are very light. Do not feel you are restricted to the recipes given but use your imagination to vary the flavors. The cakes and tarts use whole-wheat flour, and again the contents are low in fat and high in fiber.

Soufflé de Passion
PASSION FRUIT SOUFFLÉ

This wonderful soufflé is a prime example of the success of this new soufflé method. With its very delicate flavor, it should be served at the end of a meal, after cheese, as in France — the best way to finish a meal.

GLUTEN FREE
SERVES 4
PREHEAT THE OVEN TO 350°F

1 cup skim milk
1 tbsp. honey
1 tsp. butter
4 passion fruit, halved
2 eggs, separated
3 tbsp. potato starch
2 egg whites
2 tsp. light brown sugar

TO SERVE
confectioners' sugar to dust

1   Place the milk, reserving 2 tablespoons, into a saucepan with the honey and bring to the boil. Butter a 1-quart soufflé dish and put in the refrigerator for the butter to set.

2   Scoop the passion fruit flesh and seeds into a bowl, and mix with the egg yolks. Put the potato starch into another bowl with the reserved cold milk, and mix well. Add the scalded milk, whisking well, then return to the heat and boil for a minute. Pour into the bowl with the passion fruit and leave to "infuse" for 5 minutes.

3   Beat the egg whites to form soft peaks, adding 1 teaspoon of the sugar. Fold one quarter of this into the passion fruit.

4   Push through a conical sieve (to eliminate the seeds) onto the remaining egg whites, and fold together delicately.

5   Dust the soufflé dish with the remaining sugar and pour in the soufflé batter. Bake in the preheated oven for 20 minutes.

TO SERVE Dust the top with confectioners' sugar. Place the dish on a plate lined with a napkin or doily and serve *immediately*.

Gratin d'Oranges à la Maltaise
GRATIN OF ORANGES

*T*his is an ideal winter dessert, as it is warming and oranges are at their best in winter, when their vitamin C and the calcium and vitamin B of the nuts are needed most. If available, use blood oranges, which will give an even nicer flavor.

GLUTEN FREE
SERVES 4

4 oranges
1½ tbsp. honey
¼ cup water
1 slice fresh ginger root, peeled and cut into thin julienne
1 tsp. Grand Marnier
1 fresh pomegranate, halved, or 1 tsp. grenadine
¼ tsp. ground allspice
5 pistachio nuts
1 egg yolk
¼ cup Greek yogurt
¼ cup whipping cream

THE DAY BEFORE SERVING

1   Wash the oranges, scrubbing the skin with a vegetable brush or clean nailbrush to get rid of any residual chemicals. Peel and section them carefully (see page 27) and reserve the sections and juice in a china bowl. Keep the peel of two of the oranges, cut it into *julienne*, and blanch for 1 minute in boiling water.

2   Put the honey and water in a saucepan, bring to the boil and add the orange peel and ginger *julienne*. Simmer very gently for 2–3 minutes until tender, then remove from the liquid. Continue reducing the liquid until it caramelizes, then pour in the orange juice from the bowl and the Grand Marnier. Mix well and add the pomegranate seeds and juice (or the grenadine).

3   Let stand for 15 minutes until cold and then strain over the orange sections. Add the allspice, orange peel and ginger. Cover with plastic wrap and keep in the refrigerator overnight.

4   To prepare the pistachios, shell them, then plunge into a saucepan of boiling water. Simmer for 1 minute, then drain and refresh under cold running water. Put into a dish towel and rub them; most of the skin will come off but you may need to finish skinning by hand. Chop coarsely on a board, then dry in a warm oven for 3 minutes. Reserve in a cool, dry place.

THE DAY OF SERVING

Preheat the broiler to its maximum.

1   Mix the egg yolk and the yogurt together in a bowl. Thin down with some of the juice strained from the sections to form a light sauce that can coat the back of a spoon. Whip the cream, fold in and mix in the nuts.

2   Drain the orange sections and arrange them on individual heatproof plates or a round heatproof serving dish. Cover the sections and the bottom of the plate(s) with the sauce. Place under the broiler for 2 minutes or until brown, and serve immediately. Decorate with the orange zest and ginger *julienne*. Serve the remaining sauce separately.

LEFT   *Gratin d'Oranges à la Maltaise*

Oranges Soufflées
ORANGE SOUFFLÉS

*T*his recipe originally contained a large amount of cream and flour, neither of which are really necessary. Our much lighter version is served in the orange shells. Make sure you serve immediately after they come out of the oven; like any soufflé, these deflate very quickly.

GLUTEN FREE
SERVES 4
PREHEAT THE OVEN TO 350°F

4 oranges
2 tbsp. dark brown sugar
1 tbsp. potato starch
⅓ cup skim milk
1 vanilla bean
1 tbsp. Grand Marnier
2 egg whites

TO SERVE
confectioners' sugar to dust

1   Cut the oranges in half and remove the sections as you would a breakfast grapefruit. Put the sections and juice into a bowl and, using a teaspoon, remove the core and all the pith from the peel.
2   Take the sections out of the juice with a slotted spoon and place on a sheet of parchment paper on a tray and dry out for 2 minutes in the oven.
3   Mix half the sugar with the potato starch in a bowl, and form a well for the milk. Bring the milk with the vanilla bean to the boil, and slowly pour into the well, mixing well with a whisk. Return to the heat and boil for 1 minute, beating well to remove any lumps, before adding the Grand Marnier. Remove the vanilla bean.
4   Beat the egg whites until they form soft peaks, then add the remaining sugar. Mix one-quarter of the egg whites into the hot sauce, then fold the sauce gently into the egg whites. Transfer into a pastry bag with a large fluted tip.
5   Place the orange cups in a roasting pan lined with a sheet of paper and just enough hot water to cover the paper. Pipe a small amount of soufflé into the bottom of the orange cups. Divide the orange sections equally between the cups, and pipe the remaining soufflé mixture over the oranges. Bake for 10–15 minutes.
TO SERVE Remove from the oven, dust with confectioners' sugar, and serve immediately on a plate lined with a doily.

Sorbet aux Pommes
APPLE SORBET

A wonderful palate cleanser in the middle of a meal or a much appreciated end to a meal, this so-called sorbet is in fact a compromise between a sorbet and a granité, using a little more sugar than a granité, but much less than a traditional sorbet. Adjust the quantity of sugar according to the variety of apple selected.

GLUTEN FREE EXCEPT
FOR THE PANIERS
SERVES 4

1 lb. apples, washed or 3 cups
    pure apple juice
2¼ cups water

1   Cut the apples into large cubes, core and peel included.
2   Place in a saucepan with the water and sugar, bring to the boil and simmer until the apples are tender and the sugar has melted.

168

3 Mash the apples roughly, then strain through a conical sieve to separate the juice and pulp from the peel and cores.

4 Add the Calvados to the juice and pulp when it is cool.

5 You can either put the mixture into an ice cream machine or *sorbetière*, following the manufacturer's instructions, or you can make it "by hand." Set the freezer to its coldest temperature several hours beforehand, and put a shallow tray, a bowl and a fork into the freezer to chill. Pour the apple juice and pulp into the tray and freeze.

6 When the mixture is almost solid, scrape it out into the chilled bowl and mash with the fork until the largest lumps have been beaten out. Return to the tray and place in the freezer. Repeat this beating and freezing several times more for a smooth texture.

TO SERVE Use two spoons to make *quenelle* shapes (see page 26) from the sorbet and place in the *Paniers*. Serve immediately.

¾ cup sugar
2 tbsp. Calvados

TO SERVE
4 Paniers *(see page 170)*

Sorbet de l'Été
SUMMER FRUIT SORBET

---

*T*his delicious sorbet is a perfect combination of the Continental sorbet and the delicious taste of the British summer pudding. In fact we could call it "Summer Pudding Sorbet." Compared with a traditional recipe, the sugar has been cut down considerably, and an egg white added to give volume and a smooth consistency.

1 Bring the sugar and water to the boil and add the red currants. Simmer for 1 minute (timing from when the syrup starts to boil again), then remove the red currants using a slotted spoon. Reserve in a bowl.

2 Add the black currants to the still simmering syrup, and simmer for 2 minutes longer. Reserve with the red currants.

3 Add the strawberries and raspberries to the simmering syrup and take off the heat immediately. Add the red currants and black currants and leave for 5 minutes to infuse. Transfer back into the bowl to cool.

4 Reserve some of the fruit for decoration, covered with a little juice. Push the rest through a sieve or food processor to eliminate any pips.

5 When cold, either put into an ice cream machine or *sorbetière* — follow the manufacturer's instructions — or make it "by hand" (see recipe above).

6 While the mixture is still soft, add the beaten egg white and churn in the machine, or beat well by hand. Place in the freezer, in a bowl covered with plastic wrap.

TO SERVE Half an hour before serving, transfer the sorbet from the freezer to the refrigerator. When it is soft, make into *quenelle* shapes (see page 26) and place in the *Paniers* (see page 171). Decorate with the reserved fruit and juice.

GLUTEN FREE
SERVES 4

2 oz. each of raspberries and strawberries, washed and hulled
2 oz. each of red currants and black currants, washed, topped and tailed
4 tbsp. sugar
1 cup water
1 egg white

TO SERVE
1 recipe Paniers *(see page 170)*

Paniers

FEATHERLIGHT BASKETS

*Y*ou may find making these a little difficult at first, but do *persevere. Once you have the hang of it, they'll take you no time to prepare and they will make your presentation of ice cream, sorbets and fresh fruit salads so much more successful.*

The little trick of warming the egg white helps a lot in the preparation of the batter, but it does need time to rest. The batter will keep 3–4 days in the refrigerator, but remove it a few minutes before using so that it spreads more easily. It freezes perfectly too.

MAKES 8
PREHEAT THE OVEN TO 350°F

2 large egg whites
6 tbsp. unsalted butter
7 tbsp. sugar
9 tbsp. flour

1   Pour the egg whites into a bowl and place the bowl over a saucepan of hot water (122°F maximum). Prepare a baking sheet, greasing it well.

2   Soften the butter thoroughly, add the sugar and beat to a pale and creamy consistency. Add the warmed egg whites a little at a time.

3   Add the flour quickly, and mix together, but do not overwork. Allow the batter to rest for 20 minutes in the refrigerator.

4   Place approximately 1 heaping tablespoon of batter on the baking sheet, and shape it into a 6-inch round with the back of the spoon. Bake for 5–10 minutes in the preheated oven until the edges start to brown.

5   Remove from the oven immediately, and quickly place over a small inverted bowl. Use a palette knife if necessary to detach it from the sheet. Place a larger bowl on top or shape it with the fingers, and leave to cool.

6   Once you have mastered the method for this first basket — and grasped the speed at which you have to work once it is out of the oven — bake and cool the remainder in the same way.

7   Keep the baskets in a cool, dry place until ready to serve; they should be made no longer than 5–6 hours in advance. Fill at the last moment.

RIGHT *Paniers* with *Sorbet de l'Été*

Tarte aux Fraises
STRAWBERRY CUSTARD TART

A very traditional strawberry tart, but made a little healthier by using our pâte brisée, *much less sugar and egg yolks, and no butter in the* crème pâtissière (custard). *Only make this dish while strawberries are in season as the recipe is not suitable for frozen strawberries. Frozen red currants may be used for glazing, though, and if they are not available, use red currant jelly instead.*

Do not assemble more than 1 hour ahead of time, or the juice of the strawberries will run into the custard.

SERVES 6
PREHEAT THE OVEN TO 350°F

1 recipe Pâte Brisée *(see page 44)*
1 lb. fresh strawberries, washed, drained and hulled
7 oz. red currants
½ cup light brown sugar

CRÈME PÂTISSIÈRE
1 cup skim milk
1 vanilla bean
1 tbsp. whole-wheat flour
1 tbsp. potato starch
2 tbsp. light brown sugar
1 egg
confectioners' sugar to dust

1   Rest the pastry in the refrigerator for 20 minutes. Roll out thinly and line a 10-inch tart pan. Bake blind in the oven until completely cooked. Remove from the pan to cool so the bottom will firm up.

2   To make the *crème pâtissière*, reserve ¼ cup of the milk and bring the remainder to the boil with the vanilla bean in a saucepan. In another saucepan mix together the flour, potato starch and the 2 tablespoons of sugar. Beat the egg lightly in a bowl with the reserved milk, then pour it slowly into the flour mixture, mixing well with a small whisk until smooth. When the vanilla milk is boiling, pour it into the saucepan with the egg and flour, a little at a time, whisking energetically. Place the saucepan immediately over medium heat and, stirring and whisking constantly, return to the boil. Boil, stirring vigorously for 1 minute, then remove the vanilla bean (rinse it and place in a jar with sugar to use again another time).

3   Pour the *crème pâtissière* into the tart case to cool, and dust the top with confectioners' sugar to prevent a skin forming.

4   When the custard is cool, arrange the strawberries very closely together on top.

5   To make the red currant jelly, wash the fresh red currants, or if frozen, defrost in a bowl and use both fruit and juice. Detach the currants from the stalks with a fork.

6   Place the currants in a saucepan with 2 tablespoons water, cover with a lid and place over high heat to make them pop, about 2 minutes. Add the sugar and stir well, return to the high heat and bring to the boil. After 3 minutes, remove from the heat. Skim off any froth, strain and allow to cool for 5 minutes.

7   Pour slowly or brush over the strawberries. Allow the tart to set in the refrigerator for a minimum of 10 minutes.

TO SERVE Serve on a round serving dish lined with a doily.

Sorbet à l'Ananas

PINEAPPLE SORBET

*T*his sorbet proves that little or no sugar is needed in a sorbet if the combination of fruits is right. The teaspoon of sugar used here is only to stabilize the egg whites which give a smooth consistency! Both fruits contain good amounts of vitamins and fiber. Pineapple is also reputed to contain an enzyme which breaks down excess fat in the body.

GLUTEN FREE
SERVES 4

1 medium pineapple
1 orange
2 egg whites
1 tbsp. dark brown sugar
¼ cup water
2 tbsp. Grand Marnier

1   Quarter the pineapple (see page 27). Insert the blade between flesh and skin and remove the flesh. Cut it into cubes and place in a blender or food processor. Reserve the pineapple skin quarters.

2   Remove the orange zest with a zester or scorer and reserve. Section the orange (see page 27) and put the fruit into a blender or food processor with the pineapple flesh.

3   Purée together thoroughly, then place in an ice cream maker or *sorbetière*, or in a tray in the freezer, and whisk vigorously with a fork every 15 minutes until the mixture is almost solid.

4   Beat the egg whites until stiff, adding a couple of pinches of the sugar, and fold into the sorbet, while the *sorbetière* is running, or by hand. Add half the Grand Marnier and return to the freezer.

5   Prepare the zest for the decoration. Blanch for 1 minute in boiling water, then drain and return to the saucepan with the remaining sugar, the water and remaining Grand Marnier. Simmer very slowly until 1 tablespoon of liquid is left in the pan. Lay the zest on a piece of parchment paper, and allow to dry in a warm, dry place (a low oven, for instance).

TO SERVE Just before serving, put the sorbet in a pastry bag with a fluted tip, and pipe over each pineapple skin quarter. Decorate with the orange zest.

Sorbet à l'Ananas

Cygnes au Citron

CHOUX SWANS WITH LEMON MOUSSE

These choux pastry swans, filled with a lemon mousse, are delicious and impressive. Although the choux pastry contains butter, when it is divided between six people it means less than ½ ounce per person. The pastry swans could also be filled with sorbets.

The mousse contains very much less sugar, cream and egg yolk than the original recipe. It could also be shaped into quenelles (see page 26) and, along with orange and lime mousses made in the same way, served in a panier *or basket (see page 170).*

SERVES 6

PREHEAT THE OVEN TO 450°F

1 recipe Pâte à Choux *(see page 42)*
egg wash (optional)
confectioners' sugar to dust

LEMON MOUSSE
2 tsp. unflavored gelatin
1 lemon, washed
1 oz. sugar cubes (about 8 small)
2 tbsp. light brown sugar
2 eggs, separated
2 egg whites
¼ cup Greek yogurt

1   Place the choux pastry in a pastry bag fitted with a ½-inch plain tip. Place a ¼-inch tip *over* the existing tip, and pipe six figure 2s onto a baking sheet covered with parchment paper. These will be the heads and necks of the swans. Remove this tip and pipe six oval shapes for the swan bodies. Dab the shapes with a wet finger to smooth them. For a better shine, brush with egg wash.

2   Bake in the preheated oven for 5 minutes then turn the oven down to 350°F. Bake for a further 20 minutes, removing the necks after 5–10 minutes or when brown. If using a conventional oven, keep the choux bodies in the oven for an extra 5 minutes with the door slightly open (keep ajar with the handle of a wooden spoon).

3   Cut the top layer off the bodies. Cut this layer in half lengthwise to form the wings. Spoon any excess dough from the bodies and dry out in the oven if necessary. Leave to become cold.

4   To make the mousse, first soften the gelatin in 2 tablespoons of lemon juice diluted with 1 tablespoon of cold water in a small pan. Place over very low heat to dissolve, stirring constantly.

5   Dry the lemon and rub the sugar lumps over the skin to extract the oil. Place these lumps, the light brown sugar and lemon juice into a bowl with the egg yolks. Beat the bowl over a pan of hot water to make a light, fluffy batter. Add the dissolved gelatin, remove from the heat and continue whisking.

6   In another bowl beat the four egg whites until stiff. Fold gently into the mousse mixture, along with the yogurt.

7   Pour into a pastry bag.

TO SERVE Pipe the mousse into the hollowed-out bodies of the swans. Dust the wings with confectioners' sugar and place them at an angle to form the wings. Push each neck into the mousse at one end. Dust with confectioners' sugar and serve immediately on a doily-lined dish.

RIGHT *Cygnes au Citron*

Aumonières Surprise

FRUIT CRÊPES

*I*nside these little pancake packages are low-fat vanilla ice cream and delicious fruit salad. The accompanying sauce is a simple coulis of strawberries.

All the preparation can be done ahead of time, but the assembling should be done just before starting dinner, and the packages kept in the freezer until it is time for dessert.

SERVES 4

CRÊPE BATTER
⅓ cup all-purpose flour
⅓ cup whole-wheat flour
1 egg
⅔ cup skim milk
salt
sugar
grapeseed or safflower oil

VANILLA ICE CREAM
1 cup skim milk
1 vanilla bean
2 tbsp. light brown sugar
2 egg yolks
¼ cup whipping cream
¾ cup Greek yogurt

FRUIT SALAD
1 orange
½ lemon
1 tbsp. light brown sugar
⅓ cup water
¼ pineapple, peeled
4 strawberries, hulled
1 tsp. Grand Marnier

COULIS DE FRAISES
7 oz. strawberries
juice of ½ lemon
1 tbsp. confectioners' sugar

GARNISH
4 strips angelica, 5 in. long or
  2 pieces of thin licorice (to tie
    the parcels together)

1 To prepare the crêpe batter, sift the flours together into a bowl, add the bran from the sieve, and make a well in the center. Put the egg, milk, and a pinch each of salt and sugar into the well and mix these wet ingredients together well. Using a small whisk, gradually gather in a little flour at a time until it has all been worked in. The batter should be light and cover the back of a spoon thickly. If too thick, thin with a little more milk. Rest in the refrigerator for 20 minutes before using.

2 To prepare the vanilla ice cream, bring the milk and vanilla bean to the boil. Meanwhile, whisk the sugar and egg yolks vigorously until pale and fluffy. When the milk boils, add about a third of it to the egg and sugar mixture, then return the milk to the heat. Whisk the egg mixture well and pour into the boiling milk. Remove the pan from the heat immediately and stir. Replace over low heat for 2 minutes, stirring slowly, then remove from the heat again. Cover and let stand for 5 minutes for the vanilla bean to infuse its flavor. Transfer to a bowl, add the cream and place in the freezer to cool quickly, stirring once in a while. When cold, remove the vanilla bean.

3 Place the mixture in an ice cream machine, and freeze according to the manufacturer's directions. When semi-hard, add the yogurt, a spoonful at a time, then finish churning. Alternatively, make the ice cream "by hand" (follow the directions given in the recipe for *Ananas Princesse* on page 180).

4 To prepare the fruit salad, remove the zest of the orange and the half lemon with a scorer or zester. Place the shreds in a saucepan with the sugar and water, and simmer to reduce until only 1 tablespoon of liquid is left. Reserve to one side. Section the oranges (see page 27) and place with the zest in a bowl with the juice of the half lemon. Cut the pineapple into very small chunks (see pages 26–27), and the strawberries into quarters, and add both to the bowl, with the Grand Marnier. Cover and leave in the refrigerator for at least 20 minutes.

5 To prepare the *coulis*, reserve 4 strawberries for decoration, and place the remainder in a food processor or blender (or use a sieve or food mill). Add the lemon juice and confectioners' sugar. Process well for 3 minutes and reserve. If the purée is too thick, thin it with a little of the juice from the fruit salad. Reserve in a bowl and cover with plastic wrap.

6 To cook the crêpes, add a tablespoon of oil to the batter, stirring it in very gently. Heat an 8-inch crêpe pan or non-stick skillet over low heat. Add a drop of oil and wipe it around with a paper towel.

Aumonières Surprise

Add a small ladleful of batter, and spread it evenly, turning the pan in a circular motion. Cook over low heat for 2 minutes, then toss it to cook the other side (use a small metal spatula if you can't toss!). Cook for 2 minutes or until lightly colored, then reserve on a plate. Cover the plate with a lid (or another plate). Repeat until all the batter has been used. No more oil should be necessary, but you should wipe the pan with the greased paper towel between each crêpe.

7   Bring a small saucepan of water to the boil and blanch the angelica (*not* the licorice) for 2 minutes. Allow to soak and soften in the water for 15 minutes, then cut into long strips. Leave in the water until ready to use.

8   Drain the juices from the fruit salad and add to the *coulis*. Lay the crêpes on a board and place a spoonful of the fruit salad in the middle. Add a spoonful of the ice cream. Bring the sides up and tie with a strip of angelica or licorice to form a little purse. Place in the freezer to keep the ice cream solid, but for no more than 10–15 minutes or the fruit salad will be frozen too! (Keep in the refrigerator thereafter.) Make eight purses. Reserve the remaining ice cream and fruit salad in bowls to serve separately.

TO SERVE   To serve traditionally, shape the remaining ice cream into a mound on a large round serving plate and place the purses all around. Pour some of the *coulis* over the mound, and pass the remainder in a sauceboat. Halve the reserved strawberries and use to decorate. Serve the remaining salad separately.

   To serve individually, line the base of each plate with *coulis*. Place the remainder in a sauceboat to serve separately. Place two purses on each plate, and decorate with the reserved halved strawberries. Serve with the remaining ice cream and fruit salad.

Soufflé au Chocolat
CHOCOLATE SOUFFLÉ

*O*ur selection of desserts would not be complete without a traditional chocolate soufflé. Chocolate is very rich, as we all know, which is why we have removed the butter from the recipe; this makes it lighter.

Adding the orange zest oil gives a very special flavor which is similar to the Reine de Saba *on page 186. For a different flavor try adding a teaspoon of instant coffee powder to the milk or, better still, replace some of the milk with 2 tablespoons strong, fresh coffee laced with a dash of Tia Maria or Kahlua.*

GLUTEN FREE
SERVES 4
PREHEAT THE OVEN TO 350°F

1 tbsp. butter
white flour to dust
3 tbsp. potato starch
⅓ cup ground almonds
⅞ cup milk
1 vanilla bean
3 oz. semisweet chocolate,
*   broken into pieces*
2 sugar lumps
1 orange, washed
2 eggs, separated
1 tsp. Grand Marnier
2 egg whites
1 tbsp. light brown sugar

1 Grease a 3-cup soufflé dish (or four individual ramekin dishes) with the butter, and place in the refrigerator for the butter to set. When set, dust with a little flour and tap upside-down on the work surface to remove the excess.

2 Sift the potato starch and almonds together into a bowl, and make a well in the center.

3 Bring the milk and vanilla bean to the boil in a saucepan, then remove from the heat. Pour slowly into the well in the flour, mixing the flour and almonds in slowly with a whisk. Beat vigorously to get rid of any lumps. Return to the heat, bring just to the boil, then remove from the heat. Remove the vanilla bean.

4 Add the pieces of chocolate and cover the pan. Rub the sugar lumps against the orange peel to obtain the oil, then add the sugar to the saucepan and stir well to dissolve it.

5 Add the egg yolks and Grand Marnier and mix well. Cover and reserve in a warm place.

6 Beat all 4 egg whites with a whisk to form soft peaks, then add the light brown sugar. Whisk in well, then stir a third of the egg whites into the chocolate mixture. Fold in the remaining egg whites carefully with a spatula.

7 Pour the soufflé mixture into the dish, or dishes, to come three-quarters up the sides.

8 Bake the soufflés in the preheated oven, 20 minutes for a big one, 10–15 minutes for individual ramekins.

TO SERVE Serve immediately. A soufflé does not wait for guests, they wait for the soufflé!

Tarte au Fromage Blanc
CHEESECAKE

How can a cheesecake be healthy, you may well ask! Well, it took a long time to figure it out, but as we love the taste, we experimented and experimented. The cream cheese was replaced by low-fat soft cheeses and Greek yogurt, the vast amount of double cream by a small amount of whipping cream, and the refined sugar by muscovado sugar with its delicious licorice flavor.

SERVES 6
PREHEAT THE OVEN TO 350°F

Pâte Brisée *made with 2¼ cups (11oz) flour (see page 44)*
⅔ *cups golden raisins*
2 tbsp. *cognac*
1 *egg yolk*
4 tbsp. *muscovado (or dark brown) sugar*
zest and juice of 1 lemon
2 *eggs*
3 tbsp. *potato starch*
7 oz. *Ricotta (or other low-fat soft cheese)*
2 oz. *low-fat cream cheese*
⅓ *cup skim milk*
½ *cup whipping cream*
½ *cup Greek yogurt*
egg wash

TO SERVE
confectioners' sugar to dust

Tarte au Fromage Blanc

1   Allow the pastry to rest in the refrigerator for 20 minutes.

2   Wash the golden raisins, then dry on paper towels. Place them in a saucepan with the cognac, heat for 1 minute and flame. Wait for the flames to die, then cover the pan and reserve for later.

3   Whisk the egg yolk, sugar, lemon zest and juice together very well. Add the whole eggs and mix well. Add the potato starch and mix in without overworking the mixture.

4   Sieve the cheeses, add the egg mixture and whisk to a smooth paste. Mix in the milk, cream and yogurt.

5   Roll out the dough, and use to line a 9-inch tart pan with a removable bottom. Push the dough well into the edges, and cut off excess. Prick the base with a fork and line with parchment paper or foil and baking beans. Bake blind for 5 minutes in the preheated oven, then rotate and leave for 5 minutes. Remove the paper and baking beans, and bake for 5 minutes. Glaze with egg wash, and cook for 1 minute. Coat again and cook for another minute.

6   Scatter the golden raisins evenly over the pastry case. Add the cheese mixture and bake in the oven for 15 minutes. Don't be alarmed by the wobbly texture: it will set as it cools. Remove the base and sides of the pan, place the tart on a cooling rack, and leave.

TO SERVE Serve cold, sprinkled with confectioners' sugar.

Ananas Princesse
PINEAPPLE WITH STRAWBERRY ICE CREAM

This dessert is a combination of light strawberry ice cream and pineapple slices served in the pineapple shell. Double cream has been replaced by half whipping cream and half Greek yogurt, which makes the ice cream lighter and healthier; very little sugar is added (less will be needed if the strawberries are very ripe). The lemon juice both adds vitamin C and helps bring out the flavor of the strawberries.

Frozen strawberries could be used instead of fresh. Defrost in a bowl and use both the fruit and the juice in the recipe.

Never freeze the pineapple and ice cream together, the result is not good at all.

GLUTEN FREE

SERVES 4

1 tsp. unflavored gelatin
1/4 cup cold water
11 oz. ripe strawberries, rinsed, drained and hulled
1/2 cup confectioners' sugar (plus extra to dust)
1 tsp. lemon juice
1/2 cup whipping cream
1/2 cup Greek yogurt
1 small ripe pineapple
1 tbsp. Grand Marnier

TO SERVE
glacé mint leaves (see page 25)

1   Sprinkle the gelatin over cold water in a small bowl or ramekin to soften it.

2   Reserve a few strawberries for decoration, and put the rest in a blender or food processor with the sugar and the lemon juice. Process well and reserve 2 ounces of the purée for decoration.

3   Place the container of gelatin in a shallow pan of simmering water. Stir, and leave over low heat just long enough to melt the gelatin. Pour into the strawberry purée and mix well. Strain through a nylon sieve. Place in an ice cream machine and leave to churn. If you don't have a machine, put the ice cream in a shallow metal or glass dish in the freezer and whisk vigorously every 10 minutes until thick.

4   Whip the cream lightly, then add the yogurt, by spoonfuls. Reserve 1 tablespoon in a pastry bag for decoration. When the ice cream is the consistency of a thick purée, fold in the yogurt mixture and churn until well frozen or fold in gently by hand. Put the ice cream into a pastry bag fitted with a large, fluted tip, and return to the freezer.

5   Prepare the pineapple as explained on pages 26–27, leaving a thick shell. Cut the pineapple flesh into thin slices, sprinkle with the Grand Marnier, cover and reserve.

TO SERVE   No earlier than 20–30 minutes before serving, pipe a layer of ice cream into the pineapple shell, and lay a slice of pineapple on top. Repeat until the shell is full, and decorate with more ice cream to mound over the top. Dust the leafy head of the pineapple lightly with confectioners' sugar and place on top. Pour the reserved *coulis* onto a serving plate and pipe a thin circle of the reserved cream and yogurt mixture 1/2 inch inside the edge of the *coulis*. Feather with the tip of a knife. Place the pineapple in the center of the *coulis* and serve immediately with the remaining pineapple slices and ice cream in separate dishes.

RIGHT *Ananas Princesse*

Marquise à la Passion
PASSION FRUIT MERINGUE CAKE

SERVES 12
PREHEAT THE OVEN TO 350°F

6 tsp. unflavored gelatin
8 passion fruit
2 cups passion fruit or tropical fruit juice
1/2 cup light brown sugar
oil
2 tbsp. rum, preferably white
1 cup whipping cream
1/2 cup Greek yogurt

GÉNOISE
1 tsp. grapeseed or safflower oil
1/2 cup whole-wheat flour
1/3 cup dark brown sugar
2 large eggs

MERINGUE ITALIENNE
1/2 cup light brown sugar
2 tbsp. cold water
4 egg whites

TO SERVE
1 lb. strawberries, washed and hulled
2 kiwi fruit, peeled and sliced
1/2 tsp. lemon juice

*T*his is a delicious dessert to prepare for a buffet party or a special dinner party. It originally contained a lot of cream and sugar, but in reducing these we have, happily, increased the flavor of passion fruit. If no passion fruit juice is available, use mixed tropical fruit juice, as the flavor of passion fruit is usually predominant.

As it is such a lengthy recipe, prepare it the day before so that you're not too exhausted to prepare the main course and starter on the day itself!

THE DAY BEFORE SERVING

1 First prepare the *génoise*, using the ingredients listed here, and following the method outlined on page 185. Bake in an 8 × 12-inch baking pan lined with parchment paper for 10–15 minutes. Invert onto a cooling rack and allow to cool. When completely cool, split in half horizontally.

2 Cut all the passion fruit in half like grapefruit, and scoop out the flesh of 8 of the halves into a saucepan. Soften 2 teaspoons of gelatin in a small bowl with 1/3 cup of the juice. Add the sugar with 1/3 cup more juice to the saucepan and bring to the boil. Add the gelatin mixture and simmer for 2 minutes, stirring constantly. Skim off any foam and leave to cool in a bowl, stirring occasionally.

3 Wash the pan used to bake the *génoise*, rub in a little oil, and line with plastic wrap (the oil helps it to cling to the sides of the pan). When the fruit jelly is cool, pour it into the pan and place in the refrigerator to set firmly. If you don't want the seeds (although they are quite decorative), strain the jelly before pouring into the pan.

4 Scoop out the flesh of the remaining 4 passion fruit into a bowl, and add 1 cup of fruit juice. Sprinkle the remaining gelatin over 1/2 cup of the remaining juice in a small saucepan. Place over low heat until the gelatin melts, then pour into the juice in the bowl. Strain the seeds through a conical sieve. Stir occasionally.

5 Place the small remaining amount of juice in a ramekin dish with the rum. Cover, and reserve for later.

6 To prepare the *meringue italienne*, reserve 2 tablespoons of the sugar and place the remainder in a saucepan with the water. Bring to the boil, cleaning the sides of the pan well with a brush dipped in a bowl of cold water. Boil for approximately 3 minutes over medium heat, then take the pan off the heat and dip, for 1 second, into the bowl of cold water to stop the cooking. Take a small amount of the sugar syrup out with a teaspoon and place in the bowl of cold water. It should form a soft ball; if too runny, replace the pan on the heat and boil again until the right consistency is reached. Every time you take it off the heat, dip the bowl into cold water to stop the cooking.

7 Beat the egg whites until they form stiff peaks, then add the reserved sugar and beat for another minute. Still beating, add the sugar syrup in a steady flow, and beat until cool. The meringue will become thick and shiny. Reserve for later.

Marquise à la Passion

8 Whip the cream, then add the yogurt a little at a time. If the juice in the bowl has not thickened yet, place the bowl over some ice cubes and water to thicken more quickly, stirring gently all the time. Both the cream and yogurt mixture and the juice in the bowl should have the same consistency to mix properly. When ready, fold the cream, jellied juices and the meringue together using a lifting motion with a whisk.

TO ASSEMBLE
1 Pour half of the cream/jelly/meringue mixture above over the set jelly in the baking pan. Position the bottom half of the *génoise* on top and soak with the juice and rum mixture. Cover with the remaining half of the mixture, then soak the remaining half of the *génoise* with the remaining juice and rum. Place over the top, crust side up.
2 Refrigerate for at least 3 hours to set — it's best left overnight.
TO SERVE Dip the baking pan in a basin containing hot water for 10 seconds, and turn out onto a large serving board. Remove the wrap carefully, and cut the *marquise* in half lengthwise, and then across the width at 2-inch intervals to obtain twelve portions, at least.

Decorate each portion with a strawberry half, and a slice of kiwi fruit, fanned out. Purée the remaining strawberries with the lemon juice. If served on individual plates, pour a little purée over the plate and place the decorated portion on top.

Compôte de Pommes aux Oranges Confites

APPLE COMPÔTE WITH ORANGES

GLUTEN FREE
SERVES 4

*4 Golden Delicious apples,
washed*
½ cup cold water
1 vanilla bean
1 star anise
*1 slice fresh ginger root, peeled
and cut into thin* julienne

ORANGES CONFITES
4 oranges, washed
¼ cup light brown sugar
1 tbsp. dark brown sugar
1⅓ cups cold water

*Compôte de Pommes aux
Oranges Confites*

*T*his stewed apple recipe was only created to use up leftover Oranges Confites, *but it became so popular that we often prepare it regardless! So whenever you are making a recipe which uses these cooked orange slices, prepare a few more than you need, and make this deliciously simple pudding as well.*

THE DAY BEFORE SERVING
1   Prepare the *Oranges Confites.* Slice the oranges carefully. Put both sugars and the water into a pan and bring to the boil, making sure the sugars have dissolved first. Add the orange slices and cover with a circle of parchment paper and a lid. Simmer very gently for an hour. Remove from the heat and allow to cool. Refrigerate overnight.

THE DAY OF SERVING
1   Prick the skin of the apples all over with the point of a knife, then core and quarter them. Cut each quarter in half again. Place in a saucepan with the water, the juice from the *Oranges Confites,* the vanilla bean, the star anise and ginger *julienne.*
2   Place over low heat and bring very slowly to the boil, covered. Stir gently occasionally without breaking up the pieces of apple. Simmer for 5 minutes, then take off the heat.
3   Let stand to cool, still covered, for 30 minutes.

TO SERVE   Remove the vanilla bean and the star anise. (Keep the vanilla bean, discard the star anise.) Chop half the orange slices finely and add to the apples. Halve the remaining orange slices and reserve.

   Transfer the apples onto a serving dish or individual plates, using a slotted spoon, and decorate with the remaining orange slices. Serve the juices separately in a sauceboat.

Génoise aux Pommes
APPLE SPONGE CAKE

This génoise, or sponge cake, is made with half whole-wheat flour to add fiber. The finished cake is hollowed out and filled with lightly baked apples.

1 Prepare the *génoise*. Use the oil to grease a 10-inch cake pan, then cut a circle of parchment paper to line the bottom. Place in the refrigerator to set the oil, about 2 minutes. When set, dust the inside of the pan with extra flour, then bang the pan upside-down on the work surface to remove the excess.

2 Mix the wheat and white flours together and sift onto a piece of parchment paper. Mix in the bran left in the sieve.

3 Bring a saucepan of water to the boil and place the eggs and the sugars in a heatproof bowl. Whisk the eggs and sugar together vigorously until they become paler in color, about 1–2 minutes. Take the saucepan of boiling water off the heat and place the bowl over it (the bowl must touch the water). Beat well until the batter thickens and, when lifted with the whisk, it falls in a "ribbon." This will take up to 5 minutes. Take the bowl out of the pan and continue beating for 1 minute to cool. Fold the flour into the cooled batter, pouring quickly from the paper so that the batter does not collapse.

4 Pour into the middle of the prepared pan, being careful not to splash the sides, and bake for 20–30 minutes in the preheated oven. The cake is cooked when golden brown and, when pressed lightly with a finger, the top springs back. Remove from the pan immediately and cool on a cooling rack.

5 Prepare the apples. Turn the oven down to 325°F. Core the apples, then cut in half through the core. Slice across the core "bridge," keeping the half apple shape together, and place in a buttered baking pan with a tiny piece of butter and a dash of Calvados on top of each half. Pour 2 tablespoons of water into the bottom of the pan, cover with buttered foil, and bake for about 15–20 minutes. Remove and allow to cool.

6 Put the sugar and ½ cup water into a small saucepan and heat to make a syrup. Add the remaining Calvados.

TO ASSEMBLE

1 Using a small knife, cut a circle around the cake, ¾ inch in from the outside edge. Do not cut right through to the bottom. To separate the bottom, insert the knife horizontally ¾ inch from the base of the cake on one side and swing it from side to side. Do this again at the opposite side of the cake, making sure not to enlarge the openings on the outside too much. Using a fork, ease up all round the cut circle on top of the cake, and remove the whole circular section. Cut this in half horizontally.

2 Dab the syrup all around the insides of the hollowed-out cake. Place the cake on a serving plate and arrange the apple slices in the hollow in layers. Place the crusty half of the cake circle on top of the apples and dust with confectioners' sugar.

SERVES 6

PREHEAT THE OVEN TO 350°F

GÉNOISE
1 tsp. grapeseed or safflower oil
½ cup all-purpose flour (plus extra to dust)
⅓ cup whole-wheat flour
3 eggs (extra-large)
2 tbsp. light brown sugar
2 tbsp. dark brown sugar
2¼ lb. apples, washed
butter
2 tbsp. dark brown sugar
1 tbsp. Calvados
water
confectioners' sugar to dust

Reine de Saba aux Oranges Confites
CHOCOLATE CAKES WITH ORANGES

GLUTEN FREE
SERVES 4
PREHEAT THE OVEN TO 350°F

½ recipe Oranges Confites *(see page 184)*
¼ cup potato starch (plus extra to dust)
¼ cup ground almonds
1 cup skim milk
4 oz. semisweet chocolate, grated
2 tbsp. butter
2 sugar lumps
1 orange, washed
3 eggs, separated
1 vanilla bean
3 tbsp. light brown sugar
1 tsp. Grand Marnier
½ tsp. confectioners' sugar to dust

*D*o indulge once in a while in these delicious little chocolate "mushroom" cakes. The recipe has, as usual, been modified; the butter has been reduced considerably, and the flour has also been reduced to a minimum — but never forget the richness of the chocolate! The oranges make a very good decoration and are at their best slowly cooked and left overnight to marinate.

1   Sift together the potato starch and almonds.

2   Bring ¼ cup of the milk to the boil, then remove from the heat and add the chocolate and half the butter. Rub the sugar lumps against the skin of the orange to extract the oil, then add the sugar lumps to the saucepan. Cover, let it all melt together, and stir well. Meanwhile, use the remaining butter to grease four ramekin dishes. Place them in the refrigerator for the butter to set.

3   Off the heat, add two of the egg yolks, one at a time, to the chocolate mixture. Add the sifted potato starch and almonds while mixing. Beat the egg whites until they form soft peaks. Add 1 tablespoon of the sugar and whisk well. Fold the egg whites into the chocolate mixture very gently with a rubber spatula.

4   Dust the ramekin dishes with a little potato starch and tap them lightly upside-down on the work surface to remove the excess. Divide the mixture between the ramekins, and bake for 10–15 minutes in the preheated oven. Unmold the cakes as soon as they come out of the oven, and cool on a rack.

5   To prepare the *crème anglaise* sauce, bring the remaining milk and the vanilla bean to the boil. Meanwhile whisk the remaining 2 tablespoons of sugar and the egg yolk together until pale and fluffy. Pour a quarter of the scalded milk onto this, mix well and return it to the remaining milk. Cook on low heat, stirring constantly, until it thickens. Do not boil or it will curdle (if that happens, whirl it in a blender).

6   Remove the *Oranges Confites* carefully from their syrup and reserve twelve slices for decoration. Reduce the orange syrup by half (or until ½ cup is left) and mix into the *crème anglaise*. Purée the remaining orange slices (by hand or in a food processor) and add to the *crème anglaise* with the Grand Marnier. Marinate for at least 20 minutes before serving.

TO SERVE   Put four dessert plates into the refrigerator to chill. Cut the reserved orange slices in half.

Dust each little cake with confectioners' sugar (through a sieve) and place one in the center of each plate, surrounded with a circle of overlapping orange slices. Strain the *crème anglaise* through a conical sieve, discarding the chopped oranges (but keeping the vanilla). Pour a little sauce in the remaining space on the plate. Serve the remaining sauce in a sauceboat.

RIGHT *Reine de Saba aux Oranges Confites*

Rosace à l'Orange
ORANGE GATEAU

*H*ere is another delicious cake, from which a lot of sugar, butter and cream have been removed. Start preparing it 2 days in advance, by making the Oranges Confites, *the* crème pâtissière *and the* génoise. *It will not take long to assemble the cake, but make sure to chill it in the refrigerator for at least 12 hours to set.*

TWO DAYS BEFORE SERVING

1   Prepare the *crème pâtissière*. Use the ingredients listed here, but follow the method as described in *Tarte aux Fraises* (see page 172). Reserve on a plate to cool, and dust with confectioners' sugar to prevent a skin forming. When cold, cover with plastic wrap and refrigerate.

THE DAY BEFORE SERVING

1   Drain the slices of *Oranges Confites* delicately, and set aside ⅔ cup of the juice. Add 1 tablespoon of the Grand Marnier to it, and add the rest to the remainder of the juice. Reserve.

2   Use the oil to grease the pan in which the *génoise* was cooked. Line the inside with plastic wrap (the oil will help the wrap to cling).

3   Choose the best orange slices and use them to line the base and sides of the pan. Chop the remaining oranges and reserve.

4   Soften the gelatin in half of the reserved ⅔ cup juice in a small saucepan. Place over low heat just long enough for the gelatin to melt, then add to the rest of the juice. Reserve on top of a bowl with water and ice cubes to help it thicken.

5   Push the *crème pâtissière* through a sieve and add the reserved chopped oranges and thickened juice to it. They should each have the same consistency.

6   Add the yogurt to the cream, a spoonful at a time, and fold into the *crème pâtissière*.

TO ASSEMBLE

1   Cut the *génoise* into three layers horizontally.

2   Pour one-third of the orange filling on top of the oranges inside the pan, and lay over it the first layer of the cake. Soak the cake with a little of the reserved orange juice. Pour in another third of the filling, cover with the second layer of cake, and soak with juice. Pour in the remainder of the filling, and cover with the last layer of cake, soaked in juice, placed upside-down over the batter. Place a small plate on top of the cake and a heavy weight on top of that. Refrigerate for at least 12 hours to set.

TO SERVE Dip the cake pan in a bowl of hot water and invert onto a serving dish delicately. Wipe the oranges on top of the cake free of any surplus cream.

SERVES 6

1 recipe Oranges Confites (*see page 184*)
1 recipe génoise (*see* Génoise aux Pommes *page 185*)

CRÈME PÂTISSIÈRE
1 cup milk
1 vanilla bean
1 tbsp. potato starch
1 tbsp. cornstarch
1 tbsp. light brown sugar
1 egg
confectioners' sugar to dust

ORANGE FILLING
2 tbsp. Grand Marnier
2 tbsp. unflavored gelatin
1 tsp grapeseed or safflower oil
¼ cup Greek yogurt
⅔ cup whipping cream, whipped

LEFT *Rosace à l'Orange*

Tarte aux Pignons
SPINACH AND PINE NUT TART

SERVES 6
PREHEAT THE OVEN TO 350°F

Pâte Brisée *made with 1¼ cups*
   flour (see page 44)
2 tbsp. butter
11 oz. spinach leaves, cut into
   chiffonade
3 tbsp. honey
⅓ cup golden raisins
grated nutmeg
ground allspice
juice of ½ lemon
2 eggs, beaten
¼ cup pine nuts
½ cup whipping cream
⅓ cup milk

SAUCE
¾ cup Greek yogurt
2 tsp. liquid honey

Tarte aux Pignons

*N*o, the editor did not put this recipe in the wrong place; it is still a dessert, despite the spinach. Swiss chard in fact is traditional in Provence, where the recipe originates, but as it is not often available, we use young spinach leaves instead.

1 Allow the pastry to rest for 20 minutes in the refrigerator.

2 Melt the butter in a large saucepan and sauté the well dried spinach briskly over high heat. Add the honey (except for 1 teaspoon), the golden raisins, a pinch each of the spices, and the lemon juice. Leave to cool on a large plate, so that the golden raisins absorb any remaining liquid.

3 Roll out the pastry and use to line a 10-inch tart pan. Line the pastry with foil or parchment paper, and cover with baking beans. Bake blind in the preheated oven. After 10 minutes remove the paper and beans and continue baking until the dough is firm but not too brown, about 10 minutes. Brush with a little beaten egg and return to the oven for 5 minutes. Repeat this once more.

4 While the pastry is cooking, place the pine nuts on a baking sheet and toast them in the same oven until golden brown.

5 In a bowl mix the remaining beaten egg, the cream, milk, a little more nutmeg and allspice, and the reserved teaspoon of honey. Add the spinach mixture and mix together well. At the last moment add the pine nuts, then pour this mixture into the pastry case. Bake for 20 minutes.

TO SERVE Remove the tart from the pan and cool briefly on a cooling rack. Serve tepid with a little sauce made from the yogurt mixed with the honey.

INDEX

∽ACKNOWLEDGMENTS∽

I would like to thank the following people without whose cooperation this book would never have seen the light of day.

First my parents and family who always supported me in every circumstance, whatever choices I made, especially "maman" who researched a lot on my behalf for the herb section.

Very special thanks, too, to Sabine de Mirbeck-Brassart who, like a "mother," has helped me and always supported me throughout eight years of working closely together. Thank you also for the tedious task of testing the recipes without being able to let your wonderful culinary imagination take over…

Then Patrick Brassart, a very special "boss" to me, who has always fascinated me throughout my life with his ideas and enthusiasm. He took me like a "son" into his business venture…

A very big thank you to the team of staff at the school — Bertrand and Nathalie Brassart, Mandy Wagstaff, Sarah Woodbridge and Wayne Edwards. Bertrand made possible the first contacts with Swallow Books, and Nathalie helped Sabine with the testing of the dishes. The delightful presentation of the dishes in the pictures is owed to Mandy, my assistant teacher for many years, now home economist and caterer extraordinaire. Her attention to detail is remarkable and her taste exquisite. The ingredients list is due mainly to Wayne, and a lot of typing and the introduction to Sarah, but their main job was to keep the courses running and take away some of my responsibilities so that I could dedicate my time and attention to the book.

Thanks also to the team at Swallow Books, who had to cope with our continental approach (vive l'entente cordiale!) Tim Imrie, photographer; Elaine Partington, art director, and her stand-in, Dave Allen, who came to the school every weekend for two months; and Susan Fleming, who adapted my continental English!

More privately, special thanks to all my friends, whom I have neglected since I started on this book, and Betty, in particular, who had to put up with a ménage à trois — with a book!

The School would like to thank the following establishments for the loan of props: Ateliers de Ségrières, Paris; David Hicks, Paris; Faïencerie de Giens, Paris; Cristalleries Daum, Paris; Nappes Porthault, Paris; Alfriston Antiques, Alfriston, Sussex; Steamer Trading, Alfriston, Sussex.